LAW AND THE NEW

This book is unique in presenting an interdisciplinary conversation between jurists and logicians. It brings together scholars from both law and philosophy and looks at the application of 'the new logics' to law and legal ordering, in a number of legal systems. The first part explores the ways in which the new logics shed light on the functioning of legal orders, including the structure of legal argumentation and the rules of evidence. The second addresses how non-classical logics can help us to understand the interactions between multiple legal orders, in a range of contexts including domestic and international law. The final part examines particular issues in the applicability of non-classical logics to legal reasoning. This book will be of interest to scholars and students of law, jurisprudence and logic who want to deepen their understanding of the relationships between law and logic, and learn about recent developments in formal logic and their implications for legal reasoning.

H. PATRICK GLENN taught and had research interests in the areas of comparative law, private international law, civil procedure and the legal professions. He was Peter M. Laing Professor of Law at McGill University, and was a member of the Royal Society of Canada and a titular Member of the International Academy of Comparative Law. He also served as Director of McGill's Institute of Comparative Law. In 2006, Glenn received the Prix Léon-Gérin in recognition of his contributions to comparative law over his career, and in 2012, he was elected president of the American Society of Comparative Law. He died in October 2014.

LIONEL D. SMITH is Sir William C. Macdonald Professor of Law at McGill University. He has written extensively on many aspects of comparative private law and is particularly engaged with how private law understands aspects of unselfish behaviour. Smith is a member of the American Law Institute, the European Law Institute, the International Academy of Comparative Law and the International Academy of Estate and Trust Law.

LAW AND THE NEW LOGICS

Edited by

H. PATRICK GLENN
McGill University, Montreal

LIONEL D. SMITH
McGill University, Montreal

CAMBRIDGE
UNIVERSITY PRESS

CAMBRIDGE
UNIVERSITY PRESS

University Printing House, Cambridge CB2 8BS, United Kingdom

One Liberty Plaza, 20th Floor, New York, NY 10006, USA

477 Williamstown Road, Port Melbourne, VIC 3207, Australia

314-321, 3rd Floor, Plot 3, Splendor Forum, Jasola District Centre, New Delhi - 110025, India

79 Anson Road, #06-04/06, Singapore 079906

Cambridge University Press is part of the University of Cambridge.

It furthers the University's mission by disseminating knowledge in the pursuit of
education, learning and research at the highest international levels of excellence.

www.cambridge.org
Information on this title: www.cambridge.org/9781107514539
10.1017/9781316227329

© Cambridge University Press 2017

First published 2017
First paperback edition 2018

A catalogue record for this publication is available from the British Library

Library of Congress Cataloging in Publication data
Names: Glenn, H. Patrick, editor. | Smith, Lionel D., editor.
Title: Law and the new logics / edited by H. Patrick Glenn, Lionel D. Smith.
Description: New York : Cambridge University Press, 2016.
Identifiers: LCCN 2016023150 | ISBN 9781107106956 (Hardback)
Subjects: LCSH: Law–Interpretation and construction. | Law–Methodology.
Classification: LCC K213 .L393 2016 | DDC 340/.1–dc23 LC record available at
https://lccn.loc.gov/2016023150

ISBN 978-1-107-10695-6 Hardback
ISBN 978-1-107-51453-9 Paperback

Cambridge University Press has no responsibility for the persistence or
accuracy of URLs for external or third-party internet websites referred to in
this publication, and does not guarantee that any content on such websites is,
or will remain, accurate or appropriate.

This book is dedicated to Jane and Patrick Glenn
In gratitude for everything they have done
for their students and their colleagues.

LDS

CONTENTS

CONTRIBUTORS

N.W. BARBER is a Fellow of Trinity College, Oxford.

J. C. BEALL is Board of Trustees Distinguished Professor of Philosophy and Logic at the University of Connecticut (Storrs, USA), and Professor of Philosophy at the University of Tasmania (Hobart, Australia). Beall is also an Associate Research Fellow in the Arche Centre at the University of St Andrews (Fife, Scotland).

CHRISTINE BELL is Assistant Principal (Global Justice) and Professor of Constitutional Law, University of Edinburgh.

KEVIN M. CLERMONT is the Ziff Professor of Law, Cornell University.

H. PATRICK GLENN, FRSC, was Peter M. Laing Professor of Law, Faculty of Law, McGill University.

JAAP HAGE holds the Chair of Jurisprudence at Maastricht University.

ANDREW HALPIN is Professor of Law and Director of the Centre for Legal Theory at the Faculty of Law, National University of Singapore.

OREN PEREZ is a Professor at the Faculty of Law, Bar-Ilan University.

HENRY PRAKKEN is a lecturer in artificial intelligence at the Department of Information and Computing Sciences, Faculty of Science, Utrecht University and a professor of legal informatics and legal argumentation at the Faculty of Law, University of Groningen.

GRAHAM PRIEST is Distinguished Professor of Philosophy at the CUNY Graduate Center, and Boyce Gibson Professor Emeritus at the University of Melbourne.

CHAIM SAIMAN is a Professor of Law at Villanova Law School.

LIONEL D. SMITH is Sir William C. Macdonald Professor at the Faculty of Law, McGill University.

PREFACE

Hugh Patrick Glenn, who passed away in 2014, was one of the world's best-known comparative lawyers. One of the reasons for his reputation was that he did comparative law *differently*. This special voice was exemplified in what is probably his best-known book, LEGAL TRADITIONS OF THE WORLD: SUSTAINABLE DIVERSITY IN LAW. Upon its first appearance in 1998, it was awarded the inaugural Canada Prize of the International Academy of Comparative Law; the fifth edition was published in 2014. Like many great books, *Legal Traditions* found its origin in a course; in this case, a course that H. P. Glenn taught for many years at McGill's Faculty of Law, and that is still taught today.

H. P. Glenn was appointed to McGill in 1971, in the same year as Jane Matthews Glenn, both having come from doctoral studies in Strasbourg. During a long career, he published voluminously and, with Jane, visited law faculties and centres of comparative law around the world. He was a Bora Laskin National Fellow in Human Rights Law, a Killam Research Fellow and a Visiting Fellow of All Souls College, Oxford. He was a member of the Royal Society of Canada, and received in 2006 the Prix Léon-Gérin from the Government of Québec. He was posthumously awarded the Paul-André Crépeau Medal by the Quebec Division of the Canadian Bar Association.

He developed particular expertise in comparative civil procedure and comparative private international law. It was in the later part of his career that he became interested in comparative law writ large, at the level of legal traditions. This led not only to LEGAL TRADITIONS, but also to his monographs ON COMMON LAWS (2005) and THE COSMOPOLITAN STATE (2013). The latter is a truly ambitious work that aims to reassess the nature and role of the state in the modern world.

THE COSMOPOLITAN STATE reflects H. P. Glenn's growing interest in the relationship between law and logic. He sought to demonstrate that it is a mistake to think that law and legal reasoning are necessarily governed by classical logic, with its laws of the excluded middle and of non-contradiction. He thus became increasingly interested in non-classical logics.[1] These include fuzzy logics, which reject the law of the excluded middle and allow truth-values other than 'true' and 'false'. They also include paraconsistent logics, which reject the law of non-contradiction and allow the co-existence of contradictory propositions. This current of thought was related to his emerging idea that we should be less concerned with the 'conflict' of laws and more attentive to the conciliation of laws.[2] Indeed, it was part of a wider vision about law that was the product of his whole career. This vision rejected the idea of legal systems as self-contained normative orders that operate wholly independently. For Glenn, the idea of independent legal systems, with its link to what might be called classical, taxonomic comparative law, was part of a worldview that was tied to an understanding of the State and its legal system as wholly self-contained. With the benefit of a long view of history and a wide comprehension of the legal traditions of the world, Glenn rejected the monopoly of that approach. He argued for a more nuanced understanding of how legal traditions interact, using the ideas of conciliation and interpretation, as well as the insights of non-classical logic.[3]

If these propositions seem somewhat abstract, and indeed difficult to grasp for the jurist who takes classical logic for granted, a concrete example may illustrate the power and the importance of this train of thought. In Canada, as in many countries, there are legal systems that were brought by colonists, and there are Aboriginal communities who consider themselves to be governed by their own laws. The juridical version of classical logic may reel at this: since these communities are

---

[1] In addition to the present book, and its short chapter by H. P. Glenn (the origins of both of which are described below), see also *Multivalent Logic and the Rome Convention* in K. Boele-Woelki and W. Grosheide, eds., THE FUTURE OF EUROPEAN CONTRACT LAW: ESSAYS IN HONOUR OF EWOUD HONDIUS (Kluwer, 2007), 283; *Les droits privés* (Les Éditions Thémis, 2012) (the text of the 16th *Conférence Albert-Mayrand* given at the Université de Montréal); *The Cosmopolitan State* (O.U.P., 2013), particularly ch. 14; LES LOGIQUES DU DROIT INTERNATIONAL PRIVÉ, a chapter in *La conciliation des lois*, vol. 364 of the Collected Courses of the Hague Academy of International Law (Brill, 2013); LEGAL TRADITIONS OF THE WORLD: SUSTAINABLE DIVERSITY IN LAW, 5th ed. (O.U.P., 2014), particularly at 368–372.
[2] By the end of career, his own course on the subject was entitled 'Private International Law: The Conciliation of Laws'.
[3] For a careful assessment of Glenn's work, see R. Janda, *Cosmopolitan Normative Information: Patrick Glenn's Legal Theory* (2016) 1 INTER GENTES: McGILL J INTL L & LEG PLURALISM, online at http://intergentes.com/cosmopolitan-normative-information-patrick-glenns-legal-theory.

inside Canada, seen as a physical and political unit, they must be
governed by Canadian law; according to classical logic and a view of
legal systems as mutually exclusive, the only alternative would be to see
them as outside of Canada. But it is not so; scholars of Aboriginal law
note that the law that applies to Aboriginal peoples draws on both
Aboriginal and non-Aboriginal sources of law.[4] And in line with Glenn's
argument as it is set out in his contribution to this volume, it is by a
process of interpretation that these multiple legal orders can be brought
into harmony.

   In 2010–2011, Glenn held the Henry G. Schermers Fellowship of the
Hague Institute for the Internationalization of Law, and he and Jane
spent that year at the Netherlands Institute of Advanced Study in Wassenaar. He organized a workshop on *Multi-Valued Law and Multivalent
Logic* that took place at the Institute on 17–18 June 2011. This workshop
brought together a group of logicians and jurists to reflect on questions
arising out of the interactions between legal reasoning and legal orders,
and non-classical logics. It was important to Patrick that the papers given
that day be developed and published, but it was reflective of his scholarly
character that he was in no great rush. He stayed in contact with all of the
contributors, and announced in September 2014 that he had signed a
contract to publish the essays as a book, under his editorship, with Cambridge University Press. To everyone's shock, he passed away about two
weeks later.

   All of the contributors to this volume wanted to continue the project,
for its own inherent scholarly value but also to stand as a tribute to
Patrick Glenn's special brilliance. Cambridge University Press and Jane
Matthews Glenn were equally supportive of the idea. Being already a
contributor, and a colleague of both Patrick and Jane, it was an honour
for me to take on the role of co-editor. The royalties will go to the Paul-
André Crépeau Centre for Private and Comparative Law at McGill's
Faculty of Law, of which Patrick was and Jane remains a member. The
text that is included under the authorship of Patrick Glenn is derived
from a document that was found among his electronic files and that was
apparently the draft paper from which he gave his own presentation
at the workshop. It has been lightly edited for publication with the
other papers. Although it is relatively short, it touches on almost all of

---

[4] J. Borrows, *Recovering Canada: The Resurgence of Indigenous Law* (U. of Toronto
Press, 2002), esp. at 5–12; see also *Legal Traditions of the World*, note 1, at 84–85.

the currents of thought that characterized Patrick's thinking over the last decade.

We are aware that this is an unusual book, born of an unusual, but unusually thought-provoking event. We hope that it will be of interest to logicians, to jurists and to anyone who is interested in legal reasoning and legal systems. We offer the collection as a tribute to H. Patrick Glenn: a great scholar, a great thinker, a great teacher and a great colleague.

Lionel D. Smith
Faculty of Law, McGill University

PART I

New Logics in the Functioning of Legal Orders

Logics of Argumentation and the Law

HENRY PRAKKEN[1]

1 Introduction

In his LEGAL TRADITIONS OF THE WORLD (Glenn 2010), Patrick Glenn observes that the world contains many different legal traditions, often inconsistent with each other, and that even a single tradition can contain different sub-traditions that may be inconsistent with each other. Moreover, he notes that these traditions may interact with each other in complex ways. In chapter 10, Glenn raises the question of how to account for this from the perspective of formal logic. In chapter 14 of his THE COSMOPOLITAN STATE (Glenn 2013) he writes that new logics may be needed that are multivalent, paraconsistent or non-monotonic and do not adhere to the classic rules of non-contradiction and the excluded middle. In this chapter I will explore the use of one such new kind of logic, namely, logics of argumentation. It will turn out that such logics offer what Patrick Glenn is asking for without giving up classical two-valued logic. Instead, classical logic is in argumentation logics embedded in a larger formal framework, and it is this larger framework that has the desired nonstandard behavior. Thus argumentation logics provide a way to cope with inconsistent legal traditions without having to give up two-valued logic, a way that is moreover arguably close to the way lawyers think since notions like argument, counterargument and rebuttal are natural them.

Introductory textbooks to logic often portray logically valid inference as 'foolproof' reasoning: an argument is deductively valid if the truth of its premises guarantees the truth of its conclusion. In other words, if one accepts all premises of a deductively valid argument, then one also has to accept its conclusion, no matter what. However, we all construct arguments from time to time that are not foolproof in this sense but that merely make their conclusion plausible when their premises are true. For example, if we are told that John and Mary are married and that John

---

[1] Parts of this chapter are adapted from Prakken and Sartor (2009).

lives in Amsterdam, we conclude that Mary will live in Amsterdam as well, since we know that usually married people live where their spouses live. Sometimes such arguments are overturned by counterarguments. For example, if we are told that Mary lives in Rome to work at the foreign offices of her company for two years, we have to retract our previous conclusion that she lives in Amsterdam. However, as long as such counterarguments are not available, we are happy to live with the conclusions of our fallible arguments. The question is: are we then reasoning fallaciously or is there still logic in our reasoning?

The answer to this question has been given in more than thirty years of research in Artificial Intelligence (AI) on so-called logics for defeasible reasoning, partly inspired by earlier developments in philosophy and argumentation theory. At first sight it might be thought that patterns of defeasible reasoning are a matter of applying probability theory. However, many patterns of defeasible reasoning cannot be analysed in a probabilistic way. In the legal domain this is particularly clear: while reasoning about the facts can (at least in principle) still be regarded as probabilistic, reasoning about normative issues clearly is of a different nature. Moreover, even in matters of evidence reliable numbers are usually not available so that the reasoning has to be qualitative.

In this chapter an account is sketched of legal reasoning that respects that arguments can be fallible for various reasons. In short, the account is that reasoning consists of constructing arguments, attacking these arguments with counterarguments, and adjudicating between conflicting arguments on grounds that are appropriate to the conflict at hand. Just as in deductive reasoning, arguments must instantiate inference schemes (now called 'argument schemes') but only some of these schemes capture fool-proof reasoning: in our account deductive logic turns out to be the special case of argument schemes that can only be attacked on their premises.

This chapter is organised as follows. In Section 2 the notions of argument, counterargument and the relations of attack and defeat between conflicting arguments are introduced. These ingredients are combined in Section 3 into the idea of dialectical argument evaluation, which completes the general architecture of an argumentation logic. Then in Section 4 the distinction between deductive and defeasible arguments is introduced, and in Section 5 some stereotypical patterns of defeasible arguments are presented, together with stereotypical ways to attack them. Section 6 delves deeper into the formalization of argumentation logics; this section is primarily meant for more formally interested readers with some background in formal logic. Section 7 then concludes this chapter.

This chapter is intended to be a tutorial on argumentation logics and their relevance for legal reasoning. For this reason I will be sparse with references. A more formal introduction to argumentation logics with references to the literature can be found in Prakken (2011). The use of argumentation logics for modelling legal reasoning is reviewed in Prakken and Sartor (2015).

2 Arguments and Counterarguments

As just said, we assume that any argument instantiates some argument scheme. (More generally, arguments chain instantiations of argument schemes into trees, since the conclusion of one argument can be a premise of another.) Argument schemes are inference rules: they have a set of premises and a conclusion. What are the 'valid' argument schemes of defeasible reasoning? Much can be said on this and we will do so later on in Sections 4 and 5, but at least the deductively valid inference schemes of standard logic will be among them. In this section we examine how deductive arguments can be the subject of attack.

Consider the following example. According to section 3:32 of the Dutch civil code (natural) persons have the capacity to perform legal acts (this means, for instance, that they can engage in contracts or sell their property), unless the law provides otherwise. Suppose John argues that he has legal capacity since he is a person and the law does not provide otherwise. Then in standard propositional logic we can write this argument as follows:

Argument A:
Somebody is a person & $\neg$ The law provides otherwise $\rightarrow$ S/he has legal capacity
John is a person
$\neg$ The law provides otherwise
Therefore, John has legal capacity

(Here & stands for 'and', $\neg$ for 'it is not the case that' and $\rightarrow$ for 'if . . . then'.) This argument is deductively valid, since it instantiates the deductively valid argument scheme of *modus ponens*:

Modus Ponens Scheme:
$P \rightarrow Q$
P
Therefore, Q

(where P and Q can be any statement). This scheme is deductively valid: it is impossible to accept all its premises but still deny its conclusion, since the truth of its premises guarantees the truth of its conclusion.

Now does the deductive validity of argument A mean that we have to accept its conclusion? Of course not: any first lesson in logic includes the advice: if you don't like the conclusion of a deductive argument, then challenge its premises. According to section 1:234 of the Dutch civil code, minors have the capacity to perform legal acts if and only if they have consent from their legal representative. Now suppose John's father claims that John is in fact a minor and does not have such consent. Then the following deductive argument against the premise '¬The law provides otherwise' can be constructed, in two steps. First application of 1:234 results in the conclusion that John does not have the capacity to perform legal acts:

Argument B:
Somebody is a minor → (S/he has consent ↔ S/he has legal capacity)
John is a minor
¬ John has consent
Therefore, ¬ John has legal capacity

(Here ↔ stands for 'if and only if'). The double arrow expresses that when a person is a minor, then having consent is not only a sufficient but also a necessary condition for having the capacity to perform legal acts. So, since John is a minor but does not have such consent, he does not have legal capacity. This conclusion can then be used to attack the third premise of argument A:

Argument B (continued):
¬ John has legal capacity
¬ John has legal capacity → The law provides otherwise
Therefore, the law provides otherwise

Now we must choose whether to accept the premise '¬ The law provides otherwise' of argument A or whether to give it up and accept the conclusion of counterargument B. Clearly the phrase "unless the law provides otherwise" of section 3:32 of the Dutch civil code is meant to express that any place where the law expresses otherwise is an exception to section 3:32. Since argument B is based on such a statutory exception, we must therefore give up the premise of A and accept the counterargument. In this case we say that argument B not just *attacks* but also *defeats* argument A.

However, not all attacks are a matter of statutory exceptions. In our example, John might attack his father's argument B by saying that he does have consent of his legal representative since his mother consented and she is his legal representative. This gives rise to an argument attacking the third premise of argument B (before the continuation):

Argument C:
Somebody's mother consented → S/he has consent
John's mother consented
Therefore, John has consent

This time we have a genuine conflict, namely, between John's father's claim that John acted without consent of his legal representative (the third premise of argument B) and John's claim that he acted with consent of his legal representative (the conclusion of argument C). Now note that if one accepts all premises of argument C, then one must also accept its conclusion, since argument C instantiates the deductively valid scheme of modus ponens. And if one accepts argument C's conclusion, one must, of course, reject the third premise of argument B. In the latter case we say that argument C not only attacks but also defeats argument B. Let us assume that the latter is indeed the case.

In sum then, what we have so far is that all three arguments are deductively valid but that argument A is defeated by argument B on its third premise while argument B is in turn defeated by argument C on its third premise. This implies that it is rational to accept the conclusions of arguments A and C: even though A is defeated by B, it is *defended* by C, which defeats A's only defeater.

This leads to a very important insight. In order to determine what to believe or accept in the face of a body of conflicting arguments it does not suffice to make a choice between two arguments that directly conflict with each other. We must also look at how arguments can be defended by other arguments. In our example this is quite simple: it is intuitively obvious that C defends A so, since C is not attacked by any argument, both argument A and argument C (and their conclusions) are acceptable. However, we can easily imagine more complex examples where our intuitions fall short. For instance, another argument D could be constructed such that C and D defeat each other, then an argument E could be constructed that defeats D but is defeated by A, and so on: which arguments can now be accepted and which should be rejected? Here we cannot rely on intuitions but need a *calculus,* or an *argumentation logic.* Its input will be a collection of arguments plus an assessment of which arguments defeat each other, while its output will be an assessment of the *dialectical status* of these arguments in terms of three classes (three and not two since some conflicts cannot be resolved). Intuitively, the *justified* arguments are those that survive all conflicts with their attackers and so can be accepted, the *overruled* arguments are those that are attacked by a justified argument and so must be rejected; and the *defensible* arguments are those that are involved in conflicts that cannot be resolved. Furthermore, a statement is justified if it has a justified argument, it is overruled if all arguments for it are overruled, and it is defensible if it has a defensible argument but no justified arguments. In terms more familiar to lawyers, if a claim is justified, then a rational adjudicator is convinced that the claim is true; if it is overruled, such an adjudicator is convinced that the claim is false; while if it is defensible, s/he is neither convinced that it is true nor that it is false.

Before an argumentation logic can be presented, a subtlety concerning the defeat relation between arguments must be explained. Above we made a distinction between attack and defeat. An argument A *defeats* an argument B if A *attacks* B and is *not inferior* to B (according to the appropriate criteria for comparing arguments). This definition allows that two arguments defeat each other, namely, if neither argument is inferior or superior to the other. In such cases we say that the two arguments *weakly defeat* each other; otherwise (if one argument is superior to the other) we say that one argument *strictly defeats the other*. Suppose in our example that further evidence was given by both John and his father on whether John's mother consented. John presents a testimony by his brother that his mother consented, while his father presents a testimony by John's mother that she never consented:

Argument C (continued)
John's brother says that John's mother consented
What a witness says is usually true
Therefore, John's mother consented

Argument D
John's mother says that she never consented
What a witness says is usually true
Therefore, ¬ John's mother consented

(In Section 4 we return to the question of whether these arguments can be reconstructed as deductively valid and how it can be that they attack each other on their conclusions instead of on their premises.) Suppose that the court cannot find a reason why one witness testimony is stronger than the other: then it must conclude that both conflicting arguments (weakly) defeat each other.

3   Logic of Argumentation

Let us now discuss what an argumentation logic looks like. Just as in deductive logic, there is no single universally accepted one and there is an ongoing debate in AI about what is a good argumentation logic. However, we need not go into the details of this debate, since it turns out that there is a simple and intuitive definition that suffices for most applications. The idea is to regard an attempt to prove an argument justified as a *debate* between a proponent and opponent of the argument.[2] The proponent starts with the argument that he wants to prove justified and then the turn shifts to the opponent, who must provide all its defeating counterarguments. It does not matter whether they weakly or strictly defeat their target, since the opponent's task is to interfere with the proponent's attempt to prove his argument justified. For each of these defeating arguments, the proponent must then construct one strict defeater (it has to be a strict defeater since the proponent must prove his argument justified). This process is repeated as long as it takes: at each of her turns, the opponent constructs all mutual and all strict defeaters of the proponent's previous arguments, while at each of his turns, the proponent constructs a strict defeater for each of the opponent's previous arguments, and so on. The idea is that our initial argument is justified if proponent can eventually make opponent run out of moves in every of opponent's lines of attack.

This process can be visualised as follows (note that this figure does *not* model the above example but is a new, abstract example).

Note that if an argument is justified, this does not mean that the proponent will in fact win the game: he could make the wrong choice at some point. All that it means is that the proponent will win if he plays optimally. In terms of game theory, an argument is justified if the proponent has a so-called *winning strategy* in a game that starts with

---

[2] The proponent and opponent should not be seen as real human beings; they are a metaphor for the dialectical nature of the reasoning process, where both pros and cons are considered. Such a dialectical reasoning process can just as well take place in the mind of a single reasoner.

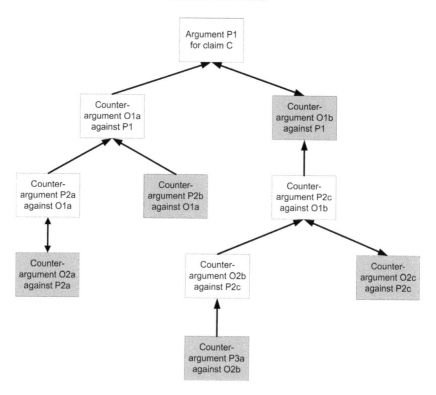

Figure 1.1:   A dialectical tree

the argument. In fact, there is a simple way to verify whether the proponent has a winning strategy. The idea is to label all arguments in the tree as *in* or *out* according to the following definition:

1. An argument is *in* if and only if all its defeating counterarguments are *out*
2. An argument is *out* if and only if it has a defeating counterargument that is *in*

In the figures *in* is coloured as grey and *out* as white. It is easy to see that because of (1) all leaves of the tree are trivially *in*, since they have no counterarguments. Then we can work our way upwards to determine the colour of all other arguments, ultimately arriving at a colour of the initial argument. If it is grey, i.e., *in*, then we know that the proponent has a winning strategy for it, namely by choosing a grey argument at each point he has to choose. If, on the other hand, the initial argument is

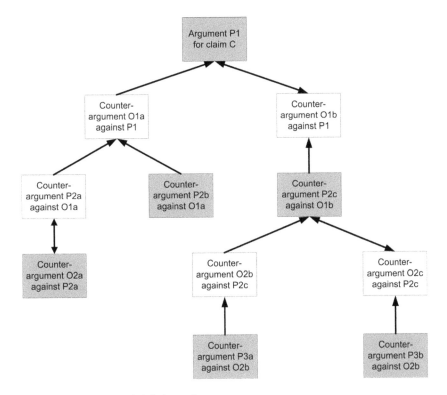

Figure 1.2:   An extended dialectical tree.

white, i.e., *out*, then it is the opponent who has a winning strategy, which can be found in the same way. So in the above figure the opponent has a winning strategy, which she can follow by choosing argument O1b at her first turn.

Suppose now that new information becomes available that gives rise to a strictly defeating counterargument P3b against O2c. Then the situation is as in Figure 1.3.

Now argument P1 is *in* so now it is the proponent who has a winning strategy, viz. choosing P2b instead of P2a when confronted by O1a. This illustrates that when new information becomes available from which new arguments can be constructed, the dialectical status of arguments may change.

It should be noted that each argument appearing as a box in these trees has an internal structure. In the simplest case it just has a set of premises and a conclusion, but when the argument combines several inferences, it

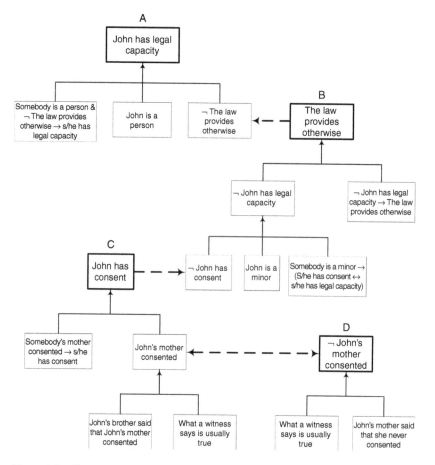

Figure 1.3: Four arguments and their defeat relations

has the structure of an inference tree as is familiar from standard logic. This is illustrated by Figure 1.3, which displays all four arguments of our example, plus their defeat relations (solid lines represent inferences while dashed lines stand for defeat relations).

Abstracted to a dialectical tree as in Figure 1.1 we obtain Figure 1.4, which shows the two game trees for arguments A and B. (Both trees are very simple, having just one branch, since neither the proponent nor the opponent has any choice.)

The tree on the left of Figure 1.4 displays the game tree for argument A: it shows that argument A is not justified, since argument A is labelled *out.* The tree on the right displays the game tree for argument B: it shows

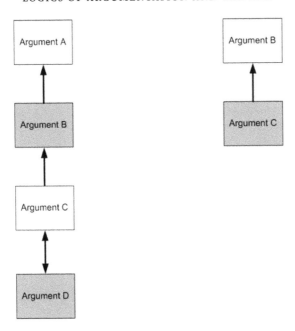

Figure 1.4:   Two abstract dialectical trees corresponding to Figure 1.3

that argument B is also not justified since it is also labelled *out*. Hence both argument A and argument B are not justified. Let us next examine whether they are defensible or overruled. Argument A has just one defeater, namely, argument B, but we have just seen that B is not justified. So A is not overruled but defensible. Argument B also has just one defeater, namely, argument C. Is C justified? No it is not: if the proponent starts a game with C, then the opponent can reply with argument D, which weakly defeats C. Then the proponent cannot find an argument that strictly defeats D (since C only weakly defeats C), so the game ends with a win for the opponent. So B's only defeater is not justified (in fact it is defensible), so B is also defensible.

4   Defeasible Rules and Generalizations

So far we have only considered deductive argument schemes and we have modelled the fallibility of arguments as the possibility of premise attack (with one exception, namely, arguments C, continued, and D, to be further discussed below). At first sight, it might be thought that this is all we need: if we adopt a suitable logic for adjudicating conclusion–premise

conflicts between arguments, then the only argument schemes we need
are those of deductive logic. However, if we have a closer look at arguments as they are constructed and attacked in practice, we see that they
can often be attacked even if all their premises are accepted. In fact, we
have already encountered one such case. Let us again look at the above
arguments for and against the claim that John's mother consented. Both
arguments used a premise 'What witness say is usually true' but from this
premise and a given witness statement it does not *necessarily* follow that
what the witness says is true. The circumstances may be unusual: for
example, the witness may have bad memory or may have reason to lie (in
our example mother might be afraid for father, if he is known to be
violent). In such cases the conclusion only *presumptively* follows, namely,
under the presumption that everything is as usual. This explains why a
rational person can accept both premises of arguments C and D but still
deny their conclusion, namely, if there is evidence that things are not
as usual.

Many factual generalisations that are used in daily life and also many
that are used in in legal proof are of this presumptive, or *defeasible*
nature. At the beginning of this chapter we gave the example *usually
married people live where their spouses live*, which can have exceptions,
for instance, when a spouse temporarily works abroad. An evidential
example is the generalisation *fleeing from the crime scene indicates consciousness of guilt*, which has exceptions in case the person fleeing from
the crime scene has another reason for avoiding the police, such as being
an illegal immigrant. Or consider *This type of radar is a reliable source of
information about speed of traffic*; but what if it has a hidden defect? Or
Confessing suspects are guilty; but what if the suspect later retracted his
confession? Not only factual generalisations are defeasible but also, for
example, interpretation rules or reasons for action. An example of a
defeasible interpretation rule in American contract law is *A statement 'I
accept . . .'* is an acceptance, but an exception was *A statement 'I accept'*
followed by terms that do not match the terms of the offer is not an
acceptance (cf. Gardner 1987). Reasons for action are also often defeasible, for example: *When I have an exam, I should study hard*; but not
necessarily, for example, when a close friend or family member is seriously ill. It has even been argued that legal rules are also defeasible, since
there can always be unforeseen cases in which a rule should be set aside
because of higher principles or unwanted consequences. A famous
example is the *Riggs v. Palmer* case in American inheritance law (discussed by Dworkin 1977), in which a grandson had killed his grandfather

and then claimed his share in the inheritance. The court made an exception to inheritance law based on the principle that no person shall profit from their own wrongdoing.

Now an important point is that the application of defeasible generalisation cannot be regarded as an instance of the *modus ponens* argument scheme, since $P \rightarrow Q$ means that *always* when P is true then Q is true, and this is not the same as saying that *usually* when P is true then Q is true. So we need a new argument scheme, called *defeasible modus ponens*:

Defeasible Modus Ponens:
If P then usually Q
P
Therefore (presumably) Q

The qualifier 'presumably' of the inference indicates that this is not a deductively valid scheme. Even if both premises are accepted, it may be rational not to accept the conclusion, namely, if there is an exception to the first premise. However, whether this is rational depends on whether an acceptable counterargument can be constructed: if this is impossible, that is, if there is no evidence that there is an exception, or this evidence is unconvincing, then an argument that instantiates the defeasible modus ponens scheme must be accepted. Now in the previous section we saw how an argumentation logic systematises this process of testing an argument in light of all possible counterarguments. The only thing left to do is to allow that an argument can be attacked not only on its premises but also on its conclusion.

In fact, a conclusion of an argument can be attacked in a stronger and a weaker way. The strong way is to build an argument with the opposite conclusion, as we did above with argument D. Such a conclusion-to-conclusion attack is called a *rebutting* attack. A rebutting counterargument may attack the final conclusion of its target but it may also attack an intermediate conclusion. For example, as Figure 1.3 shows, argument D above attacks argument C by rebutting its intermediate conclusion that John's mother consented. However, sometimes an argument can be attacked in a weaker way, namely, by saying that the premises, even if true, do not support their conclusion in the case at hand, because the case at hand is an exceptional case. Consider again the factual generalisation *What witnesses say is usually true*: if, for example, it turns out that the witness has a poor memory, this is a reason not to infer that what he says is true, but of course, this does not imply that the opposite of what he says is true. This weaker form of attack is often called *undercutting* attack.

Undercutting counterarguments do not attack a premise or the conclusion of their target but instead deny that the scheme on which it is based can be applied to the case at hand. Obviously, such a denial does not make sense for deductive argument schemes. In sum, while deductive arguments can only be attacked on their premises, presumptive arguments can also be attacked on their conclusion and on their inference steps.

5   Presumptive Argument Schemes

Our analysis can be further refined. When looking at defeasible rules or generalisations, we see that often they are not just specific statements about the world but conform to certain reasoning patterns. For instance, evidential arguments are often based on stereotypical evidential sources, such as expert or witness testimony, observation or memory. Other evidential arguments apply the scheme of causal abduction: if we know that A causes B and we observe B, then in the absence of evidence of other possible causes we may presumptively conclude that it is A that caused B. It is important to note that arguments based on such patterns speak about states of affairs in general: unlike specific generalisations like 'summer in Holland is usually cool' or 'fleeing from a crime scene typically indicates consciousness of guilt' they express general ways of obtaining knowledge from certain information. Nobody would dispute these ways in general; at most their application to specific cases is disputed on the grounds that there is an exception. For these reasons it is natural to regard such patterns not as conditional premises of a *defeasible modus ponens* argument but as independent presumptive (or defeasible) argument schemes. The idea of presumptive argument schemes has been developed in the fields of informal logic and argumentation theory. The standard reference is Walton (1996). In this section I discuss some schemes that are common in legal reasoning, to start with the argument scheme from witness testimony:

Argument Scheme from Witness Testimony:
Person *W* says that *P*
Person *W* was in a position to observe *P*
Therefore (presumably), *P*

As explained in the previous section, the use of presumptive argument schemes in an argument gives rise to two new ways of attack, namely, rebutting and undercutting attack. For example, an application of the scheme from witness testimony can be rebutted by an application of the same scheme to a contradicting witness. Undercutting attacks are in fact based on the idea that a presumptive argument scheme has typical exceptional circumstances in which it does not apply. For example, a witness testimony is typically criticised on the witnesses' truthfulness or the functioning of his memory or senses. In general, then, each argument scheme comes with a set of *critical questions* which, when answered negatively, give rise to undercutting counterarguments (or sometimes to rebutting counterarguments). For example, the Witness Testimony Scheme is often given the following critical questions:

Critical Questions to the Argument Scheme from Witness Testimony
W1: Is the witness truthful?
W2: Did the senses of the witness function properly?
W3: Does the memory of the witness function properly?
A related scheme is the scheme from expert testimony:

Argument Scheme from Expert Testimony:
Person E is an expert in domain D
Person E says that P
P is within domain D
Therefore (presumably), P

Obvious critical questions are:

Critical Questions:
E1: Is the expert truthful?
E2: 'is P consistent with what other experts say?'
E3: 'is P consistent with known evidence?'

Note that the second and third question do not point to undercutting attacks: E2 points to rebutting applications of the same scheme, while E3 points to rebutting applications of any scheme with the opposite conclusion.

Another important scheme for legal evidential reasoning is causal explanation, which is a form of abduction:

Argument Scheme from Causal Explanation:
P causes Q
Q is observed
Therefore (presumably), P is the case

(Weaker variants of this scheme can be obtained by replacing the first premise with 'P usually causes Q' or 'P can cause Q'.)

Critical Questions:
C1: Can Q be caused by something else?
C2: Does P also cause something else which is known not to be the case?

Here is an example of this scheme and its critical questions:

An Abductive Argument:
This type of gun fires this type of bullet.
A bullet of this type was found at the crime scene.
Therefore, (presumably) the victim was shot at with this type of gun.

Critical question C1 can be used, for instance, when other types of guns also fire this type of bullet, while question C2 can be used as follows:

A Rebuttal of the Abductive Argument:
This type of gun usually causes this type of wound.
The victim had a different type of wound.
Therefore (presumably) the victim was not shot at with this type of gun.

This argument instantiates the following scheme:

Argument Scheme from Causal Refutation:
P usually causes Q
Q is not observed
Therefore (presumably), $\neg P$

The use of presumptive argument schemes is not confined to reasoning about the facts. For instance, arguments from practical reasoning (reasoning about what to do) often conform to the 'argument scheme from consequences':

Argument Scheme from Good Consequences:
If A is brought about, then good consequences may plausibly occur.
Therefore (presumably), A should be brought about.

An application of the argument scheme from consequences may be criticised by pointing at other ways than A to realise the same consequences or at negative consequences brought about by realising A:

Critical Questions:
GC1: Are there other ways to bring about the good consequences?
GC2: Does A also bring about bad consequences?

The scheme also has a negative version:

Argument Scheme from Bad Consequences:
If A is brought about, then bad consequences may plausibly occur.
Therefore (presumably), A should not be brought about.

Critical Question:
BC1: Does A also bring about good consequences?

In legal reasoning a typical way in which the schemes from consequences are used is in so-called teleological interpretation arguments. For example:

> If the term 'personal data' of the Dutch Data Protection Act is interpreted to include email addresses, then new legal measures against spam become possible, which is good.
>
> Therefore, the term 'personal data' of the Dutch Data Protection Act should be interpreted to include email addresses.

An argument using the positive version of the argument scheme from consequences may be rebutted by an argument using the negative version, such as:

> If the term 'personal data' of the Dutch Data Protection Act is interpreted to include email addresses, then new legal measures against spam become possible, which may result in a massive increase in litigation, which is bad.
>
> Therefore, the term 'personal data' of the Dutch Data Protection Act should be interpreted not to include email addresses.

We next list, without illustration, argument schemes for two further common forms of presumptive reasoning. The first is (enumerative) induction, which defeasibly infers generalisations from a collection of observations. This scheme can be formulated differently depending on the strength of the conditional connection:

Argument Scheme from Induction:
Most (all) observed P's were Q's.
Therefore (presumably), most (all) P's are Q's.

Critical Questions:
I1: Is the number of observations large enough?
I2: Was the selection of observations biased?

The following scheme is for analogical reasoning, a form of reasoning often used in the law.

Argument Scheme from Analogy:
Cases that are relevantly similar should be decided in the same way.
Cases *C1* and *C2* are relevantly similar.
Therefore (presumably), cases *C1* and *C2* should be decided in the same way.

Critical Questions:
A1: Are there also relevant differences between the cases?
A2: Are there relevant similarities with other cases that are decided differently?

But more sophisticated formulations of analogy are possible.

To give a final illustration of reasoning with argument schemes and their critical questions, consider an alleged murder case in which an accused called Bob claims he killed in self-defence and produces a witness called Roy, who testifies that the victim threatened the accused with a knife. The Witness Testimony Scheme can then be instantiated as follows (using an intermediate reasoning step to infer the second premise of the scheme):

Argument A:
F1: Roy says that the victim threatened the accused Bob with a knife.
F2: Roy was there when the killing took place.
G1: If W is there when an event E takes place, then W is in the position to observe event E.
Therefore, Roy was in the position to observe whether the victim threatened the accused Bob with a knife.
Therefore (presumably), the victim threatened the accused Bob with a knife.

Let us represent critical questions that point to undercutting counter-arguments as rules with a consequent ¬Name, where 'Name' is a place-holder for the name of the undercut argument scheme. Then, for instance, critical question W1 of the Witness Testimony Scheme can be represented as follows:

W1: ¬ Witness W is truthful → ¬ Witness-Testimony-Scheme

Suppose next that it becomes known that the witness is a friend of the accused. Then if it is believed that friends of accused persons, when testifying, try to protect their friend and that this means that they are not truthful, an undercutter of this argument can be constructed in three steps.

Argument B:

G2: If Witness W is a friend of accused A, then usually Witness W tries to protect accused A

F3: Witness Roy is a friend of accused Bob

Therefore (presumably), Witness Roy tries to protect accused Bob

R1: Witness W tries to protect accused $A \rightarrow \neg$ Witness W is truthful

Therefore, $\neg$ Witness Roy is truthful

W: $\neg$ Witness W is truthful $\rightarrow \neg$ Witness-Testimony-Scheme

Therefore, $\neg$ Witness-Testimony-Scheme

This argument could in turn be attacked, for instance, by attacking its premise F3 or by arguing that there is an exception to the defeasible generalisation G2.

Finally, how many presumptive argument schemes are there? Here the classical logician will be disappointed. One of the main successes of modern formal logic has been that an infinite number of valid deductive inferences can be captured by a finite and even very small number of schemes. However, things are different for defeasible inference: many different collections of presumptive argument schemes have been proposed; the above schemes are just a few examples of schemes. Moreover, while some schemes, such as abduction and the scheme from consequences, can arguably be used in any domain, other schemes may be domain-dependent. For instance, it can be argued that in legal contexts the witness and expert schemes have a different form and different critical questions than in ordinary commonsense reasoning.

6   Logic of Argumentation Formalised

Readers of this chapter who are interested in formal logic may want to know more about how an argumentation logic can be formally defined. For these readers I now discuss in more detail how the account of an argumentation logic developed throughout this paper can be formalised. I will do so by summarising a formal framework for argumentation logics as developed in AI; some aspects will not be presented in their full formal detail but will be semi-formally sketched. I start with the formalisation of the structure of arguments and the nature of attack and defeat, and then I discuss a fully abstract approach to the dialectical evaluation of arguments.

6.1   The Structure of Arguments and the Nature of
Attack and Defeat[3]

In the previous sections, arguments were depicted as trees of inferences where the inferences apply either deductive (or 'strict') or presumptive (or 'defeasible') argument schemes (or 'inference rules'). Informally, that an inference rule is strict means that if one accepts all its antecedents, then one has to accept its consequent *no matter what*, while that an inference rule is defeasible means that if one accepts all its antecedents, then one has to accept its consequent *if one has no good reason not to accept it*.

This notion of an argument can be formalised assuming the following elements:

- A *logical language L* containing a negation symbol ¬.
- Two sets of *strict* and *defeasible inference rules Rs* and *Rd*. Each inference rule is of the form $a_1, . . .,a_n$ *strictly/defeasibly implies c,* where $a_1, . . .,a_n$ and c are well-formed formulas from L. The formulas $a_1, . . .,a_n$ are called the *antecedents* and c is called the *consequent* of the rule.

Arguments are then inference trees, where the nodes are well-formed formulas from the logical language L and the links between the nodes are applications of strict or defeasible inference rules. More formally, for any node n, if $n_1, . . .,n_k$ are all children of n, then there exists an inference rule in Rs or Rd of the form $n_1, . . .,n_k$ *strictly/defeasibly implies c*. The starting points of an argument (the nodes not derived by applying an inference rule) are called the argument's *premises* and all other nodes are called its *conclusions*. The premises of an argument are assumed to be taken from a, possibly inconsistent, *knowledge base* (the available information, from wherever it originates). A conclusion that is not used as an antecedent of another inference in an argument is called the argument's *final conclusion*; the other conclusions are its *intermediate conclusions*.

For example, argument C in Figure 1.3 has three premises, *John's brother said that John's mother consented, What a witness said is usually true* and *Somebody's mother consented → S/he has consent*; it has one intermediate conclusion *John's mother consented*; and a final conclusion *John has consent.*

---

[3] This subsection is based on the ASPIC+ framework presented in Prakken (2010). Some definitions of ASPIC+ are here slightly changed for ease of explanation. The changes do not make a difference for the outcome of argument evaluation.

Note that this notion of an argument does not commit to a particular logical language. For L any logical language can be chosen, such as the language of propositional logic, first-order predicate logic or deontic logic. The strict rules over L can be based on the semantic interpretation of L by saying that Rs contains all inference rules that are semantically valid over L (according to the chosen semantics). So, for example, if L is chosen to be the language of standard propositional logic, then Rs can be chosen to consist of all semantically valid inferences in standard propositional logic (whether such an inference is valid can be tested with, for example, the truth-table method).

The defeasible rules Rd cannot be based on the semantic interpretation of L, since they go beyond the meaning of the logical constants in L. Consider, for example, defeasible modus ponens, discussed in Section 4: 'if P then usually Q' and 'P' do not together deductively imply Q, since we could have an unusual case of P. In other words, defeasible inference rules are deductively invalid. They can instead be based on insights from epistemology or argumentation theory. For example, Rd could be filled with presumptive argument schemes as discussed above in Section 5.

Arguments can be *attacked* in three ways: on their premises, on conclusions of their defeasible inferences and on their defeasible inferences themselves:

- An argument A *undermines* an argument B if a conclusion of A contradicts a premise of B.
- An argument A *rebuts* an argument B if a conclusion of A contradicts a conclusion of B that is derived with a defeasible inference rule.
- An argument A *undercuts* an argument B if a conclusion of A says of some defeasible rule used in B that it is not applicable.

Undermining and rebutting attacks can be resolved by looking at the relative strength of arguments:

- An argument A *successfully undermines* an argument B if A undermines B and A is not weaker than B with respect to this conflict.[4]
- An argument A *successfully rebuts* an argument B if A rebuts B and A is not weaker than B with respect to this conflict.

These definitions presuppose that the relative strength of arguments can be determined. This may not be trivial and may even be the subject of

---

[4] Here we say 'with respect to this conflict' since in general two arguments may simultaneously attack each other in several ways.

arguments and counterarguments. However, in this chapter we do not go into the details of this issue and simply assume that some definition of the relative strength of arguments is given.

Undercutting attacks succeed irrespective of the strength of arguments, since undercutters state exceptions to inference rules. Then:

- An argument A *defeats* an argument B if A successfully undermines B, successfully rebuts B or undercuts B.

Let us illustrate these notions with the arguments in Figure 1.3.

- The logical language L in the example is that of standard propositional logic.
- The strict rules Rs are all propositionally valid inferences.
- The set of defeasible rules Rd contains the defeasible-modus-ponens rule discussed in Section 4.
- Arguments A and B only use strict inference rules, so they can only be attacked on their premises. Argument C first uses a defeasible rule, namely, defeasible modus ponens, and then uses a strict rule, namely, standard modus ponens. So C can be attacked on its premises, on its conclusion that mother consented and on the application of defeasible modus ponens to derive that conclusion. Finally, argument D uses defeasible modus ponens and can therefore be attacked on its premises, its conclusion and its inference.
- Argument B successfully undermines argument A, since B's final conclusion contradicts a premise of A and since (as assumed above in Section 2) B is stronger than A with respect to this conflict since B provides a statutory exception to the legal rule that is A's first premise (A's third premise in fact assumes that there is no such exception). So B strictly defeats A.
- Argument C undermines argument B since B's final conclusion contradicts a premise of A. Moreover, in Section 2 we assumed for unspecified reasons that B is stronger than A with respect to this conflict, so C successfully undermines B and so strictly defeats B.
- Arguments C and D rebut each other since they have contradictory conclusions *John has consent* and $\neg$ *John has consent*, both derived with a defeasible inference rule. Furthermore, in Section 2 it was assumed that no reason can be found why one witness is more reliable than the other, so both arguments are equally strong with respect to this conflict. So they successfully rebut each other and hence (weakly) defeat each other.

6.2   *Dialectical Evaluation of Arguments*[5]

As explained in Section 2, in order to determine whether an argument can be accepted, it does not suffice to make a choice between two arguments that directly conflict with each other but we must also look at how arguments can be indirectly defended by other arguments. One way to formalise this idea is to fully abstract from the internal structure of the arguments and from the reasons why they defeat each other. Thus in the example of Figure 1.3 we just say that there are four arguments *A*, *B*, *C* and *D* and that *B* defeats *A*, *C* defeats *B* while *C* and *D* defeat each other. This can be conveniently depicted as a directed graph, which from now on will be called a *defeat graph*.

The task now is to determine which arguments in this graph can be accepted and which must be rejected given their various defeat relations. From now on we will speak of the task of labelling nodes in the graph with either the label *in* or the label *out* (but not both). Clearly, not any labelling will do but they must satisfy some conditions. It turns out that the same conditions can be used as above in Section 2:

1. An argument is *in* if and only if all its defeating counterarguments are *out*
2. An argument is *out* if and only if it has a defeating counterarguments that is *in*

However, this time we do not apply these conditions to labellings of a game tree, to see which party has a winning strategy in a game, but to labellings of the defeat graph.

Let us see if in Figure 1.5 argument *A* can be labelled *in*. To make *A in*, by condition (1) all defeaters of *A* must be *out*, so *B* must be *out*. To make *B out*, condition (2) requires that it has a defeater that is *in*, so *C* must be *in*. In turn, to make *C in*, condition (1) requires that *D* must be *out*. And to make *D out*, condition (2) requires that it has a defeater that is *in*, so *C* must be *in*. At first sight, the definition would here seem to turn out to be circular, but this is not true: all we need is to find a labelling that satisfies conditions (1) and (2) and if we choose the labelling as depicted in Figure 1.6, this is the case (here grey nodes stand for the label *in* and white nodes for the label *out*).

---

[5] This subsection is based on Dung (1995) and later work extending it. See Prakken (2011) for a brief overview.

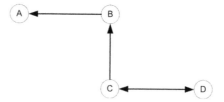

Figure 1.5:   A defeat graph (and a 'grounded labelling')

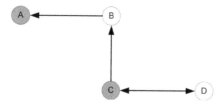

Figure 1.6:   A 'preferred' labelling of the defeat graph

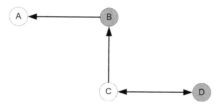

Figure 1.7:   An alternative 'preferred' labelling of the defeat graph

However, this is not the only possible labelling that satisfies our two conditions. Since the defeat relation between C and D is symmetric and since neither C nor D is defeated by any other argument, we can just as well label C *out* and D *in*. But if we do so, then B must be labelled *in* (since all its defeaters are now *out*) while A must be labelled *out* (since it now has a defeater that is *in*). This alternative labelling is depicted in Figure 1.7.

Thus the labelling approach captures that often in argumentation alternative reasonable positions can be defended. However, this is not yet all to the labelling approach, since we are not forced to assign a label to arguments C and D: if we do not assign any label to these two arguments, then this also satisfies conditions (1) and (2): that C is not labelled *in* is justified by condition (1), since not all defeaters of C are labelled *out*. And that C is not labelled *out* is justified by condition (2), since there exists no defeater of C that is labelled *in*. However, the choice not to label C and D implies that A and B can also not be labelled: B cannot be labelled *in* since it has a defeater which is not labelled *out* and B cannot be labelled *out* since it has no defeater that is labelled *in*. For the same reasons A cannot be labelled. This third labelling that satisfies conditions (1) and (2) is in fact the labelling depicted in Figure 1.5.

The three alternative labellings are induced by two alternative policies for labelling a defeat graph. The labellings of Figures 1.6 and 1.7 are induced by the policy to label as many arguments *in* as possible, while the labelling of Figure 1.5 is induced by the policy to abstain from labelling a node *in* whenever possible. In formal argumentation theory such policies for labelling defeat graphs are called 'argumentation semantics' and the policies to, respectively, maximise and minimise the sets of arguments that are labelled *in* are called, respectively, *preferred* and *grounded semantics*.[6] In fact, these semantics correspond to, respectively, a 'brave' and 'cautious' attitude in taking positions in argumentation (sometimes also called a 'credulous' and 'sceptical' attitude).

Since defeat graphs can have more than one labelling, a single labelling does in general not suffice to determine whether an argument is dialectically acceptable (with respect to a given semantics). Only if an argument is labelled *in* in all possible labellings according to the given semantics can it be said to be dialectically acceptable according to that semantics. In fact, a distinction can be made into three dialectical statuses of arguments. Let S be any given argumentation semantics. Then an argument A in a defeat graph D is:

1. *S-justified* if and only if A is labelled *in* in all S-labellings of D
2. *S-overruled* if and only if A is labelled *out* in all S-labellings of D
3. *S-defensible* otherwise.

These statuses can be carried over to conclusions of arguments as follows. A well-formed formula P for which an argument exists in D is:

4. *S-justified* if and only if P is the conclusion of some S-justified argument
5. *S-overruled* if and only if all arguments that have P as conclusion are S-overruled
6. *S-defensible* otherwise.

---

[6] No further meaning should be attached to the terms 'preferred' and 'grounded'. Also, the term 'semantics' is here used in a different way than in deductive logic, where it is used for the meaning of a formal language.

In our example, if S is either grounded or preferred semantics, then all arguments are defensible: in grounded semantics since they all have no label and in preferred semantics since all four arguments are labelled *in* in one preferred labelling and *out* in another preferred labelling.

Finally, what about the relation with the argument game that was sketched in Section 3 for determining the dialectical status of a given argument? It has been shown that this game corresponds to grounded semantics in that the proponent in the game has a winning strategy for a given argument just in case that argument is labelled in in the grounded labelling.

6.3   Labellings versus Positions

More can be said about the positions that can be taken in argumentation. It can be shown that every defeat graph has a unique grounded labelling but (as shown by our example) defeat graphs can have multiple preferred labellings. This makes preferred labellings particularly interesting from a philosophical point of view, since they combine a foundationalist and coherentist view on knowledge. Very briefly, *Foundationalists* argue that something is knowledge if it can be derived (in some sense) from undisputed givens, while coherentists claim that something is knowledge if it is part of an (in some sense) coherent system of cognitions. To see how preferred semantics combines the two views, let us call any set of arguments from a defeat graph a *position*. Then we define a position P as *coherent*[7] if and only if

1. P is conflict-free (i.e., no argument in P defeats an argument in P); and
2. P defends all its members (i.e., all defeaters of a member of P are defeated by a member of P)

In our example, the smallest coherent position is the empty set but this position is, of course, not very interesting. Two more interesting positions are the sets $P1 = \{A,C\}$ and $P2 = \{B,D\}$: both are conflict free (no defeat relations within the sets) while they both defend all their members against defeats from outside: in position $P1$ argument C defends A against B while C defends itself against D; and in position $P2$ argument D defends both B and itself against C. So both $P1$ and $P2$ are coherent. From this it follows that positions $\{C\}$ and $\{D\}$ are also coherent (although

---

[7] Dung (1995) calls sets satisfying these conditions 'admissible'.

not maximally coherent). However, positions {A} and {B} are not coherent: {A} does not defend A against B while {B} does not defend B against C. Furthermore, position {A,D} is incoherent since it does not defend A against B. Finally, any other position is not conflict-free.

The following properties of positions can be proven:

- If position P is coherent, then there exists some labelling of the defeat graph satisfying labelling conditions (1) and (2) (with respect to any semantics) in which all arguments in P are labelled *in*.
- If an argument A is S-justified or S-defensible (according to any given semantics S) then A is included in at least one coherent position.
- If two coherent positions P1 and P2 both only contain arguments that are labelled *in* in the grounded labelling, then their union P1 ∪ P2 is also coherent.

The first two properties state relations between labellings and positions: the first one implies that every coherent position is included in the set of all *in*-arguments of at least one possible labelling. The third property in fact says that grounded semantics does not allow for alternative coherent positions (in the sense that their union is incoherent). By contrast, as our example shows, preferred semantics does allow for alternative positions that are internally coherent but jointly incoherent. Now preferred semantics combines the foundationalist and coherentist views in the following way: any argument must be based on premises taken from the knowledge base, while to be justified or defensible it must be part of a coherent position.

7   Conclusion

To return to our question in the introduction, we have seen that there is indeed logic in defeasible argumentation: the form of arguments must fit a recognised argument scheme (whether deductive or defeasible), and the dialectical status of an argument must be determined in a systematic dialectical testing procedure. On the other hand, what cannot be provided by a logic for argumentation are the standards for comparing conflicting arguments: these are contingent input information, just like the information from which arguments can be constructed.

Let me finally return to Patrick Glenn's suggestion that to make logical sense of the fact that the world contains many different legal (sub) traditions, often inconsistent with each other and interacting in complex ways, new logics may be needed that are multivalent, paraconsistent or non-monotonic and do not adhere to the classic rules of non-contradiction and the excluded middle. In this chapter I have explored the use of one such new kind of logic, namely, logics of argumentation. It turns out that, even if such a logic includes classical two-valued logic as its strict core (the set of strict inference rules for constructing arguments), the resulting logic is (at least) three-valued: each conclusion of an argument has one of the three statuses *justified*, *defensible* or *overruled*. Another way to capture the multiplicity of legal traditions is in the notion of a coherent position discussed in Section 6.3: in general a body of legal information gives rise to multiple *positions*, each internally coherent but mutually conflicting. Argumentation logics are also clearly *non-monotonic*: For example, an argument that is justified on the basis of given information can become defensible or even overruled if new information gives rise to new counterarguments. Argumentation logics are also *paraconsistent*: if two arguments have contradictory conclusions, this does not lead to trivialisation as in classical logic but gives rise to two rebutting arguments; at most one of these arguments can be in the same position but both arguments can be in alternative positions. Finally, argumentation logic *invalidates the law of non-contradiction* in that two statements P and $\neg P$ can both be defensible, and it *invalidates the law of the excluded middle* in that it is not the case that for any statement P, either P or its negation $\neg P$ is justified. In sum, argumentation logics satisfy all the properties that according to Patrick Glenn may be needed to capture the multiplicity of legal traditions.[8] Moreover, argumentation logics are arguably close to how lawyers think, since notions like argument, counterargument and rebuttal are natural them.

References

Dung, P. M. (1995), *On the acceptability of arguments and its fundamental role in nonmonotonic reasoning, logic programming and n-person games*. ARTIFICIAL INTELLIGENCE, 77: 321–357.

Dworkin, R. M. (1977), TAKING RIGHTS SERIOUSLY. Cambridge, MA: Harvard University Press.

Gardner, A. von der Lieth (1987), AN ARTIFICIAL INTELLIGENCE APPROACH TO LEGAL REASONING. Cambridge, MA: MIT Press.

---

[8] Strictly speaking this only holds for argumentation logics that are well-defined but explaining this goes beyond this chapter.

Glenn, H. P. (2010), LEGAL TRADITIONS OF THE WORLD, 4th edn. Oxford: Oxford University Press.

(2013), THE COSMOPOLITAN STATE. Oxford: Oxford University Press.

Prakken, H. (2011), *An overview of formal models of argumentation and their application in philosophy*. STUDIES IN LOGIC 4: 65–86.

(2010), *An abstract framework for argumentation with structured arguments*. ARGUMENT AND COMPUTATION 1: 93–124.

Prakken, H. & Sartor, G. (2009), *A logical analysis of burdens of proof*, in: H. Kaptein, H. Prakken, B. Verheij (eds.), LEGAL EVIDENCE AND PROOF: STATISTICS, STORIES, LOGIC, Aldershot: Ashgate Publishing, p. 223–253.

(2015), *Law and logic: a review from an argumentation perspective*. ARTIFICIAL INTELLIGENCE 227: 214–245.

Walton, D. N., (1996), ARGUMENTATION SCHEMES FOR PRESUMPTIVE REASONING. Mahwah, NJ: Lawrence Erlbaum Associates.

2

Conjunction of Evidence and Multivalent Logic

1 Introduction

Nonclassical logic offers promise of a less conflictual and more conciliatory approach to legal problems than the dichotomia of classical logic provides. Nonclassical recognition of the vagueness of legal concepts and of the reality that not all propositions are either completely right or completely wrong would indeed seem a step forward. The late H. Patrick Glenn argued that these theoretical insights could bridge the gaps between the world's divergent legal traditions.[1] He further argued that nonclassical logic already works to reconcile the seemingly inconsistent legal elements within a particular tradition.[2] I want to go a bit further to argue that nonclassical logic, and multivalent logic in particular, is necessary to understanding and performing legal factfinding.

Probability theory gauges the odds of a proposition being either completely true or completely false. Our mentality's instinctive acceptance of this classical bivalence, in preference to employing multivalent logic, plays a problematic role in the law. A prime illustration lies in the law's infamous conjunction paradox. Consider how the best-known statement of that paradox assumes the applicability of probability's product rule:

---

* I thank Larry Alexander, Adrienne Clermont, Oskar Liivack, and Don Mathias for helpful comments. I draw part of my argument from Kevin M. Clermont, STANDARDS OF DECISION IN LAW: PSYCHOLOGICAL AND LOGICAL BASES FOR THE STANDARD OF PROOF, HERE AND ABROAD (2013), which more fully documents the subject and broadens its reach considerably. This essay addresses the most disputed point in the book's general theory.

[1] See H. Patrick Glenn, LEGAL TRADITIONS OF THE WORLD 361–385 (5th edn 2014). But cf. Graham Priest, *Where Laws Conflict: An Application of the Method of Chunk and Permeate*, in LAW AND THE NEW LOGICS 168 (H. Patrick Glenn & Lionel D. Smith eds., 2016) (reading Glenn to embrace only multivalent logic and arguing that a paraconsistent, modal logic would perform better).

[2] See GLENN, *supra* note 1, at 372–373, 379–385.

We purport to decide civil cases according to a more-probable-than-not standard of proof. We would expect this standard to take into account the rule of conjunction, which states that the probability of two independent events occurring together is the product of the probability of each event occurring separately. The rule of conjunction dictates that in a case comprised of two independent elements the plaintiff must prove each element to a much greater degree than 50%: only then will the plaintiff have shown that the probability that the two elements occurred together exceeds 50%. Suppose, for example, that a plaintiff must prove both causation and fault and that these two elements are independent. If the plaintiff shows that causation is 60% probable and fault is 60% probable, then he apparently would have failed to satisfy the civil standard of proof because the probability that the defendant *both* acted negligently and caused injury is only 36%.

In our legal system, however, jurors do not consider whether it is more probable than not that all elements occurred in conjunction. Judges instruct jurors to decide civil cases element by element, with each element decided on a more-probable-than-not basis. Once jurors have decided that an element is probable, they are to consider the element established, repress any remaining doubts about it, and proceed to consider the next element. If the plaintiff proves each element by a preponderance of the evidence, the jury will find in his favor. . . . Thus, jurors may find a defendant liable even if it is highly unlikely that he acted negligently, that is, the conjoined probability of the elements is much less than 50%. In such cases, the verdict fails to reflect a probable account of what happened and thus fails to minimize the cost of judicial errors. . . .

. . ..

. . . Although courts direct juries to consider and decide each element seriatim, juries do not consider each item of evidence seriatim when deciding whether a given element is proved. The jury must decide each element by looking at all of the evidence bearing on proof of that element. Thus, although the jury does not assess the conjunction of the elements of a case, it does decide each element by assessing the conjunction of the evidence for it.[3]

---

[3] Charles Nesson, *The Evidence or the Event? On Judicial Proof and the Acceptability of Verdicts*, 98 HARV. L. REV. 1357, 1385–1388 (1985) (footnotes omitted). Professor Nesson saw the paradox as illustrating his broad thesis that the law's process of proof aims at generating acceptable statements about past events and thus at projecting behavioral norms to the public, rather than at reaching probable conclusions in a search for truth:

> Application of the more-probable-than-not test to each element produces the most acceptable conclusion as to that element. The conjunction of these conclusions constitutes a story that is more probable than any other story about the same elements. Suppose, for example, that the elements of a story are A and B, and A (70%) is more probable than not-A (30%), and B (60%) is more probable than not-B (40%). The conjunction (A & B) (42%) may not

The implications are profound but boggling. Allowing recovery on a 36% showing of causation *and* fault seems not only unfair but inefficient. How embarrassing for the law! Going beyond embarrassment, though, the conjunction paradox undermines one of civil procedure's most fundamental principles: where possible, the parties should receive equal treatment. Yet, refusing to multiply probabilities would seem to disadvantage defendants.

For another boggle, ponder the apparent criticality of how exactly the ancients (and moderns) divided our causes of action (and defenses) into elements: the more subdivisions, the lower the conjunctive probability that would suffice for victory.[4] And yet: "Anyone who has ever litigated a real case knows the exact opposite of the conjunction paradox is true: the more disputed elements the plaintiff has to prove, the *less* likely the plaintiff is to prevail [because] the jury will find at least one element to be less likely than not."[5]

Many clever legal academics over the last century also have lamented that the law illogically ignores the product rule for conjunction or have tried to explain away the legal practice.[6] Few have questioned their assumption that ignoring the product rule is illogical. I do.

be more probable than its negation (not-(*A* & *B*)) (58%). But the conjunction (*A* & *B*) (42%) is more probable than any other version: (*A* & (not-*B*)) (28%), ((not-*A*) & *B*) (18%), or ((not-*A*) & (not-*B*)) (12%). The application of the more-probable-than-not standard of proof on an element-by-element basis will produce the single most probable story.

    Ibid. at 1389–90 (footnotes omitted).

[4] *See* James A. Henderson, Jr., Fred Bertram & Michael J. Tőke, *Optimal Issue Separation in Modern Products Liability Litigation*, 73 Tex. L. Rev. 1653, 1655–1659, 1667–1675 (1995).

[5] David A. Moran, *Jury Uncertainty, Elemental Independence and the Conjunction Paradox: A Response to Allen and Jehl*, 2003 Mich. St. L. Rev. 945, 946–947, 950; *see* Jef De Mot & Alex Stein, *Talking Points*, 2015 U. Ill. L. Rev. 1259 (arguing that repetitive chance of error by the factfinder on multiple findings unavoidably disadvantages plaintiffs).

[6] An early rendition of the paradox lies in the innovative Jerome Michael & Mortimer J. Adler, The Nature of Judicial Proof 140–143 (1931) (also identifying preponderance with the >0.5 standard for the first time, according to John Leubsdorf, *The Surprising History of the Preponderance Standard of Civil Proof*, 67 Fla. L. Rev. 1569, 1579 n.45 (2015)). More recent scholars reflexively invoke the paradox. *E.g.*, Dale A. Nance, The Burdens of Proof 74–78 (2016); Ronald J. Allen & Sarah A. Jehl, *Burdens of Persuasion in Civil Cases: Algorithms v. Explanations*, 2003 Mich. St. L. Rev. 893; Alon Harel & Ariel Porat, *Aggregating Probabilities Across Cases: Criminal Responsibility for Unspecified Offenses*, 94 Minn. L. Rev. 261 (2009); Jason Iuliano, Essay, *Jury Voting Paradoxes*, 113 Mich. L. Rev. 405 (2014); Jonathan J. Koehler & John B. Meixner, *Decision Making and the Law: Truth Barriers*, in 2 The Wiley-Blackwell Handbook of Judgment and Decision Making 749 (Gideon Keren & George Wu eds., 2015); Michael S. Pardo, *Group*

I see the general problem as how to deal with a *partial truth* about the *real world* that will persist unavoidably in *factfinding*.[7] First, by "partial truth" I do not mean the odds of something being eventually revealed to be an absolute truth, but rather I mean a belief that expresses a degree of certainty about the state of the real world represented by the evidence and that lies somewhere between holding the thing completely false and holding it completely true. Second, the "real world" is the world as perceived by humans and described by natural language. Third, I refer to "factfinding" in its broad sense, as covering anything that a court or other entity subjects to a proof process in order to establish what the entity will treat as truth. It would include application of law to fact, as well as pure fact. And it would extend far beyond the courtroom, say, to factfinding by historians as they construct a believed narrative of the French Revolution by resolving the issues they choose to resolve.[8]

I address the problem in three steps. The initial step is recognition that classical logic cannot treat partial truths, because it assumes all facts are either completely false or completely true. It consequently has no tool for combining partial truths. Factfinders need such a tool.

In the next step comes realization that multivalent logic developed to handle partial truths. Multivalent logic offers factfinders a way forward, a way to deal with things that will forever be uncertainly stuck partway between false and true. I establish that deciding how to proceed in a world of persisting uncertainty (including how to combine uncertainties) logically differs from predicting how uncertainty will resolve itself into certainty (including how to calculate the chance of multiple events occurring together). I then uncover signs that the law intuitively but appropriately employs multivalent logic for its factfinding.

Finally this essay will be ready to show how the law uses multivalent logic to resolve the conjunction paradox. To repeat, my basic argument is that *estimated probabilities* mathematically differ from *partial truths*: a betting question of how likely two fleetingly glimpsed cards will turn out to be both black is fundamentally different from the law's question of

Agency and Legal Proof; or, Why the Jury Is an "It," 56 Wm. & Mary L. Rev. 1793 (2015); Ariel Porat & Eric A. Posner, *Aggregation and Law*, 122 Yale L.J. 2 (2012). For a dismantling of the related aggregation paradox, see Kevin M. Clermont, *Aggregation of Probabilities and Illogic*, 47 Ga. L. Rev. 165 (2012).

[7] *See* D. Michael Risinger, *Searching for Truth in the American Law of Evidence and Proof*, 47 Ga. L. Rev. 801 (2013) (treating the necessary philosophical assumptions).

[8] *See* Giorgio Resta & Vincenzo Zeno-Zencovich, *Judicial "Truth" and Historical "Truth": The Case of the Ardeatine Caves Massacre*, 31 Law & Hist. Rev. 843 (2013).

whether both fact *A* and fact *B* occurred given that we will never learn the facts with certainty but we believe each fact more likely than not occurred. Even though classical logic can tell us that the smart bet is against two black cards being turned up, it cannot handle the second question. Only multivalent logic can show that the conjunction of partially proved fact *A* and fact *B* is more likely than all other stories combined. First, its critical contribution is not to picture, say, 60 cases of *A* and 40 cases of not-*A*, but to picture a single case of 0.60 *A* that will serve as a basis for making decisions – and likewise for *B*. The output of combined evidence should be another partial truth, not the odds of absolute truth if somehow knowable. Second, because of imperfect evidence, the partial beliefs in *A* and *B* do not imply any complementary belief in not-*A* or not-*B*. Logic then tells us to combine the partial beliefs by linking them together without discounting for the nonproven contradictions, so that the smart belief lies in the story of both *A and B* having occurred.

To resummarize the three steps, Section 2 introduces logic systems, as illustrated by classical logic. Section 3 will lay out multivalent logic, explaining why it is an effective way to express likelihood in factfinding. Section 4 will finally explain how using multivalent logic to conjoin likelihoods dissipates the law's conjunction paradox.

2   Logic Systems

The way a logician begins to work is to assume a basic representation of the world, then specify a small group of operators that suffices to generate an internally sound and complete logic system, and finally test the system to see if it makes sense of our world and hence can be useful. Logic is therefore more of an art, around the edges, than the laity would guess.

2.1   Assumptions

One must begin with "genuine logical truths," or basic assumptions about the world. For our purposes, the key assumption of classical logic is that every proposition must either be true or be false, an assumption called the principle of bivalence.[9]

The point of this essay will be that this key assumption, rather hidden from view, has a huge impact on a very practical problem that the law must confront: conjoining evidence. We are commonly unaware of the assumptions on which our reasoning rests, to say nothing of their effects.

---

[9] *See* Theodore Sider, LOGIC FOR PHILOSOPHY 2, 72–3 (2010).

So, uncovering the impact of classical logic's encoding facts in binary form, rather than as partial truths, is no easy task.

Because the impact derives from an underlying assumption, this essay will not involve merely pointing out some obviously mistaken logical step. Understanding the impact will necessarily be the more subtle endeavor of tracing the misleading effects of an implicit assumption. Yet acknowledging this subtlety should at least restrain the reader from dismissing my argument out of hand, as by saying that common sense obviously dictates multiplying probabilities.

2.2   Operators

One constructs any system of logic by stipulating a small but adequate number of logical operators, such as set theory's intersection (or propositional logic's conjunction or ∧ or AND), union (or disjunction or ∨ or OR), and negation (or ~ or ¬ or NOT).[10]

Classical logic's bivalent system, which recognizes only the two values of true and false, stipulates the following functions for conjunction and disjunction:

truth(x AND y) = 1 if both x and y are true, but 0 otherwise

truth(x OR y) = 1 if either x or y is true, but 0 otherwise

Another way to state these two functions is this:

truth(x AND y) = minimum(truth(x), truth(y))

truth(x OR y) = maximum(truth(x), truth(y))

A different format in which to stipulate an operator is by truth table. The one for negation indicates that the negative of 1 is 0, and vice versa:

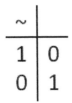

Those three operators generate an internally sound system. All things bivalently logical then flow from them.

---

[10] *See* ibid. at 25, 35–7, 67–80.

2.3   Testing

One can generate a logic system from any adequate group of operators. It
will be internally sound on a formal level, but it will not be useful unless
the operators make sense in our world as we understand it. What makes
sense translates into the philosophical question of whether their results
constitute "genuine logical consequences." But philosophers have to punt
on this question, saying that operators make sense if their consequences
appear to make sense to us.[11]

There are many signs that classical logic makes a lot of sense. For
example, it plays nicely with traditional probability theory. This mathematical tool supplements classical logic, allowing it to account for random
uncertainty. Frequentist probability can express the chance of whether a
repetitive event will occur this particular time, all the while assuming it
will occur or not occur on an all-or-nothing basis. First, the likelihood of
an event implies the complementary likelihood of its nonoccurrence.
Betting odds, like 60/40, carry that implication, because under the bivalent assumption whatever turns out to be not true will be false. Second,
for the conjunction of bivalent events, probability's product rule makes
sense too.

Some people assert that probability cannot handle one-time events.
However, subjective probability theory allows classical logic to speak of
the likelihood of a single event. A subjective probability measures an
individual's personal judgment, grounded on the evidence, about how
likely the particular event is to occur or has occurred. The theory is

> "based on the notion that it makes sense to ask someone what he would
> do if offered a reward for guessing correctly whether any proposition,
> designated X, is true or false. If he guesses that X is true under these
> circumstances, we say that *for him* the subjective probability of X, written
> $P(X)$, exceeds fifty percent. Symbolically, $P(X) > .5$. If he would be equally
> satisfied guessing either way, then we say that, for him, $P(X) = .5$."[12]

Upon expanding the measure into a complete scale of probabilities
from 0 to 1 and postulating the usual assumptions and logical operators,
subjective probabilities follow most of the rules of frequentist
probabilities.

[11] *See* ibid. at 1–2, 6–11.
[12] Laurence H. Tribe, *Trial by Mathematics: Precision and Ritual in the Legal Process*, 84
HARV. L. REV. 1329, 1347 (1971) (citing the innovative work of Leonard J. Savage, FOUN-
DATIONS OF STATISTICS (1954)); *see* Steven G. Vick, DEGREES OF BELIEF 1–54 (2002).

Classical logic will break down, nonetheless, when the principle of bivalence no longer holds – as in the task of factfinding. The process of proof investigates a world that is not a two-valued world where disputed facts are either true or false. Instead, a good portion but not all of the real world is a vague, imprecise, or many-valued world, where partial truths exist. Or, we might never know whether a disputed fact is certainly true or false, so that any absolute truth remains inaccessible to factfinders' minds. Therefore, humans can accurately represent certain things in the world, such as historical fact, only as partial truths.

Factfinders might properly find that Tom was a 0.60 tortfeasor, but not that a 60% chance exists that, when they somehow unearth the truth, he was certainly a tortfeasor. That is, the law should concern itself with partial truth, a degree of truth the factfinders construct in a world of varied uncertainty. Versions of nonclassical logic can handle this measure.

3   Nonclassical Logic

Nonclassical logic looks and sounds much like standard logic, but has altered some classical assumptions. Most commonly, new versions of logic reject the assumption of bivalence. These multivalent systems are the versions of special interest to lawyers.

If propositions are not bivalent, so that both x and not-x can be true and false to a degree, then one can show that sometimes x equals not-x, which is a rather disquieting contradiction. Fashioning multivalent logic thus faced some challenges.

The first move in developing this new logic built on the branch of modern philosophy, beginning with Bertrand Russell's work, that had struggled with the problem of vagueness.[13] Work on vagueness addresses matters such as the famed sorites paradox of ancient Greece ("sorites" comes from the Greek word for heap):

---

[13] Bertrand Russell, *Vagueness*, 1 AUSTRALASIAN J. PSYCHOL. & PHIL. 84 (1923); *see* Bertrand Russell, *The Philosophy of Logical Atomism, in* LOGIC AND KNOWLEDGE 175, 180 (Robert Charles Marsh ed., 1956) ("Everything is vague to a degree you do not realize till you have tried to make it precise, and everything precise is so remote from everything that we normally think, that you cannot for a moment suppose that is what we really mean when we say what we think.").

- Premise 1: if you start with a billion grains of sand, you have a heap of sand.
- Premise 2: if you remove a single grain, you still have a heap.
- If you repeat the removal again and again until you have one grain of sand left, then you will by logic still have a heap. But there is no heap. Thus, heap equals non-heap.

Two true premises appear to yield an absurd conclusion. At some point the heap undeniably became a non-heap. Was there a fixed boundary? No, this is not a way out, at least according to most philosophers.

A different path taken in the attempt to avoid the sorites paradox led to the embrace of many-valued logic.[14] This multivalent form of logic boldly declines the simplification offered by two-valued, or bivalent, logic built on a foundation of true/false with an excluded middle. It instead recognizes partial truths. Both a proposition and its opposite can be true to a degree. In other words, sometimes you have neither a heap nor a non-heap, but something that falls in between, with the proposition "this is a heap" being both true and not true.

Multivalent logic may be new, but it has an extended history of forerunners. Threads of it have troubled thinkers since before Aristotle embraced bivalence. Multivalent logic has enjoyed a recent flowering, perhaps inspired by the development of quantum mechanics.[15]

One particular bloom known as fuzzy logic finds its roots in the seminal 1965 article by Berkeley Professor Lotfi Zadeh.[16] His critical contribution was to use degrees of membership in a *fuzzy* set running from 0 to 1, in place of classically strict membership in a *crisp* set classified as no/yes. Yet fuzzy logic is not at all a fuzzy idea. It became a formal system of logic, one that is by now highly developed and hence rather rarefied.[17]

---

[14] See generally J. C. Beall & Bas C. van Fraassen, POSSIBILITIES AND PARADOX: AN INTRODUCTION TO MODAL AND MANY-VALUED LOGIC (2003); R. M. Sainsbury, PARA-DOXES 56–63 (3rd ed. 2009).

[15] See Grzegorz Malinowski, Many-Valued Logic and Its Philosophy, in 8 HANDBOOK OF THE HISTORY OF LOGIC 13 (2007).

[16] L.A. Zadeh, Fuzzy Sets, 8 INFO. & CONTROL 338 (1965); see Didier Dubois, Francesc Esteva, Lluís Godo & Henri Prade, Fuzzy-Set Based Logics—An History-oriented Presentation of Their Main Developments, in 8 HANDBOOK OF THE HISTORY OF LOGIC 325, 432 (2007).

[17] See Petr Hajek, Fuzzy Logic, in THE STANFORD ENCYCLOPEDIA OF PHILOSOPHY (Edward N. Zalta ed., 2010), available at http://plato.stanford.edu/archives/fall2010/entries/logic-fuzzy/ (discussing also the varying versions of fuzzy logic).

I do not mean to suggest that fuzzy logic resolves the sorites paradox or all the other philosophical problems of vagueness (or that it is especially popular with philosophers). I am suggesting that fuzzy logic is a very useful tool for some purposes. Of course, it has become so well-known and dominant outside the philosophy department because of its countless practical applications, especially in consumer electronics. But its theory is wonderfully broad, extending easily to assessing likelihood. Indeed, of the various nonclassical models for handling uncertainty, fuzzy logic seems to capture best the kinds of uncertainty that have generated the conjunction paradox.[18]

3.1 Fuzzy Logic's Basics

Fuzzy logic measures element x's degree of membership in a particular fuzzy set. The degree may take any value throughout the whole interval $[0,1]$, rather than just the value of 0 or 1. This range allows a more complete and accurate expression of membership, when membership is imprecise.

Take as an example the set A of men from five to seven feet tall. This would be a crisp set. Membership of x in A, represented by $\chi_A(x)$, is not vague. The values of χ_A can be only 0 or 1, at least if we ignore complications at the nanoscale level.

Contrast the set H of men somewhere near six feet tall. It is a fuzzy set. Membership of x in H, represented by $\mu_H(x)$, is imprecise. The values of μ_H may start at 0 for a tiny person, but they soon increase by some function to a value of 1 at precisely six feet, and then start decreasing. The membership function could be linear, but it can take on any shape.

So shortish Tom Cruise might be completely in set A but have a degree of membership in set H of 0.5. The following figure represents these two sets, with (a) representing the crisp set of men from five to seven feet tall and (b) being one representation of the fuzzy set of men somewhere near six feet tall:[19]

---

[18] *See* Liu Sifeng, Jeffrey Forrest & Yang Yingjie, *A Brief Introduction to Grey Systems Theory*, *in* 2011 IEEE INTERNATIONAL CONFERENCE ON GREY SYSTEMS AND INTELLIGENT SERVICES 1, 6 (2011).

[19] The figure comes from Timothy J. Ross & W. Jerry Parkinson, *Fuzzy Set Theory, Fuzzy Logic, and Fuzzy Systems*, *in* FUZZY LOGIC AND PROBABILITY APPLICATIONS 29, 30 (Timothy J. Ross et al. eds., 2002).

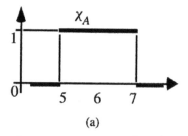 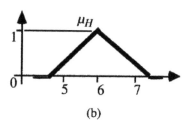

(a)   (b)

Important to note is the role of qualifying language in the prior example as a means of expressing membership. *Evaluative linguistic expressions* are words like small, medium, and big; another example is about, roughly, or near, when used in contrast to not-at-all or really. These words may not be a large part of our natural language. Yet, they are a very important part. They do a lot of work. People use them all the time to evaluate a thing or situation, to communicate their evaluation, and thereafter to perform classification, decisionmaking, and other tasks.

People employ *linguistic hedges* to modify their evaluations further. Words such as very or extremely, and fairly or almost, are examples. Obviously, these distinctions are imprecise. But they are supposed to be imprecise, and they work quite well in real life. These words allow people to create and share a gradated scale for their evaluations. Research suggests that such verbal categories can work better than numerical translations.[20]

Whether by words or numbers, fuzzy logic better comports to our view of the real world than does classical bivalent logic. In the real world, boundaries of things often appear indistinct, thus making important or even essential the human ability to process fuzzy information.

3.2   Fuzziness Versus Traditional Probability as a Means of Expressing Likelihood

The new logic especially illuminates the way for people to express their view of evidence in connection with applying a standard of proof.[21]

---

[20] *See, e.g.,* Alf C. Zimmer, *Verbal vs. Numerical Processing of Subjective Probabilities, in* DECISION MAKING UNDER UNCERTAINTY 159, 180 (Roland W. Scholz ed., 1983).

[21] My interest in this essay is not so much the factfinders' initial processing of evidence, but rather the subsequent steps that enable a standard of proof's application to assessed evidence. Application of a standard of proof is a step largely separable from evidential argument. *See* CLERMONT, *supra* note *, at 123–9. Although psychologists can tell us something about how humans process evidence, they have contributed almost nothing on how humans would apply standards of proof, leaving the dispute to logicians so far.

I therefore propose considering a broad version of fuzzy logic as the legal model for human expression of likelihood, in preference to assuming a probability-based bivalent view.[22]

A few anticipatory words of qualification are in order. I am not an anti-probabilist. I am not arguing against a probabilistic approach if "probabilistic" carries its capacious sense of accepting uncertainty and mathematically accounting for it. I am arguing against traditional probability theory as appended to a bivalent view of the world. What I am proposing is a nontraditional means for expressing uncertainty in a way that accounts for vagueness.

Describing different uncertainties. Both a traditionally probabilistic description and a fuzzy one can be accurate statements, but they describe different states. The key distinction is that traditional probability depends on the existence of a crisply bivalent world in which the decisionmaker must commit all belief to two possible outcomes, while fuzzy logic accepts an imprecisely multivalent world in which the decisionmaker could retain uncommitted belief.

On the one hand, probability is a way to describe *occurrence odds.* It can measure the chance that the event will occur, or has occurred. On the other hand, fuzziness is a way, for example, to describe *event precision.* It measures what occurs – actually, the degree to which the event occurs – which can be vague. For an illustration of occurrence odds, an act might be completely blameworthy, but there was only a 60% probability of the act's commission. For an illustration of event imprecision, the act might instead have been only 0.70 blameworthy.

Probability is a mathematical supplement used to account for that one kind of uncertainty regarding whether an event will occur or has occurred in a bivalent world. In contrast, fuzziness can measure as well

---

Fortunately, fuzzy logic is compatible with any method used initially to process pieces of evidence that reinforce or undermine each other. For example, it would accept factfinders' using intuitive techniques in a nonquantitative and approximate fashion to evaluate and combine evidence on a factual element, as they pursue the abductive task of seeking truth while they interlace inductive premises and perform deductive testing of interim conclusions. *See* Edmund M. Morgan, *Introduction to Evidence, in* Austin W. Scott & Sidney P. Simpson, CASES AND OTHER MATERIALS ON CIVIL PROCEDURE 941, 943–945 (1950).

[22] *See* Vilém Novák, *Modeling with Words,* www.scholarpedia.org/article/Modeling_with_words (2008) ("Mathematical fuzzy logic has two branches: fuzzy logic *in narrow sense* (FLn) and fuzzy logic *in broader sense* (FLb). FLn is a formal fuzzy logic which is a special many-valued logic generalizing classical mathematical logic.... FLb is an extension of FLn which aims at developing a *formal theory of human reasoning.*").

the uncertainty of vagueness. An additional advantage lies in that fuzziness is not a supplement. By expressing uncertainty as a degree of membership, it builds its inclusive measure of uncertainty right into the basics of the fuzzy logic system.

Here is another contrast. Probability conveys what we believe, when in possession of only partial information, about whether an event will occur or has occurred. With more information, the uncertainty in the probability will lessen, and when the event's occurrence becomes known the probability will morph into a value of 1 or 0. In contrast, fuzziness can convey all the information we will ever have about an event, which ends up expressed as a partial truth. Indeed, if we were to acquire more information about the situation, it would usually increase the fuzziness of set membership, because any crisp lines would become harder to maintain. That is, as one acquires more information about the world, one perceives a greater need to measure fuzziness in lieu of bivalent categorization.

The reader might see the distinction I am drawing as being between future events and past facts. But that is only a partial differentiation. Probabilism and fuzziness can each handle both future and past events. A more complete differentiation would be between the expected outcome upon revelation and the degree to which an event appears to occur.

Yet, probabilism and fuzziness can describe much more than events. So, a better distinction is between crisp and fuzzy sets, regardless of whether the sets consist of events, characteristics, or other things. Maybe another example would help to show the range. If a classical probabilist says, "There is a 30% chance that Tom is tall," the speaker supposes that Tom is either tall or not tall, and on the available evidence he thinks that it is only 30% likely that Tom would end up in the tall category upon accurate measurement. But when a fuzzy logician says, "Tom's degree of membership within the set of tall men is .30," the speaker means that Tom is not very tall at all. Both can be accurate and informative statements. But the difference between them is real and considerable. It derives from the fact that the classical probabilist is assuming bivalence, so that one is tall or not, while the fuzzy logician is speaking of a world where one can be more or less tall.

Fuzzy logic extends easily to degrees of truth. Envisage the fuzzy set of true facts. For a particular proposition, one can assess one's belief in its degree of membership in that set, express the belief in words drawn from a gradated scale of likelihood, and then act upon the result. Here is a coarsely gradated scale that utilizes natural language and captures imprecision in beliefs better than speaking in terms of decimals: (1) slightest possibility, (2) reasonable possibility, (3) substantial possibility, (4) equipoise, (5) probability, (6) high probability, and (7) almost certainty. The fuzzy logical system can thereby adapt itself to imaging belief in external truth in the way the law does.

Bases for choosing between models. Probabilism and fuzziness are not fully interchangeable, even though people tend to treat them so. People use probability loosely for any sort of uncertainty. They use it to express fuzziness, but it is inappropriate for that purpose.

The choice between probabilism and fuzziness is important. The kind of statement one can make will depend on the choice made. "You paint one picture of the world if you say there is a 50% chance that an apple sits in the refrigerator. You paint a different picture if you say half an apple sits in the refrigerator."[23]

Which model to use, traditional probability or fuzzy logic, therefore depends on what one is trying to describe.[24] If the fact in question is or is assumed to be nonvague, and thus readily distinguishable from its opposite, and its expected occurrence is subject only to random uncertainty, then probability might be appropriate because of its simplicity. For a probability example: will I pick a black ball from the urn? However, if the fact is vague, and most facts in the world are vague, fuzzy logic is the way to go. For a fuzzy example: how black is this grayish ball?

I am coming to the choice the law has made. But at this point, it is natural for the reader to jump to the conclusion that the law in its factfinding usually wants to know if an apple is in the refrigerator, not whether it is half eaten. The court wants to know if Tom was or was not the alleged perpetrator. Just to slow the reader up, however, I point out that in legal factfinding no one is ever going to be able to look inside the refrigerator. Also, I can pose another example that makes it much less clear which sort of statement the law usually seeks. Think of a somewhat sloppily drawn circle: is it more appropriate to say (i) there is a 90% probability that it is a perfect circle or (ii) it has a 0.90 membership in the set of circles?[25] An analogy to the circle would be the law's trying to

---

[23] Bart Kosko, FUZZY THINKING: THE NEW SCIENCE OF FUZZY LOGIC 15 (1993).

[24] *See* Mark Colyvan, *Is Probability the Only Coherent Approach to Uncertainty?*, 28 RISK ANALYSIS 645 (2008); Bart Kosko, *Fuzziness vs. Probability*, 17 INT'L J. GEN. SYS. 211 (1990).

[25] *See* KOSKO, *supra* note 23, at 44–46 (using this image).

determine fault, when degrees of fault are the reality. But also analogous would be causation, coercion, consent, good faith, intent, and a host of other legal issues. After all, Bertrand Russell saw all of natural language as vague. Many, many legal issues are fuzzy concepts, in that they draw indistinct lines, most often unavoidably – and many of these fuzzy concepts are subjects of proof through litigation.[26]

So, the important choice between probabilism and fuzziness seems a difficult one. Bearing on the bases for that choice, however, five advantages of fuzzy logic deserve consideration. They carry the day in all but the simplest situations.

First, fuzzy logic is more accurate than probability whenever one encounters uncertainty other than random occurrence uncertainty. The world exhibits multiple kinds of uncertainty, including the uncertainty characterized as vagueness and also the indeterminacy resulting from scarce information or conflicting evidence. Fuzzy logic picks up the extra information about all these uncertainties, extra information often expressed in natural language. Probability has the advantage of bivalent simplicity, but it will often be misleading in the real world of fuzziness.[27]

Second, another advantage of fuzzy logic is that it is the more inclusive system. Many-valued logic subsumes two-valued logic. The two-valued logic of probability demands the existence of sets with strict membership classifications, an in-or-out characteristic symbolized respectively by values of either 1 or 0. But fuzzy logic, as a form of many-valued logic, neither requires nor forbids that anything be of an on-or-off nature, true or false, completely inside a set or outside that set. So crisp sets are one kind among all fuzzy sets. Classical logic is a special case of multivalent logic. The world of black or white is merely an extreme case of all worlds shaded in grays. Therefore, fuzzy logic can handle crisp sets.

---

[26] *See* LeRoy Fibre Co. v. Chi., Milwaukee & St. Paul Ry. Co., 232 U.S. 340, 354 (1914) (Holmes, J., concurring partially) ("I do not think we need trouble ourselves with the thought that my view depends upon differences of degree. The whole law does so as soon as it is civilized.").

[27] *See* Kosko, *supra* note 23, at 25–26 ("The question is not whether the glass is half empty or half full. If we had to say all or none, the question is, is the glass full or empty. [Either answer is a half-truth.] That is the real state of the world. We don't mean that there is a 50% probability that the glass is full. We mean half a glass. If for some cultural reason we limit what we say to the two bivalent options of all or none, true or false, yes or no, then we pay the price...."); ibid. at 33 ("At the midpoint you cannot tell a thing from its opposite, just as you cannot tell a half-empty glass from a half-full glass.").

Third, in many situations, a single fact is subject both to occurrence odds and to event imprecision. Although traditional probability theory can say little on how to reason about things that are in any way not completely true or false, fuzzy logic can handle the more mixed and complex situations. Returning to the prior example of occurrence odds, an act might be completely blameworthy, but there was only a 60% chance of the act's commission. Regarding event imprecision, it might be that the act was only 0.70 blameworthy. What about a 60% chance of a 0.70 degree of blameworthiness? Then, these two kinds of uncertainty need to be integrated. Fuzzy logic provides the needed common currency.

Fourth, a decision may rest on a number of facts, some of which demonstrate only occurrence odds, while others show some event imprecision as well. Any need in decisionmaking to combine these factfindings counsels the use of one logic system, because we cannot coherently countenance two different kinds of degree of belief.[28] Fuzzy logic can effortlessly express even a traditional probability as membership in a set, that is, it can represent probability as the degree to which the imagined trials of an experiment would belong to the set of positive results. This capability allows easy combination of a randomly uncertain measure with a vaguely imprecise measure, in accordance with fuzzy logical operators. So again, fuzzy logic provides the needed common currency, and classical logic does not.

Fifth, and most importantly, most facts that look to involve only occurrence odds are more complicated than they appear. Most factfindings are not predicting the discovery of absolute truth, but instead estimating a partial truth with which to live. A 60% chance of an act's occurrence, when we have no way of discovering the absolute truth about the one-shot past event, is epistemically indistinguishable from a 0.60 blameworthy act. Both are constructed measures of an individual's judgment, based on the evidence available, about how likely a particular proposition is to be true. Each represents not a chance, but a degree of truth.

---

[28] *See* Nicholas J. J. Smith, *Degree of Belief Is Expected Truth Value, in* CUTS AND CLOUDS: VAGUENESS, ITS NATURE, AND ITS LOGIC 491, 494 (Richard Dietz & Sebastiano Moruzzi eds., 2010) (cataloging the difficulties that would come from entertaining both probabilities and degrees of belief, when the two underlying logic systems employ different operators; and in particular contending that "uncertainty-based degrees of belief and vagueness-based degrees of belief" must be treated as equivalents).

In sum, the flexibility of fuzzy logic suggests its use for every kind of fact and for combining evaluations of different facts. It handles facts exhibiting multiple kinds of uncertainty, and not only factual events but also categorical constructs. Fuzziness can handle all the kinds of facts subject to proof.

3.3   The Law's Choice

My primary concern in this essay is to unearth the logic that the law employs when it actually tells its factfinders what to do. I submit that the law treats all measures of truth simply as fuzzy sets. In its instructions to factfinders, the law does not distinguish when to use probabilism from when to use fuzziness. It speaks in terms of a common currency, mixing the questions of whether and how much an event occurred. Regardless of the nature of the issue, the standard of proof deals only in degrees of truth.

Another reason to suppose that the law speaks in fuzzy terms of degrees of membership is that it would be wise to do so. Degrees of truth behave more appropriately than probabilities in a world filled with various kinds of uncertainty. Asking for a single measure of uncertainty for occurrence and blameworthiness of an act makes sense in fuzzy logic. Relying instead on the mathematical supplement of the probability calculus would be so awkward and incomplete as to destroy sense.

To be more specific, all five of fuzziness's advantages are in play on the kinds of issues confronting the law. Imagine that the law is trying to determine if Tom was at fault. Ours is not a crisp world, so the law is often not interested in establishing that the truth value of an element is a 1 or a 0. Instead, it wants to ascertain whether the element has a sufficient truth value for the purpose at hand.[29] Indeed, in Tom's case we shall never know the answer as a 1 or a 0. Therefore, we should not be worrying too much about specifying the chance of a 1 turning up. Moreover, the factfinder might entertain thoughts of both randomness and vagueness, for example, both a sense that Tom was 0.60 likely to be the person who acted and also that the actor was at fault to a 0.70 degree. Given that some issues in a case might demand the more inclusive measure of imprecision,

---

[29]   Of course, we would worry about the fuzzy measure being closer to 1 for criminal liability, where the "sufficient" truth value is more demanding than in civil cases. The nature of the different standards of proof is the subject of my book. On the criminal standard, see CLERMONT, *supra* note *, at 26–31, 213.

coherency requires that a single inclusive measure apply to every issue. Therefore, fuzzy logic is the logical answer.

By calling for recognition that the law has chosen fuzzy logic, which I do in the hope of making many legal practices easier to comprehend, I am not calling for a major shift in conceiving the standards of proof. After all, fuzzy logic is not antithetical to classical logic. Fuzzy logic is more general, and it moves its measure of uncertainties into the basics of the system, rather than leaving their treatment to some sort of mathematical afterthought. All I am saying is that the law appreciates that more kinds of uncertainty than occurrence odds are at play. The law therefore uses a logic appropriate to the task.

My nonradical move does not even call for an overhaul of legal language or imagery. I am not saying that if we recognize the role of multivalence, we need to abandon the probability idiom. The idiom can be quite expressive in the realm of standards of proof, as it roughly communicates the odds of a fact being true. Nonetheless, when plunging to the depths, we need always to remember that the legal foundation is ultimately fuzzy in nature. Traditional probability's problems at the depths appear most obviously upon trying to conjoin facts.

4   Dysfunction of Conjunction

We are all so used to employing classical logic that it becomes a huge challenge to think in terms of multivalent logic's partial truths. Switching logical systems requires an act of will and self-control. But certain problems, like conjunction, demand the use of multivalent logic.

Let me begin with an image that is intended to shake up the usual pattern of thinking. Think of a series of three posters in varying degrees of gray, affixed side by side. Say that they are 0.80, 0.60, and 0.70 black, respectively. When you look at the whole, how gray is the mural that the posters constitute? It is at least 0.60 black. It certainly is not $0.80 \cdot 0.60 \cdot 0.70$ = 0.34 black, which would entail a miraculous lightening of the mural's color. For some purposes, then, the product rule is inappropriate.

Now, let each poster represent our belief, based on testimony and the like, of whether three corresponding posters in a past world without grays were either white or black. The product rule yields the small probability of all three actually being black, if we could somehow uncover the past posters. But if we cannot uncover them, so that we have to live with uncertainties, then our belief of their having been black does not involve multiplying beliefs into a miraculously bleached whiteness. Instead, it involves piecing the gray pieces together into a bigger gray pattern.

Is the law interested in the odds of the absolute truth if it were knowable or in our best evidence-based estimate of truth in a world where uncertainties will persist? The law should be interested in the latter, in how sure we are that the events happened. We need to move on with life while making the right decisions about what happened in the past. Our best estimate of the past is represented by the current color of the gray mural.

4.1   Fuzzy Logic's Operators

The basic operators for fuzzy logic are the usual, except that they must extend to give results for values between 0 and 1.[30] Thus, the AND and OR functions work this way for sets in fuzzy logic, when x and y can take any value from 0 to 1:

$$truth(x \text{ AND } y) = minimum(truth(x), truth(y))$$

$$truth(x \text{ OR } y) = maximum(truth(x), truth(y))$$

The negation operator carries over as the calculation of the complement.[31]

So, let A be one fuzzy set and B be another fuzzy set in the universe. The two sets might be independent, in the sense that the degree of membership in one set has no effect on the degree of membership in the other set, but they need not be. Designate the membership of element x in A as truth(x), and the membership of element y in B as truth(y). Then, the truth of the conjunction equals the smaller of the truth of x and the truth of y, by the so-called MIN operator. For a more specified example of how fuzzy logic thus injects set theory's mathematical techniques into propositional logic, let A be the set of tallness in men and B be the assumedly independent set of smartness in men. So, if Tom is a 0.30 member of A and a 0.40 member of B, then Tom is a 0.30 member of the set of (tallness AND smartness). Tom's degree of membership in the

---

[30] See Brian R. Gaines, *Fuzzy and Probability Uncertainty Logics*, 38 INFO. & CONTROL 154 (1978) (showing that the operators for fuzzy logic and probability theory are the same until the assumption of the excluded middle comes into play).

[31] Cf. Richard Bellman & Magnus Giertz, *On the Analytic Formalism of the Theory of Fuzzy Sets*, 5 INFO. SCI. 149, 155 (1973) (showing that the fuzzy negation operator has no unique meaning and that the "borderline between S and 'not S' is no longer sharp").

intersecting set does not decrease below the lower of his tallness and smartness levels.

As for justifying those logical operators, there are several signs that fuzzy logic makes sense. To begin, fuzzy logic does not produce nonsensical results. We have a partial truth and another partial truth, and we want to express the conjunction as a partial truth. On the one hand, the MIN rule in fuzzy logic avoids having the value of a conjunction exceed the value of any element. On the other hand, the MIN rule also avoids having the conjoined value be surprisingly low. More than that, it affirmatively makes sense as the way for conjoining multivalent values. Tom would seem to fall at 0.30 on the scale of tallness combined with smartness.[32]

---

[32] The proof goes as follows. Reasoning backward from what is necessary for a system to make sense, I posit the following:

$$x \wedge x = x \tag{1}$$
$$x \vee x = x \tag{2}$$
$$x \wedge y \leq x \tag{3}$$
$$x \vee y \geq x \tag{4}$$

while associativity and distributivity need to prevail as well,

$$(x \wedge y) \wedge z = x \wedge (y \wedge z) \tag{5}$$
$$x \vee (y \wedge z) = (x \vee y) \wedge (y \vee z) \tag{6}$$

Then, using (2) and (3),

$$x \wedge (x \vee y) = (x \vee x) \wedge (x \vee y) \leq x$$

and, using (4) and (6),

$$x \vee (x \wedge y) = (x \vee x) \wedge (x \vee y) \geq x$$

and their having been shown to be equal, and both $\leq$ and $\geq x$,

$$x \wedge (x \vee y) = x \vee (x \wedge y) = x \tag{7}$$

Now, designate y as the lesser or equal of the two truth values x and y. There should be a z such that $x \wedge z = y$, which allows the final conversions with the use of (7) and of (5) and (1), respectively:

$$x \vee y = x \vee (x \wedge z) = x = \text{MAX}(x, y)$$
$$x \wedge y = x \wedge (x \wedge z) = (x \wedge x) \wedge z = x \wedge z = y = \text{MIN}(x, y).$$

See Bellman & Giertz, *supra* note 31, at 152–155 (proving that the MIN and MAX operators "are not only natural, but under quite reasonable assumptions the only ones possible" for fuzzy sets); D. Dubois & H. Prade, *A Review of Fuzzy Set Aggregation Connectives*, 36 INFO. SCI. 85, 89–92 (1985) (showing that conjoined membership must of

4.2   Fuzziness Versus Traditional Probability
as a Means of Conjoining Likelihoods

The reader should nevertheless be sensing that something odd is afoot. After all, the classical probability operator for AND is multiplication of the probabilities of independent events. But fuzzy logic tells us to apply the MIN operator even for independent events.[33] The two logic systems thus represent a choice.

At bottom, fuzzy logicians are arguing that their logic makes more sense than classical logic in certain circumstances. "There are many reasons to get interested in nonclassical logic, but one exciting one is the belief that classical logic is *wrong* – that it provides an inadequate model of (genuine) logical truth and logical consequence."[34] The argument is that classical logic, by assuming bivalence, assumes one too many logical truths. Like Euclidean geometry and Newtonian physics, classical logic is very useful, but it is an oversimplification that can give wrong answers on the edges where its assumptions no longer hold.

Applying different rules. Think of a room with ten men, each estimated to be 5'6" tall. We might think of each as 0.30 tall. What would we term the tallness of the ten men as a group? It would not be 0.30 to the tenth power, a very tiny number yielded by the product rule to reflect the remote chance of them all turning out to be truly tall.

Now if the room has ten men, with three "short" men 5'6" or below and three "dumb" men, then one man picked at random has a .09 chance of being both short and dumb, assuming independence. If that is what we want to know, the product rule applies. For random uncertainty in a bivalent world, the probability operator will give the right answer. The probability operator will make most sense in connection with frequentist probabilities. Still, the uncertainty could concern unique events, because one can speak of the subjective probability of x and y turning out to be true = 1 rather than false = 0. That is, the probability operator is not invalid in all cases.

Nor is the probability operator inconsistent with the fuzzy operator. The two just contemplate different contexts. Indeed, the two are

---

course be either less than or equal to the minimum membership, but that accepting a value less than that minimum would produce nonsensical results).

[33] For interdependent events, the probability operation for conjunction is P(A) multiplied by P(B|A), so it is still multiplicative. Meanwhile, fuzzy logic tells us still to apply the MIN operator, a process that is so much easier to comprehend and apply.

[34] SIDER, *supra* note 9, at 72.

fundamentally consistent, because traditional probability is a special case of fuzzy logic's more general theory of uncertainty. If the world were crisp, so that x and y will appear randomly as either 1 or 0, then the probability and fuzzy operators are equivalent. The MIN rule reduces to the product rule, if one assumes random bivalence and then adds an assumption of independence. The chance of complete conjunction of currently unknown independent variables – the chance that x and y will both appear as 1, or completely true – will be the product of their individual probabilities in either logic system.

Thus, the probability operator is fine, as long as its assumptions hold. However, remember that there are multiple kinds of uncertainty. If one tries to deal with the variedly uncertain real world, the assumptions fail and the MIN rule's more inclusive approach to conjunction often becomes appropriate. In a fuzzy world, the probability operator retreats to a specialized role, applying only in a narrow setting. In sum, one theory generalizes the other and so is better for certain tasks.

Bases for choosing between rules. Because both a multiplicative rule and the MIN operator can give correct, but sometimes different, answers, they must be giving answers to different questions or, rather, questions resting on different assumptions. The product of probabilities is answering a question different from what the conjunction of degrees of truth is answering.

The desired nature of answer will determine which question to ask and, hence, whether the product rule or the MIN operator is appropriate to apply. What do you want to know? The product of two probabilities gives the chance of two things, which can take only a value of 1 or 0, coming up as 1 in independent trials under random conditions. The MIN operator measures the intersection of truth sets, telling you how much to believe two propositions put together.

First, as a thought experiment, ponder the correct question to ask when one wants to know if Tom is tall and smart. Begin with the earlier example's two membership statements – Tom is a 0.30 member of A and a 0.40 member of B – which mean something like "Tom is not so tall" and "Tom is not so smart."

Calculation by the product rule would be appropriate for certain kinds of decisions (and bets), but seems inappropriate for determining one's belief in Tom's membership in the set of tallness and smartness. The chance of a tall and smart Tom according to the product rule is 0.12, so that the probabilistic result is lower than both truth(x) and truth(y). It yields, "Because Tom is not so tall and Tom is not so smart, Tom is very likely a very short and/or very dumb man." Mathematics alone have made him very short and/or very dumb. Multiplication of probabilities gives the chance that Tom is both completely tall and completely smart, but does not work if what we want to know is the degree to which he is both tall and smart. The inappropriateness becomes much more obvious as one combines more and more elements in the calculation. The product calculation will approach 0.00, even if all of the values are high. What is Tom's membership in the set of tall, smart, rich, famous, and strange men? The product rule implausibly suggests well under 0.05.

The MIN operator yields instead a 0.30 belief in that intersection of tall and smart men (or tall, smart, rich, famous, and strange men). A fuzzy combination will go no lower than the minimum truth value. The fuzzy combination of tall and smart says, "Because Tom is not so tall and Tom is not so smart, Tom is not such a tall, smart man." That answer is correct. In other words, a fuzzy intersection of many fairly true propositions is fairly true, not almost completely untrue.

Second, one might try to classify a thing as a chair and as a red object. If the thing has some of the characteristics of a chair[35] and some pinkish hue, one would give it, perhaps, a 0.60 membership in the set of chairs and a 0.51 membership in the red set. Now, if one had to give it a membership in the class of red chairs, one would say 0.51 for this reddish chair-like thing. One would not apply the product rule to say 0.31.

Third, when would one apply the product rule for probabilities? One would do so when things are completely chairs or not and red or not, and you cannot see the thing, but you have an idea of the likelihood of chairness and redness – and therefore also of nonchairness and nonredness. To compute the chances of what bivalent values one will see when the thing is uncovered, and seen clearly as a chair or not and red or not, one would use the product rule.

Fourth, many other sorts of situations call for the product rule, including many legal situations. In manipulating and evaluating statistical evidence, the factfinder would often use it. In calculating the odds of multiple future events, the product rule would be appropriate.[36]

---

[35] *See* H. G. Wells, A MODERN UTOPIA 381 (1905) ("I would undertake to defeat any definition of chair or chairishness that you gave me").

[36] *See infra* text accompanying note 51.

4.3   The Law's Choice

Once lawmakers have in mind the difference between the product rule and the MIN operator, they have to decide which they should apply. Here our lawmakers have explicitly chosen fuzzy logic, across the board. By phrasing the instruction to factfinders so as to require applying the standard of proof element-by-element, the law reveals that it has adopted the MIN operator.[37] That instruction does not ask the factfinder any overall question: it does not ask the bottom line for whether the plaintiff should recover or ask what the overall likelihood is. It does not give instructions on how to combine independent or interdependent findings, which would otherwise be necessary. Instead it tells the factfinder to determine whether an element is likely enough and, if so, to proceed afresh to the next element. If the factfinder finds all the elements to exist, it is a rule of law and not the factfinder that says the plaintiff shall recover.

I further submit that the law's choice was a wise one. There is a proper realm for the straightforward application of the MIN rule, just as there is a proper realm for the product rule. Applications of the standard of proof fall into the former realm.

Imagine again that the law is trying to determine if Tom himself was at fault, that is, whether the perpetrator was Tom and whether the perpetrator was at fault. A number of features of this compound question demonstrate why the law has chosen fuzzy logic to calculate conjoined likelihoods. First, at one level the two parts of the determination are different, the former being a factual event and the latter a legal construct; the law needs commensurable measures to combine them, which is attainable because at a deeper level the two findings are epistemically indistinguishable. Second, in establishing truths, the law should not be worrying too much about the chance of a truth value of 1 repetitively turning up; instead it should ascertain whether the string of elements has a sufficient

---

[37] *See* 3 Kevin F. O'Malley, Jay E. Grenig & William C. Lee, FEDERAL JURY PRACTICE AND INSTRUCTIONS: CIVIL § 104.01 (6th ed. 2011):

> Plaintiff has the burden in a civil action, such as this, to prove every essential element of plaintiff's claim by a preponderance of the evidence. If plaintiff should fail to establish any essential element of plaintiff's claim by a preponderance of the evidence, you should find for defendant as to that claim.

Of course, the pattern jury instruction also verbalizes the process implicitly imposed on the judge when acting as factfinder.

truth value. Third, applying the product rule to the subjective likelihoods for legal factfinding seems illogical; we want to know if Tom's fault is sufficiently true, not the much lower chance of somehow revealing the perpetrator certainly to be Tom and also revealing the perpetrator to be completely at fault.[38]

Not only is the MIN rule the right mathematical tool for the standard of proof, but also its application makes the process of proof much simpler and more understandable. First, if we put aside the imperfections of evidence for the moment, we can see that applying the standard of proof element-by-element comfortably works out to be equivalent to applying the standard to the whole story conjoined by the MIN rule. The whole story will meet the standard of proof if and only if each element meets the standard of proof. So, if the factfinder in actual practice approaches the

---

[38] Some logicians have suggested the illogic of the product rule in this context. *See* Didier Dubois & Henri Prade, *A Set-Theoretic View of Belief Functions: Logical Operations and Approximations by Fuzzy Sets*, in CLASSIC WORKS OF THE DEMPSTER-SHAFER THEORY OF BELIEF FUNCTIONS 375, 403 (Ronald R. Yager & Liping Liu eds., 2008) (rejecting the application of "arguments deriving from the study of statistical experiments"). Major philosophers concur. *See* Bertrand Russell, HUMAN KNOWLEDGE: ITS SCOPE AND LIMITS 359–361 (1948) (arguing that his "degrees of credibility" do not follow the rules of traditional probability); Susan Haack, *The Embedded Epistemologist: Dispatches from the Legal Front*, 25 RATIO JURIS 206, 217–218 (2012) (arguing comparably that her "degrees of warrant" do not follow the rules of traditional probability); John MacFarlane, *Fuzzy Epistemicism*, in CUTS AND CLOUDS: VAGUENESS, ITS NATURE, AND ITS LOGIC 438, 443–49 (Richard Dietz & Sebastiano Moruzzi eds., 2010) (arguing against the product rule and in favor of the MIN rule). The line of argument of the latter, that the product rule here "just seems wrong," is worth quoting from ibid. at 444 (footnote omitted):

1. If classical semantics is correct for vague discourse, then borderline propositions are either true or false; no finer distinctions are made.
2. If borderline propositions are either true or false, then (since we don't know which truth value they have) our attitudes toward them must be attitudes of uncertainty-related partial belief.
3. If our attitudes towards borderline propositions are attitudes of uncertainty-related partial belief, they ought to obey norms of probabilistic coherence.
4. We regard the propositions Jim is tall, Jim is bald, and Jim is smart as independent. That is, we don't think Jim's being bald (or smart, or bald and smart) would make it any more likely that he is tall, and so on.
5. Probabilistic coherence demands that our credence in the conjunction of several propositions we take to be independent be the product of our credences in the conjuncts.
6. But it is not the case that we ought to have much less credence that Jim is bald and tall and smart than we have that he is bald.
7. Therefore, classical semantics is not correct for vague discourse.

case holistically by constructing an overall story, that practice would not directly endanger the standard of proof. The apparent criticality of the number of elements additionally melts away. The law splits the case into parts and tells its factfinder to proceed part-by-part only to make the path to decision more comprehensible and rigorous. Second, some of the proof process within elements is similar to the proof process between elements. For separate findings within elements, the factfinder should use the fuzzy operator for conjunction. Because the MIN rule applies to each set of evidence to be conjoined, it does not matter logically where the law draws formal lines between elements, or whether any required fact technically constitutes an "element" of a claim.[39] Third, it does not matter whether the combined constituent facts are independent or interdependent. The same MIN rule applies to both independent and interdependent facts.

Explanatory introduction. Reactions of colleagues have convinced me that explanatory elaboration, even in multiple ways, is necessary. Most law professors have never thought about conjunction of elements until one explains the conjunction paradox to them. Apparently, the law's application of the standard of proof element-by-element accorded completely with their common sense up to that very moment.[40] Then suddenly and ironically, the law professors' "common sense" demands the application of the product rule and the condemnation of law as illogical.[41]

---

[39] *See* L. Jonathan Cohen, THE PROBABLE AND THE PROVABLE 267 (1977) ("So on the inductivist analysis, if the plaintiff gains each of his points on the balance of probability, he can be regarded as gaining his case as a whole on that balance ..., without any constraint's being thereby imposed on the number of independent points in his case or on the level of probability at which each must be won."). "Element" would therefore best serve merely as a synonym for a finding necessary to a cause of action or defense under the substantive law. Yet, as the definition of element rightly broadens, application of a multiplicative rule for conjunction would render the plaintiff's proof burden virtually impossible to carry. Thus, another argument for the MIN rule emerges.

[40] In fact, an occasional philosopher rejects use of probability's product rule on the very ground that the law's proceeding element-by-element is so obviously sensible. *See* Susan Haack, EVIDENCE MATTERS 62–63 (2014).

[41] Exceptions exist. Some professors rely on the future/past distinction between ex ante probabilities, used to make predictions of what you will eventually know, and ex post probabilities, used to decide what actually happened even though you will never know for sure. They then say that if you are placing a bet predicting whether two randomly uncertain events will independently happen together, multiply their probabilities. But if you are looking back to the past, then you need a different operator. You are no longer trying to figure the odds of two things being sure, but rather how sure you are that one thing happened while you remain somewhat sure that the other happened. "The ex post probability for complete instantiation of the causal law is equal to the lowest ex post

My cited technical arguments[42] do not suffice in dissuading the professors from turning on the law's traditional element-by-element approach and dismissing multivalent logic's contrary lesson. Nor do they bow to eminent logicians and philosophers who have argued the inapplicability of traditional probability theory.[43] What I need, then, is an accessible common-sense explanation of conjunction in the law, which no one has hitherto produced. It is all so subtle.

The essence of the common-sense explanation entails realizing that factfinders do not announce the odds of an element being true or false. They instead give their degree of belief in the element's truth. Those two measures are different quantities. Factfinders sense their beliefs and disbeliefs based on the available evidence. They might believe a fact more than they disbelieve it, even if they would not be willing to bet on it as the truth if the truth could somehow be revealed. The evidence-based belief might be quite weak, while the bet must commit total belief to either yes or no.

To flesh out that explanation, let me begin with the law professors' sudden yearning to apply the product rule. If element A is 60% likely and element B is 70% likely, if both A and B either occurred or did not, and if the law wants to allow recovery only if A and B both occurred, then their assertion that the plaintiff should lose on this 42% showing makes superficial sense.

My opening defense is that this result seems to be tough on plaintiffs. Multiple elements would stack the deck against real-world plaintiffs, who must live with the imperfections of available evidence. Imagine some plaintiff's having proven four elements each to 70%. That plaintiff has done a really good job of presenting a strong case. The plaintiff has well established each element before passing to the next one. The plaintiff has done exactly what we should demand. Yet this plaintiff would lose under the product rule with a miserable 24% showing. What happened? How did a strong case become a sure loser? Regardless of how, plaintiffs would lose apparently strong cases they arguably should win. Moreover, defendants at fault would not be receiving a corrective message. These errors would detrimentally affect economic efficiency.

---

probability for instantiation of any constituent element." Richard W. Wright, *Proving Facts: Belief Versus Probability*, in EUROPEAN TORT LAW 2008, at 79, ¶ 45 (Helmut Koziol & Barbara C. Steininger eds., 2009).

[42] *See supra* note 32.   [43] *See supra* note 38.

Philosophical explanation: provability is the aim. The law should not be interesting itself in the probability of the elements all turning out to equal 1, as if the veil on perfect knowledge could be lifted. If every event and thought were somehow videotaped, then we would be partially living in an ascertainably bivalent world, and the law's approach to standards of proof might be inappropriate. But the law should not counterfactually imagine the real world to be a videotaped one. The law should not ask the odds of the elements bivalently and conjoinedly existing on a nonexistent videotape.

The law instead should ask how well the burdened party has proven its case. The law wants to know whether the state of our knowledge based on proof justifies recovery. The factfinder needs to operate on the resulting internal beliefs about the external world, rather than pretending that certainty is attainable. Forming a belief as to what happened, rather than a prediction about a veil-lifting that will never happen, is the aim. Provability, not probability, is therefore the law's concern.

Fuzzy expression of provability comes in terms of membership, to a degree, in the set of true propositions, with the degree measured as a truth value. Probability can tell the odds of two black cards turning up. Which image fits the factfinding endeavor: set theory or the betting table? I submit that the standards of proof are looking for provability based on set theory. In a sense, traditional probability crisply deals with the "provably probable," while fuzzy logic vaguely deals with the "probably provable."[44]

This key distinction between probability and provability was at the heart of L. Jonathan Cohen's almost impenetrably brilliant book entitled *The Probable and the Provable.*[45] For inspiration this Oxford philosopher looked to the law as an example of practical reasoning. He then constructed on the basis of inductive reasoning a whole system of inductive probability. His exercise justified what the law was doing intuitively. His book, I now see, constitutes a sophisticated proof of what I have independently postulated in the roughly equivalent but more understandable terms of fuzzy logic.

He argued that the task of the law court is to decide what is provable. Importing traditional probability into the project, including the product

---

[44] *Cf.* David A. Schum, THE EVIDENTIAL FOUNDATIONS OF PROBABILISTIC REASONING 243 (1994) (crediting this phrasing to Judea Pearl, *Bayesian and Belief–Functions Formalisms for Evidential Reasoning: A Conceptual Analysis, in* READINGS IN UNCERTAIN REASONING 540, 571 (Glenn Shafer & Judea Pearl eds., 1990)).

[45] COHEN, *supra* note 39.

rule, produces a whole series of anomalies. To avoid the anomalies, his conjunction rule for inductive probability is the MIN rule: "The conjunction of two or more propositions . . . has the same inductive probability . . . as the least" likely conjunct, because "betting odds" are inapplicable to "unsettlable issues."[46]

Thus, if two wholly unrelated facts are each likely true, then their conjunction is likely true. Provability of one element does not detract from the provability of another. An easily provable *A* and an easily provable *B* mean that it will be easy to prove *A* and *B* together. If you believe *A* and you believe *B*, then you should believe the story of *A and B*. The intersection of sets can represent the interaction of a cause of action's elements, and the MIN rule governs the intersection of sets. Accordingly, if the plaintiff proves element *A* to 60% and *B* to 70%, then the probability of the overall case's being in the set of (*A* AND *B*) is 60%.

Mathematical explanation: complementarity is not contradiction. Perhaps pure philosophy convinces few of anything. But its underlying mathematical arguments are harder to ignore.

"Unsettlable" may suggest that the critical feature of factfinding's partial truths is their being findings about one-shot events that will never convert into absolute truths. Therefore, the law should employ the mathematical technique for turning partial truths into a conjoined partial truth.

I now observe that a consequence of this unsettlable trait is that in the real world where the evidence available is always incomplete, inconclusive, ambiguous, dissonant, or untrustworthy, partial truths normally do not imply a measure of their own contradiction. A belief in *x* normally does not imply anything about the belief in not-*x*, other than that the contradiction cannot be more likely than the belief's complement, or one minus the belief. The degrees of belief are nonadditive, meaning that the beliefs in *x* and not-*x* will normally not add to one.[47]

On the basis of available evidence the factfinder assembles reasons to believe. The law tells the factfinder that it can, and should, leave a good part of belief uncommitted. The factfinder would need proof or inference of the contradiction before generating any belief in it. In other

---

[46] Ibid. at 89–91, 265–267 (arguing that the law's interest in provability means that probability's product rule should not apply).

[47] *See* Rolf Haenni, *Non-Additive Degrees of Belief, in* DEGREES OF BELIEF 121, 121–127 (Franz Huber & Christoph Schmidt-Petri eds., 2009); Ron A. Shapira, *Economic Analysis of the Law of Evidence: A Caveat,* 19 CARDOZO L. REV. 1607, 1613–1616 (1998) (distinguishing additive from nonadditive).

words, given scarce information or conflicting evidence, the factfinder forms a belief in a proposition, while leaving a lot of belief uncommitted and without necessarily forming any belief in the proposition's contradiction. The factfinder then compares the affirmative belief to any belief in the contradiction, pursuant to the imposed standard of proof. At no point does the factfinder need to decide whether to bet on the existence of fact.

In contrast, the bettor has a different task. The "evidence" for making the bet is deemed complete. The bettor cannot retain uncommitted belief. The bettor must judge the likelihood of truth, with the complement (one minus the likelihood) being the contradictory likelihood of falsehood because, under the bivalent assumption, whatever turns out not to be true will be false. In other words, betting odds imply the complementary likelihood of the contradiction.

Logicians have indeed identified this aspect of contradiction as a determinant of how to conjoin: the product rule applies only where the convincingness of a proposition implies the complementary likelihood of its contradiction.[48] The product rule critically depends on the assumption that one minus x is the probability of falsehood. Because a partial truth from factfinding does not measure falsehood, one should not account for contradiction in combining partial truths. The provability of one fact does not detract from the provability of another fact. Thus, one should combine beliefs by stringing them together into a chain, with the conjunction of beliefs being as likely as the weakest link. One looks to the weakest link because the unsureness represented by the weakest belief's complement overcomes the stronger links. Meanwhile, the disjunction of the complements is, by the MAX rule, as big as the biggest complement, which represents the peak of unsureness.

Imagine that Tom is believed 60% likely the perpetrator, and the perpetrator 70% at fault. In all but fanciful or rare civil cases, a 70% finding on fault does not imply a 30% chance that fault was not in play. It merely means that the evidence is currently strong enough to move the belief in fault up to 70%. The 30% complement represents not only the vagueness of the fault concept but also what is not known because of imperfect evidence. For any part of that 30% to constitute a belief that fault was not in play would demand proof or inference of nonfault. The 70% finding suffices because the law allows incomplete proof.

---

[48] *See* COHEN, *supra* note 39, at 34, 167–169, 220–222, 265–267.

Fault proven to 70% will never convert to 1 or 0, so that the 70% figure represents a partial truth that will forever remain partial. We should not further account for nonfault. The 30% complement does not suggest hypothesized findings of nonfault, but rather merely nonfindings. Fault having satisfied the standard of proof, further reliance on the 30% figure by the decisionmaker would represent only reliance on nonfindings. If the perpetrator did an act that was 70% wrongful and therefore liability-creating, and if Tom is 60% likely the perpetrator, the 60% figure means that it is 60% likely that Tom is the person who was 70% at fault. We thus have a 60% chance of Tom's being legally at fault, just as the MIN rule would say. The law just asks the burdened party to convince on each of his or her elements, and thus convince on his or her whole case. The relevant inquiry comprises whether the weakest element meets the standard of proof, given that all the other elements would simultaneously be stronger. Therefore, if a 60% belief in identification is the weakest link in the case, we can say that all the other elements are more likely than not to exist and so liability exists.

The 40% and 30% complements represent possibilities, not probabilities. The defense of (not-A OR not-B) is at most 40% possible, according to the MAX rule for disjunction of each element's complement. That is, the belief in the overall claim is stronger than its complement (all the possibilities that some or all elements failed).

Now consider, by contrast, the product rule. Multiplying the chances, to get 42%, delivers only an inaccurate measure of the chance of full findings on both identity and fault. Most of the remaining 58% actually represents unsureness or uncommitted belief. Rather than calculating the minimal chance of somehow both revealing the perpetrator certainly to be Tom and revealing the perpetrator to be completely at fault, we should want to know if Tom's fault is sufficiently true.

While the MIN rule thus seems the obvious choice if either issue is a matter of event imprecision,[49] I think the product rule would be inappropriate even if both factfinding percentages measure only what look like

---

[49] Even easier to justify applying the MIN rule is the situation where both issues involve event imprecision. Imagine that Tom admits to being the perpetrator, but the two fuzzy issues are how wrongful was his known act and how much was the known act causal. Let us say that the evidence establishes at least 70% wrongful and 60% causal. Note that the 30% and 40% complements, respectively, do not represent the odds that the act did not occur or the odds that there was no fault or causal link. Instead, the 70% and 60% figures represent the degree of truth that the known act fits into the legal categories of fault and causation. No one combining the two figures would leap to thinking the likelihood of

occurrence odds. Most people would agree that having different operators for different kinds of elements, leading to some weird hybrid
calculation unknown to current law, would be more than awkward. But
I am going further, arguing that the MIN rule is the right approach for all
factfinding, not just a convenient one.

The reason for its being the right approach is that, as already explained,
a 60% belief in an actor's identity in the factfinding context is epistemically indistinguishable from a 60% wrongful act. Both are constructed
measures of an individual's judgment, based on the available evidence,
about how likely true a particular unsettlable proposition is. Each represents not a chance, but a belief. Therefore, two findings that look like
occurrence odds conjoin not as chances do, but as beliefs do.

Moreover, neither a 60% belief in the actor's identity nor a 60%
wrongful act implies a complementary belief in its contradiction. Let us
consider a different representation of belief and contradiction.[50] Even

---

causal fault is 42%. One would instead tend to say the combined story is as strong as its
weakest element, or 60%.

[50] *See supra* note 31 and accompanying text. I have previously surveyed the various theories
on how to handle uncertainty, and explored the ones that best image how the law
contemplates uncertainty: for the purposes of expressing imprecise evidential assessments
in probability-like terms and conjoining separate findings, fuzzy logic is the optimal
theory; for the purposes of understanding how to apply the standards of proof, the
compatible theory of belief functions is more expressive. *See* CLERMONT, *supra* note *,
at 147, 149–151, 201–220 (explaining, and preferring, belief functions as a way to account
for imperfect legal evidence and to apply the standards of proof); *cf.* ibid. at 162–63
(discussing so-called ultrafuzzy sets as a way to handle imperfect evidence, but acknowledging that the logical operators for ultrafuzzy sets become complicated), 202–03
(describing possibility theory as a way to exploit the compatibility of fuzzy logic and
belief functions); Hans Rott, *Degrees All the Way Down: Beliefs, Non-Beliefs and Disbeliefs, in* DEGREES OF BELIEF 301, 306 (Franz Huber & Christoph Schmidt-Petri eds., 2009)
(seeing the inductive probability of COHEN, *supra* note 39, as a variation on belief
functions). First, belief functions work in the following way. The factfinder applies the
standard of proof to its belief in each element. The standard of proof requires the
factfinder to ignore uncommitted belief and then compare the affirmative belief in an
element to any belief in its contradiction. Accordingly, talk of x and not-x filling the range
from 0 to 1 is a tad misleading. Instead, we should be talking of whether the smallish
belief sufficiently exceeds its smallish contradiction. This realization makes application of
any multiplicative rule for conjunction in normal factfinding even more nonsensical.
Incidentally, the conjunction paradox dissolves by application of belief function theory
similarly to the way it does under fuzzy logic. *See* Kevin M. Clermont, *Trial by Traditional
Probability, Relative Plausibility, or Belief Function?*, 66 CASE. W. RES. L. REV. 353,
385–391 (2015) (discussing also the alternative of imprecise probability theory). Second,
the factfinder could convert its beliefs into the fuzzy values of x and not-x, which would
be normalized beliefs scaled up so as to add to 1. In a civil case, x would have to exceed
0.5. The imperfections of evidence would find expression in the third dimension of

when factfinding entails a yes-or-no issue, the complement represents
not contradiction but instead what is not known. Proof of the contradiction may have also come in, generating a contrary belief. The indeterminate zone between a belief expressed as Bel(Tom) and any belief in its
contradiction expressed as Bel(notTom) represents uncommitted belief.
The "possibility" of Tom being the perpetrator is the sum of affirmative
belief and uncommitted belief. The betting odds would fall in the uncommitted zone.

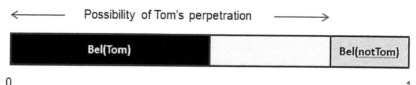

0   1

I do not deny that in specific situations, the law could face the task of
computing betting odds. The situations would arise where the law does
not want the decider to retain uncommitted belief. An example would be
computing expected costs of granting or denying a preliminary injunction. The law wants the judge to bet on the path promising the lower
costs. The proper betting strategy would involve the probability calculus,
multiplying conjectured harm by probability of harm. (Perhaps more
interesting, however, is how most courts resist that unfamiliar task,
insisting on deciding motions for preliminary injunction by some opaque
multifactor test.)[51]

Economic explanation: efficiency is an aim. As a practical matter, we
want to know what to do with the partial truths we find. The law com-
mands the use of the mathematically sound way to conjoin partial truths,
here the MIN rule. Does this approach minimize expected error costs?

First, imagine a half-truth. Proof of an element to 0.50 produces a half-
truth, which will never convert by revelation into something other than a
half-truth. A half-truth conjoining with a near certainty yields, by the
MIN rule, a half-truth in the universe of overall stories covering the two
elements.

Second, and more tellingly, that half-truth conjoining with a separate
half-truth yields an overall story that is halfway convincing, rather than

ultrafuzzy logic. *See* SCHUM, *supra* note 44, at 267 ("we could, if it were necessary, grade
the force of evidence in fuzzy terms with reference to" belief functions).
[51] *See* Richard H. Field, Benjamin Kaplan, Kevin M. Clermont & Catherine T. Struve,
Materials for a Basic Course in Civil Procedure 121–127 (11th ed. 2014); *see also supra*
text accompanying note 36.

merely a quarter-truth. The overall story is as likely as its less likely element, just as mathematical theory tells us. But it is not math that inspires us humans, or inspired the law, to follow the MIN rule. The rule is the natural way of thinking when in possession of partial truths.[52] The law acts optimally in light of the fuzzy facts that it possesses, rather than on the basis of the odds of absolute facts it will never obtain. If a historian thought it likely that Danton did this and very likely that Robespierre later said this, it would never occur to anyone to multiply the probabilities. Instead, one would naturally conclude that it was likely that Danton did this *and* Robespierre said this. Danton *and* Robespierre, or fault *and* causation, should each be judged by their weaker element. The law adopted this accurate way of thinking long before any legal academic worried about the product rule.

Third, imagine in place of the two elements a long string of elements each shown to be half-proven. In combining these partial truths, the boundaries of elements do not matter, because the storyteller is simply connecting pieces to establish an overall partial truth. The storyteller simply joins constructed beliefs together, rather than multiplying them. The chain of beliefs is as strong as the weakest link. Thus, the result is a halfway-convincing overall story, not the infinitesimally likely story suggested by the product rule's measure of the odds of every element being revealed as 1.

If each element of a cause of action passes the standard of proof, the story of liability will not only be the most believable story, but will be more believable than all the stories of nonliability combined. To minimize error in these circumstances, the law should decide in conformity with the stronger chain. Giving the plaintiff a recovery and the defendant a loss would be economically efficient. Refusing to accept the MIN rule's version of the overall truth will always involve choosing a lesser truth at some step in telling the combined story of a series of two or more elements. If the law were to deny liability because of some attraction to bivalent probability theory, more often than not the law would be in error. Therefore, deciding on the basis of betting odds would increase the error rate.

---

[52] Empirical testing is sketchy. *See* Rami Zwick, David V. Budescu & Thomas S. Wallsten, *An Empirical Study of the Interpretation of Linguistic Probabilities, in* FUZZY SETS IN PSYCHOLOGY 91, 114–116 (Tamás Zétényi ed., 1988) (indicating experimentally that people do not naturally use the product rule for partial truths).

The critical insight, again, is that establishing a betting strategy for turning over cards is a fundamentally different task from constructing a story with separate, uncertain elements. Tasks so different demand different logical operators. Classical logic can handle only things that assumedly can reveal themselves to be either true or false. Fuzzy logic is the correct tool for handling beliefs. In constructing a story, one should piece the likely elements together, not multiply their likelihoods. Therefore, fuzzy logic's MIN rule is the tool that will minimize errors and optimize efficiency in legal factfinding.

Explanatory summary. As a means of simplification, traditional probability limits its reach to only absolute truths, giving the odds of obtaining an assessment of 1 rather than 0. If one has to place a bet on the two outcomes, the mathematically sound way to conjoin these odds of absolute truth is a multiplicative rule.

But the law needs to deal with partial truths, which will never be proved beyond a partial degree of belief and that do not imply any belief in their own contradiction. If one recognizes multivalence, one can deal with an assessment standing as a partial truth. The mathematically sound way to conjoin partial truths is the MIN rule. Therefore, recognition that a party can prove an element only as a partial truth leads to the law's element-by-element approach.

Here is the key to the conjunction paradox: *a partial truth fundamentally differs from betting odds and so they conjoin differently.* Betting treats something that will either happen or not happen, so that the betting odds of its happening imply the odds of its not happening. A partial truth conveys only how much one believes a proposition, not a degree of truth of any contrary position.

Instinctive resistance to the MIN rule for partial truths derives from residual yearning to apply the familiar multiplicative rule of traditional probability, even to the problem of fuzzy provability that it cannot handle. We tend to forget that mathematical constructs operate only within their assumed system. When an assumption no longer prevails, one cannot apply the rules built on the assumption. Multivalence calls for new math. The law had to move up to MIN.

There is more at work in obscuring the picture for many people. Even if one acknowledges that the multiplicative rule should apply only in its assumed system, one may not always intuitively sense the subtle shift in a problem's setting from a bivalent assumption to a multivalent reality in which the middle is no longer excluded. The shift can be almost imperceptible.

When finding facts, it is not so easy to see the need for expanding the palette from black and white to include multivalent grays.

The bottom line is this: *the product rule does not apply within the standard of proof.* Multivalent logic answers the proof question that bivalent logic cannot, namely, how to proceed most accurately to the next step when a fact must remain partially proven. Therefore, degrees of truth behave more appropriately than bivalent probabilities for the purposes of the standard of proof.

5   Conclusion

The conjunction paradox is troubling only if theory really calls for applying the product rule. But theory does not. Factfinders do not formulate odds; they form degrees of belief. A justified true belief in A of 0.60 represents 60% of full knowledge, not a 60% chance of A being completely true. How should anyone combine such beliefs? If the factfinder believes A and believes B, then it rightly believes the story of A *and B*. This method of conjunction is indeed how we construct, in life and in law, a system of beliefs.

That is to say, sound theory invokes the MIN rule. To use the opening example, if the plaintiff shows that causation is 0.60 true and that fault is 0.60 true, then he has shown to 0.60 that the defendant *both* acted negligently and caused the injury – not 36%. The belief in the conjunction matches the least likely element, which has already passed the standard of proof. My argument to that conclusion ran this way:

1. Factfinders must deal with partial truths, that is, propositions that will never be proved beyond a partial degree of belief and that do not imply any belief in their own contradiction.
2. Classical logic, by its assumption of bivalence, refuses to recognize partial truths.
3. Consequently, classical logic has no tool to conjoin, or otherwise combine, partial truths.
4. By contrast, multivalent logic handles elements that are provable as partial truths.
5. Multivalent logic demonstrates that the truth of the conjoined elements equals the minimum of the truths of the elements, so that a narrative is as strong as its weakest link.
6. The law has intuitively embraced this multivalent logical operator.

7. If each element in a cause of action is proved as more likely than not, then the truth of the conjunction is more likely than not.

Thus, there is no conjunction paradox. It implodes under the force of multivalent logic. By following multivalent logic's rules for factfinding, the law appears to have known all along what it was doing.

3

One God, No State, and Many Legal Arguments

Multivalent Logic in Jewish Law

CHAIM N. SAIMAN[1]

1 Introduction: One God, One Answer

While speculating about the central message of the Hebrew Bible is dangerous, surely, proclaiming the truth of the monotheistic God and eradicating idolatrous polytheism, are some of its core themes. Viewed from the perspective of duality and multiplicity, a casual reader will likely conclude that the Bible maintains a rather bivalent view of the world. Following the God is good, worshiping idols and false gods is bad. This reflects what we might call a procedural view of bi-valence. That is, if there are two options A & B, if A is correct than B is perforce wrong. Examples of this thinking can be found in many places, including chapter 30 of Deuteronomy:

> See, I set before you today life and prosperity, death and destruction. For I command you today to love the LORD your God, to walk in obedience to him, and to keep his commands, decrees and laws; then you will live and increase, and the LORD your God will bless you in the land you are entering to possess.

> But if your heart turns away and you are not obedient, and if you are drawn away to bow down to other gods and worship them. I declare to you this day that you will certainly be destroyed. You will not live long in the land you are crossing the Jordan to enter and possess.[2]

---

[1] The text of this article closely tracks the talk given at the workshop that is the genesis of this collection which took place in the Summer of 2011 in Wassenaar, the Netherlands. The citations and style reflect the oral origins of this paper. In the years since, I have greatly expanded on these ideas which are reflected in my book HALAKHAH: THE RABBINIC IDEA OF LAW (forthcoming, Princeton University Press).

[2] Deuteronomy 30:15–18.

Yet, the Biblical worldview also entails second, more substantive, version of bi-valence. This is bound up in the monotheistic claim that there is One, as opposed to many, Gods. Contrary to the prevailing view of the time, the Bible argues that there is one source of life, one source of truth, one source of meaning, and one source of revelation; claims that strongly contrast with the polytheistic view which holds there are many sources of life, meaning and truth. In broad strokes, polytheism would seem to resonate with multivalence, whereas the Bible's universal mono-theism may offer the strongest form of bi-valence imaginable.

This central idea is reflected in many aspects of Jewish law and life, and is neatly summarized in the *havdala* ceremony – a short prayer recited at the conclusion of Shabbat each Saturday night. Liturgically, this prayer gives each Jew marching orders as he exits from the holy space of Shabbat to the mundane zone of workweek. The liturgy sets up a series of dichoto-mies, as follows:

> Blessed are You, Lord, our God, King of the Universe who distinguishes between:
>
> Sacred and the secular
> Light and darkness
> Israel and the nations
> The seventh day and the six days of work
>
> Blessed are You, Lord, who distinguishes between the sacred and secular.

As a compact summary of Jewish theology, one could surely do worse, and for centuries, Jews have begun each week praising God for creating sharp, bright line and mutually exclusive distinctions. Following these premises, Jewish law is replete with bivalent distinctions between Jew and non-Jew, permitted and prohibited, kosher and non-kosher, pure and impure, male and female, and so on. Further, because-Jewish law tends to favor a bivalent framing that generates clear distinctions, the halakhic corpus contains few of the multifactor balancing tests known to American law.

Judaism, of course, is not unique in maintaining that it possesses Divinely revealed truths, as to one degree or another, every religion makes this claim. More unique, however, is that so much of Jewish life, theology and culture, are conceptualized in legal form. Take for example the laws of Shabbat. Like Jews, Christians also maintain a concept of the Lord's day of rest. But only Jewish law seeks to define this rest in terms of thirty-nine formalized categories of prohibited labors which examine in fine-grained detail which actions are permitted and prohibited.[3] This pattern carries through many areas of Jewish life which halakhah regulates through a bivalent legal categories.

2 "One thing God has spoken, two things I have heard"[4]

The story however, is considerably more complex. For all its adamance about universal monotheism, Jewish law is not generally understood as universal. For the most part, it is for Jews only. Thus, whereas Christian readings tend to view the revelation of the Ten Commandments at Sinai as declaring universal moral laws,[5] the rabbinic tradition follows the plain sense of the Biblical text and understands the covenant at Sinai as a particularly Jewish event. Because God makes His covenant with Jews and not anyone else, Jewish law applies to Jews and no one else. In this way the universal absolutism assumed by monotheism is at least partially muted, since by definition other laws govern the nations outside the covenant. When combined with the idea of chosenness, this monotheism yields its own form of multivalent logic.

Yet the issue penetrates even deeper into the substantive core of Jewish law, or halakhah, as it is known, for at least three reasons. First, on closer inspection, many of the core distinctions within Jewish law complicate the claim that the legal order is divided into bivalent classifications of holy/mundane; permitted/prohibited; and guilty/innocent.

Secondly, the Talmud, the central text of halakhah, displays a unique toleration, perhaps even celebration, of the multiplicity of interpretations and opinions of Jewish law.[6] So while on the one hand the Talmud is constantly engaged in the process of searching for the correct legal answer, in another sense, it constantly draws more voices and interpretations into the legal conversation, making it nearly impossible to arrive at a single conclusion.

---

[3] See Chaim Saiman, *Jesus' Legal Theory—A Rabbinic Interpretation*, 23 JOURNAL OF LAW AND RELIGION 97, 106–116 (2007).

[4] Psalms 62:12.

[5] See for example, John Witte Jr., LAW AND PROTESTANTISM at 113–114, 125–127 (Cambridge, 2002).

[6] A more complete bibliography on the literature of pluralism in Jewish law can be found in Richard Hidary, DISPUTE FOR THE SAKE OF HEAVEN, LEGAL PLURALISM IN THE TALMUD 13–36 (Brown University, 2010).

Finally, anyone familiar with the practices of Jewish law knows that, as Patrick Glenn predicted, its lived reality is far from bivalent.[7] Over time, a number of multivalent categories have emerged allowing halakhah to develop and interact with surrounding legal systems. In this way, halakhah displays an openness to alternative normative orders, which at first glance is hard to square with its foundational claim that halakha is founded on the absolute truth of the Divine Lawgiver. The remainder of this essay elaborates on each of these claims.

3   *Galut* (Exile): The Real and the Ideal

One of the most interesting features of halakhah is the degree to which it consistently understands itself as operating under sub-optimal conditions. Ideally, Jewish law is administered in the context of a sovereign Jewish state, wherein the Temple stands in Jerusalem, and the Sanhedrin – the halakhic Supreme Court – is the ultimate legal authority. The Mishnah and Talmud describe a system that operates under clear hierarchical lines, where any controversial issue arising in the lower courts was directed up_to the Sanhedrin, where it was conclusively resolved by majority vote.[8]

Halakhah as we know it however, never quite operated in this fashion. By the time the Mishnah emerged in the second century, these neat lines of authority no longer functioned. Further, many historians have serious reservations as to whether the actual Sanhedrin that sat in Jerusalem ever followed the intricate procedural details set forth in the Mishnah and Talmud.[9] And moreover, even on the Talmud's own account, the Sanhedrin, and indeed the entire system of lower courts beneath it, only attains the full scope of its regulatory authority when the Sanhedrin sits in the Temple compound.[10] As a result, following the destruction of the Temple 70 CE, the Sanhedrin described in the Mishnah no longer exists, and for the past two millennia Jewish law operated without of its core

---

[7] H. Patrick Glenn, LEGAL TRADITIONS OF THE WORLD, 1112–1119 (Oxford, 3rd edn 2007).

[8] See Mishnah Sanhedrin 11:2–4; Talmud Sanhedrin 86b; 88a–b.

[9] See for example David Goodblatt, THE MONARCHIC PRINCIPLE: STUDIES IN JEWISH SELF-GOVERNMENT IN ANTIQUITY (Tübingen: Mohr Siebeck, 1994); Joshua Efron, STUDIES ON THE HASMONIAN PERIOD, 290–300 (Brill, 1987). See also the discussion and sources collected by Catherine Hezser in THE SOCIAL STRUCTURE OF THE RABBINIC MOVEMENT IN ROMAN PALESTINE, 186–190 (Mohr-Siebeck, 1997).

[10] Talmud Sanhedrin, 52b; Avoda Zara 8b; Maimonides, MISHNEH TORAH, *Laws of Sanhedrin* 14:11–14.

institutions: the Temple, the priesthood, the Sanhedrin, the monarchy and the prophets. This theological and political condition is known as *galut*, or exile, wherein, on account of sin, the Jewish nation is bereft of its spiritual and political bearings. In *galut*, Jews are consigned to merely "muddle through" history until such time that God will redeem His people and restore their political and legal institutions "as in the days of yore."

Later in the Talmudic period we encounter the discontinuation of *smikha* or what is known as rabbinic ordination. Jewish law understands that true ordination – which traces back from student to teacher all the way to Moses – cannot function outside the Land of Israel.[11] The institution currently referred to as ordination is a mere stand-in, a concession to necessity that aids in the muddling through, but is not vested with the authority of true Mosaic ordination.[12] Moreover, because only "Mosaicly" ordained judges can serve as "real" halakhic judges on "real" halakhic courts, contemporary courts are themselves stand-ins that lack the judicial authority granted to the judges that adjudicate in formal courts of Jewish law.[13]

This point is driven home in the daily prayer service, where observant Jews remind themselves *three times* each day that they live in a state of personal, political and legal exile. Thus, no matter how wise and just the current crop of rabbinic judges, they are not the "real" ultimate authorities of halakhah, as the liturgy stresses:

> Restore our judges as at first
> And our counselors as at the beginning
> And remove from us sorrow and sighing.

The core idea is that the true, and ideal halakhah is something that is prayed for but not yet manifest. In the meantime however, Jews plod though best as they can, dealing with the facts presented to them. This way of thinking had a profound effect on Jewish law, particularly, in those areas of halakhah where the impact of *galut* registers most strongly. One of the most famous of these doctrines is known as *dina de'malkhuta dina* (DMD), effectively translated as the "law of the kingdom is valid law."[14]

---

[11] See generally, MISHNEH TORAH, *Laws of Sanhedrin*, chapter 4.
[12] See ARBA TURIM, *Hoshen Mishpat* §2 and SHULKHAN ARUKH, *Hoshen Mishpat* §2.
[13] See MISHNEH TORAH, *Laws of Sanhedrin*, 5:9–17. ARBA TURIM, *Hoshen Mishpat* §1 and SHULKHAN ARUKH, *Hoshen Mishpat* §1.
[14] See generally, Menachem Elon, *JEWISH LAW: HISTORY, SOURCES, PRINCIPLES* Vol. 1 62–74 (JPS, 1994); ENCYCLOPEDIA TALMUDIT Vol. 7 295–308 (Hebrew). The most comprehensive

In its most basic application, DMD allows Jews to accommodate the actions of the ruling (non-Jewish) government within the parameters of halakhah. Thus, suppose the government exercises its taxing or eminent domain authority by condemning a Jew's Jewish land and using the trees to build a bridge for public use. The Talmud initially wonders whether another Jew is permitted to use the bridge, since the bridge-crosser would be complicit in the theft of the wood and land from the condemned landowner. The Talmud nevertheless permits using the bridge, on the theory that the state's act of eminent domain is legally valid. Thus, even though the state's action is probably *not* valid under internal principles of halakhic property law, they may nevertheless be justified under the alternative principle of DMD.[15]

While DMD began its career as a defense to claims of conversion and theft, in time, it introduced several different possibilities for Jewish legal multivalence. At its most basic level, DMD holds that what is considered correct Jewish legal practice will shift based on the secular jurisdiction where Jews reside. More significantly, it allows the norms mandated by the civil state to (depending on the theory of DMD), become incorporated into halakhah or even circumvent some of its otherwise binding rules. In other words, rather that just the bivalent options of permitted/prohibited, there many now be a third category, prohibited as per formal halakhah, yet permitted under DMD.[16]

The size, scope, and application of the DMD principle has long been the subject of debate. Maximalists argue that DMD enables the entire legal regime of the modern administrative state to be incorporated into Jewish law. As a result, (i) secular law prevails in cases of conflict, at least with regard to financial matters, and (ii), violations of secular law may entail religious as well as civil consequences. In modern times, this doctrine has / enabled Jews to act as full participants in the modern state, notwithstanding the conflict between state and Jewish law.

The minimalist view, by contrast, sees DMD as the limited right of the state to tax its citizens and institute modest forms of public regulation. Here the theory is much thinner, stating only that in exile, Jews must follow the basic ground rules of the ruling society so as to not stir up trouble.

---

treatment of the subject remains Shmuel Shilo, Dina de-Malkhuta Dina (Jerusalem Academic Press, 1974) (Hebrew).

[15] Talmud, Bava Kamma 113a–b.

[16] See Joel Roth, *Crossing the Bridge to Secular Law: Three Models of Incorporation*, 12 Cardozo L. Rev. 753 (1991).

However, anytime the eye of the sovereign is, or could be persuaded to, look elsewhere, Jewish law takes precedence over state law.[17]

A second, somewhat lesser known doctrine of Jewish civil law is known as *"kim li."* Literally, *kim li* means, "I hold of." This doctrine is employed by a civil defendant who may claim, "I hold of the opinion of Rabbi X," in a case where the opinion of Rabbi X is useful to the defendant's view of the case.[18]

As in the case of DMD, the size and scope of *"kim li"* is debated. The basic point, however, is that in the absence of judicial power to decide between the various positions of Jewish law, the defendant can claim that, since plaintiff bears the burden of proof, plaintiff must demonstrate that the opinion of Rabbi X is rejected. Since the court does not have the formal authority of Mosiac ordination, however, it cannot conclusively rule against Rabbi X. Thus plaintiff cannot meet his burden of proof and defendant wins.

Like DMD, *kim li* allows for a certain form of multivalence. Within the zone of acceptable *kim li* claims, each person can more or less author his own law. The defendant can force the court to accept his interpretation as correct, or at the very least, prevent the plaintiff from showing the opinion is not correct. *Kim li* assumes that in the exilic era, certain legal questions cannot be resolved, and the law must resign itself to enforcing the status quo.

Like DMD, *kim li* is less a statement of halakhic principle, and more a practical concession to exilic circumstance. Yet each of these doctrines allows Jewish jurists, to draw a line between the "real" and formal halakhah, which reflects the One Truth the One God revealed to His people, and the conditions of exile where Jews muddle through using whatever tools are available. From the perspective of bi and multivalence, however, these doctrines transition halakhah from a legal regime that assumes that are either absolutely correct or incorrect answers, to a system where the answer changes based on jurisdictional and procedural considerations.

3.1   Divine Authority and Stateless Law

A second source of halakhic multivalence emerges from the fact that the touchstone of halakhic authority lies not in a state or a political entity but

---

[17] See Elon, supra note 14.

[18] For an overview of this topic, see Ezra Batzri, *DINNEI MAMONOT*, Vol. 4 at 134–208 (HaKtav Institute, 1982) (Hebrew).

a theological commitment to God and his Torah. This difference is
manifest in how each system structures its central questions. At bottom,
state based systems are interested in one primary question: Is X's conduct
legal, and if not what actions will the state take in response? Jewish
law, by contrast, is focused in a different type of question: "Am I right
with God, and am I living in the way He has commanded?" To answer
this latter question Jewish law employs a number of legal distinctions
that further blur the lines between the bivalent categories of legal/
illegal.[19]

For example, in the realm of the positive commandments, one typically encounters the distinction between *lekhathila* vs. *bediavad*. Though
typically translated as the difference between *ex ante* and *ex post*, the
operative meaning is something closer to ideal vs. reluctantly acceptable
standards of performance. Thus, when a person has fulfilled an obligation *lekhathila*, he has discharged his duty in the ideal manner. By
contrast, *bediavad* performance implies that while the duty has been
minimally satisfied, performance is sub-optimal. By way of example,
the core requirement to recite the daily prayer known as *Shema* applies
from roughly 45 minutes before sunrise until the third hour of the day.[20]
While these times established the baseline, halakhah maintains both
more and less ideal modes of performance. The optimal time is just
moments before sunrise, such that one completes the prayer as the sun
rises. One who does so, performs in this manner, exceeds expectations
and obtains great spiritual reward.[21] By contrast, one who recites the
prayer too early (anywhere from 72–45 minutes before sunrise), or too
late (after the third and until the fourth hour after sunrise), discharges his
duty, though only reluctantly. Finally, recitation earlier or later these last-
mentioned times fails to discharge the duty at all.[22]

The structure of the laws of *Shema* demonstrates the differences
between the architecture of state law and halakhah. Because state law
is geared towards enforcement by an external agent, it often speaks in in
the bivalent dichotomy of discharged/not discharged. The laws of
Shema however, maintain a spectrum ranging from nonperformance
(after the fourth hour, or prior to 72 minutes before sunrise), reluctant

---

[19] A general overview of this topic can be seen in Aaron Kirschenbaum, EQUITY IN JEWISH
LAW—BEYOND EQUITY: HALAKHIC ASPIRATIONALISM IN JEWISH CIVIL LAW (Ktav
Publishing, 1991).
[20] SHULKHAN ARUKH, *Orakh Haim* § 58.   [21] Ibid.   [22] Ibid.

performance (between the third and fourth hour), full performance (45 minutes before sunrise till the third hour of daylight), and optimal performance (moments before sunrise). Within this structure, it is difficult to disentangle the bivalent requirements of the law (discharge/not discharge) from the religious motivation to stand right in the eyes God.

This line of thought is not limited to *ex-parte* questions of religious observance, however, and has implications for contract and tort law as well. Take for example the halakhic equivalent to the common law tort doctrine of "proximate cause." In one class of cases, the defendant's action are deemed too remote to establish liability in human courts, yet the Talmud rules that the tortfeasor is nevertheless liable under the "Laws of Heaven."[23] In terms of Jewish civil law as administered, the defendant is not liable, but because halakhah is also a religious system, the court tells the defendant he has not met his obligation in God's eyes until he renders payment. In some instances, the community will either enforce social sanctions until such obligations are met, or else, permit the plaintiff to engage in in self help to and seize defendant's assets.[24]

The same logic can be applied in the other direction. In general, halakhah requires an employer to pay her employee the wage as soon as the contract term is completed.[25] Failure to do so is sinful and entails a religious violation, but this prohibition, however, only applies when the employer has cash on hand. If the employer does not have the funds available no prohibition attaches, though the wage debt is certainly owed.[26]

But what exactly does it mean for the employer to have the necessary funds?" Must it be cash on hand, or is the employer required to sell or leverage assets? Can she rely on incoming accounts receivable? Must she take out a loan, and if so at what rates? As a minimal baseline, the *bediavad* answer to these questions is generally "no," and in each case

---

[23] Talmud, Bava Kamma 56b. See also Kirschenbaum, supra note 19 at 137–179.

[24] See Shlomo Luria, YAM SHEL SHLOMO to Bava Kamma 6:6 (sixteenth century), as well as sources cited in ENCYCLOPEDIA TALMUDIT Vol. 7 382–96; Kirschenbaum, supra note 19 at 159–60; 163–65.

[25] Mishnah, Bava Metzia 9:12; Talmud, Bava Metzia 110b–111a.

[26] See Chaim Saiman, *Talmud Study, Ethics and Social Policy: A Case Study in the Laws of Wage-Payment as an Argument for Neo-Lamdanut*, 25 JEWISH LAW ASSOCIATION STUDIES 225–261(2014).

the employer is excused from violating the religious prohibition. Yet anyone aiming for more optimal halakhic compliance will likely strive and answer these questions in the affirmative. This creates an array of legal categories that are more complex than the bivalent liable/not liable framework which prevails in state legal systems.[27]

A final example is demonstrated by the Talmud's story of Rabbah and his casks of wine, which proceeds as follows:[28]

> Rabbah b. Hanan's casks of wine were broken by porters.
> He took their clothing [as collateral for the obligation to pay for breaking the wine casks].
> The porters went and reported this to Rav
> Rav said to Rabba b. Hanan, "give them their clothing!"
> Rabbah b. Hannan asked Rav "is this the law?"
> Rav answered, "Yes. [citing Proverbs. 2:20]
> *In order that you shall go in the path of good people.*"
> Rabbah gave the porters their clothing.
>
> The porters then said to Rav:
> "We are poor, and we have labored the entire day,
> we are starving and have nothing to eat."
> Rav said to Rabba, "pay them their fee!"
> Rabba asked of Rav, "is this the law?
> Rav answered, "Yes. [citing the continuation of Prov. 2:20]
> *And you shall keep the ways of the righteous.*"

Both the implications, and even the precise text of this story are debated by classical as well as modern scholars.[29] Specifically, was Rav ruling as a judge and applying the strict letter of the law, or was giving religious or moral guidance, telling Rabbah "for *you* this is the law." When this story is assimilated into the surrounding legal framework, the latter view emerges as more cogent. A number of medieval authorities thus understood Rav as ruling against Rabbah because: (i) Rabbah was wealthy and Rav was pushing him to act charitably; or (ii) because as Rav's student, Rabbah was being judged morally rather than legally; or

---

[27] Ibid. at 251–52.   [28] Talmud, Bava Metzia 83a.

[29] See for example, Moshe Silberg, TALMUDIC LAW IN THE MODERN STATE, 118–123 (United Synagogue Books, 1972); Ephraim E. Urbach, THE SAGES: THEIR CONCEPTS AND BELIEFS 330–331 (Harvard, 3rd ed. 1987); Shmuel Shilo, *On One Aspect of Law and Morals*, 13 ISRAEL LAW REVIEW 359, 377–387 (1978); Hanina Ben-Menahem, JUDICIAL DEVIATION IN TALMUDIC LAW: GOVERNED BY MEN NOT RULES, 74–79 (Harwood, 1991); Aaron Kirschenbaum, EQUITY IN JEWISH LAW—HALAKHIC PERSPECTIVES IN LAW: FORMALISM AND FLEXIBILITY IN JEWISH CIVIL LAW, 121–123 (Ktav, 1991).

(iii) that if Rabbah wanted to be a member in good standing of the rabbinic community, he must hold himself to higher standards. Whatever the exact interpretation, this Talmudic discussion thinks about legal rules spectrally, along a range of different standards of compliance, rather than through the bivalnet categories of liable/not liable.

In sum, because halakhic authority is vested in the belief in God and His Torah, rather than the power of the state, Jewish law maintains a categories that offer different rules for various levels of religious commitment rather than the bivalent legal/illegal. When the law's central question is not "is this conduct legal" but, "am I right with God," the issue is less susceptible to the bivalent analysis that animates state law.

3.2 Is Halakhah Really Jewish Law?

A third factor of halakhic multivalence relates to the different roles halakhah plays within Jewish society. Though in many ways, halakhah is correctly defined as Jewish law, this definition fails to capture the entire range of how halakhah is conceptualized by its adherents. Rabbinic theology maintains that study of halakhah is a method of Divine worship, and on some accounts, the central way that a Jew comes to know God.

Since this is a somewhat unfamiliar and difficult concept, I will proceed by way of example:

The Book of Deuteronomy, discusses the procedure undertaken when the corpse of a murder victim is found in the deserted area between two towns.[30] The court is to measure the distance from the corpse to the nearest town, and once the closest town is identified, the elders perform an expiation ceremony that absolves the community of responsibility for the unsolved murder.

In the Mishnah and Talmud, the measurement process is seen as a core element of the expiation ritual, and the Rabbis become interested in technical surrounding details. Specifically, what if the corpse is found between two? The Mishnah records:[31]

> From which part of the corpse do they measure?
> Rabbi Eliezer says, from his navel
> Rabbi Akiva says, from his nostrils.

---

[30] Chapter 21:1–9.   [31] Mishnah, Sotah 9:4.

As a statement of legal regulation, this is a fairly ridiculous passage. First, in order for the obligation towards this ceremony to be triggered, the victim must be murdered and found in rather particular ways.[32] Second, on the Mishnah's own account, the ritual was abolished prior to the destruction of the Temple – well before the lifetime of Rabbis Akiva and Eliezer.[33] Finally, for this Mishnah to be relevant in practice, one would have to assume that, in addition to all the other conditions, the corpse was perfectly equidistant between two towns, save the 18 inches of space between the navel and the nose. (Where in the town you measure from is not discussed).

Upon closer examination, however, the laws regarding the unidentified murder victim seem more expressive than regulatory.[34] Here we find a concise example of how the Talmudic rabbis use halakhic categories to carry out a theological discussion that touches on the conceptual or perhaps ontological center of a human being. What is the essence of Man: the nose (face) or the navel (gut)? This query itself can be understood in several ways: Is Man primarily a spiritual, as the nostrils represent where God blew His life into Adam,[35] or is Man centered as his navel, where the physical body is created from?

The Talmud itself broaches such a reading, as follows:[36]

> What are they arguing about?
> One master [R' Akiva] holds:
> The primary element of life is in his nostrils.
> And one master [R' Eliezer] holds:
> The primary element of life is in his navel.

The Jerusalem Talmud presents a similar idea in these terms.[37]

> Rabbi Eliezer says:
> From his navel—from the place that the fetus is created
> Rabbi Akiva says:
> From his nostrils—the place where the face is recognized.

---

[32] For example, the victim must be found outside of the town and dead on the ground. If the body was buried in the ground or under a pile of stones, or found floating on the water or hung on a tree, the expiation procedure is not undertaken. Likewise, the victim must be murdered in particular ways. A choked or poisoned victim does not qualify, since the body must be pierced by a sword or other metal weapon. See Maimonides, MISHNEH TORAH, *The Laws of Murder*, 9:11.

[33] Mishnah, Sotah 9:9.

[34] This matter is discussed at length in Yishai Rosen-Tzvi, THE MISHNAIC SOTAH RITUAL: TEMPLE, GENDER AND MIDRASH (Brill, 2012).

[35] Genesis 2:7.   [36] Talmud, Sotah 45b.   [37] Jerusalem Talmud, Sotah 9:3.

These two passages make clear that the Mishnah's issue is not how we measure the corpse of a man, but how we measure the essence of Man. In the Christian context, this question would be interpreted theologically. In the modern academy it belongs in the humanities, social sciences or increasingly, neuropsychology. For the Rabbis, however, it is a matter of halakhah, as halakhah encompasses these very questions.

Note however, that the halakhic-legal context is not divorced from the theological message it imparts, as the expiation ceremony is designed to draw attention to the uniqueness of the human being. When an animal carcass lays at the side of the road, Jewish law does not mandate any response. But when a human is killed, the entire body politic is engaged. The Talmud even records a view whereby the King and the Great Sanhedrin – the highest ranking officials in the polity – are personally involved in the process. All this begs the question: Why is a human corpse different? And this is precisely the halakhic debate between Rabbis Akiva and Eliezer.

But while halakhah presents this matter as irrepressibly "legal," it is not the sort of issue that can be conclusively resolved by a court. The question, is much bigger than that. Thus, to the extent Jewish law is about social regulation, it might require bivalent answers. But because halakhah is also rabbinic way of discussing theology, philosophy, self-identity and group filiation, it inevitably entails multivalence.

This idea is neatly summarized by one of the most famous texts in canon relating to the theory of Talmudic legal thought.[38]

> R. Abba reported in the name of Samuel.
> For three years the students of Shammai and Hillel debated–
> Each side claimed the law was in accord with their view.
>
> Eventually a heavenly voice went out to declare,
> "That these and those [both views] are the words of the Living God.
> But the halakhah is in accord with the students of Hillel."

In response, the Talmud asks

> But if these and those are the words of the Living God,
> Why does the halakhah follow the students of Hillel?

The Talmud answers:

> Because they were congenial and humble.
> And would study their view and the view of the students Shammai.

---

[38] Talmud, Eruvin 13b.

> Moreover, they would mention the opinion of Shammai prior to their own opinion.

This text can serve as a basis for a conference on multivalence in its own right,[39] but for present purposes, I focus on how the Talmud's posits different layers of truth. At first, is truth as it stands before God. This realm of halakhah tolerates and perhaps even celebrates multivalence. But the Talmud recognizes, that at the level of legal practice decisions must be made, and for this reason the law runs in accord with Hillel. The Talmud, however, does not offer any substantive mechanism for determining which view is correct. Rather, since both positions are conceptually valid, the choice of Hillel over Shammai is based on the personal disposition and educational philosophy of its bearer, rather than on a claim of halakhic truth.

Hence a third source of Jewish legal multivalence stems from the fact that in addition to being law, halakhah is the collective project of generations of jurists, lawyers, rabbis and thinkers who employed the legal idiom to understand God's message. While some areas are clearly given over to the bivalence that is necessary for a functioning regulatory regime, others (explicitly or implicitly) serve as teaching models, examples, and explorations of enduring questions. When implemented as regulation, halakhah must inevitably favor one opinion over the other, but at the level of assessing ideas and concepts, the Talmud recognizes that other views may be equally valid.

4   How Does God Talk to Man? On the Nature of Divine Revelation

One final source of Jewish legal multivalence, which in many ways ties together the strands developed above, relates to the nature of God's Revelation itself. At the outset we assumed that because Jewish law was the product of God talking to Man, it must contain a single revealed truth that rejects all others. This bivalent view is captured in Deuteronomy's

---

[39] See, for example, Michael Rosenzweig, *Elu Va-Elu Divrei Elokim Hayyim: Halakhic Pluralism and Theories of Controversy*, 20 TRADITION 4–23 (1992); Avi Sagi, *Both are the Words of the Living God, A Typological Analysis of Halakhic Pluralism*, 65 HEBREW UNION COLLEGE ANNUAL 105 (1995); Avi Sagi, ELU VA-ELU: A STUDY ON THE MEANING OF HALAKHIC DISCOURSE (Hakibbutz Hameuched, 1996) (Hebrew); Aviezer Ravitsky, *Tolerance in the Jewish Religious Tradition*, in BETWEEN AUTHORITY AND AUTONOMY IN THE JEWISH TRADITION (SAFRAI AND SAGI EDS., Hakibbutz Hameuched, 1997) (Hebrew); Gilbert Rosenthal, *"Both These and Those": Pluralism within Judaism*, 56 CONSERVATIVE JUDAISM 3–20 (2004).

warning, "*behold I have placed before you life and goodness, death and evil*,[40] and remains the operative assumption of many halakhic jurists. Yet this position must contend with the prevalence of debate within the Talmud. After all, if God revealed the answers at Sinai, why have Jews spent the last 2000 years arguing about them?

In his seminal work, PEOPLE OF THE BOOK, the philosopher Moshe Halbertal categorized several traditional approaches to this question.[41] The most conservative approach, which Halbertal labels the "retrieval model," was summarized by the twelfth century philosopher, Abraham ibn Duad, as follows:[42]

> The purpose of this Book of Tradition is to provide students with the evidence that all the teachings of our rabbis of blessed memory, namely, the sages of the Mishnah and the Talmud, have been transmitted: each great sage and righteous man having received them from a great sage and righteous man... as far back as the men of the Great Assembly, who received them from the prophets, of blessed memory all. Never did the sages of the Mishnah, teach anything, however trivial, of their own invention...
>
> Now should anyone infected with heresy attempt to mislead you, saying: "It's because the rabbis differed on a number of issues that I doubt their words," you should retort bluntly and inform him that he is a [heretic] and that our rabbis of blessed memory never differed with respect to a commandment in principle, but only with respect to its detail; *for they had heard the principle form their teachers, but had not inquired as to its details since they had not waited upon their masters sufficiently.*

In the retrieval model, correct answers to all questions of Jewish law were revealed by God to Moses at Sinai, and from there, transmitted rabbi-to-student down through the ages. As time went on however, the quality of the students decreased as they neglected to inquire to the details of each law. Because correct answers were forgotten, later scholars had to reconstruct (and debate) the original legal rules. On this theory, the Talmud, is the record of attempts to restore the lost legal data, and the project of legal reasoning, to recover initially revealed truths.

Though this is a prominent, perhaps dominant view, a different understanding of Revelation and halakhic debate has always existed

---

[40] Deuteronomy 30:15.

[41] Moshe Halbertal, PEOPLE OF THE BOOK: CANON, MEANING AND AUTHORITY 50–72 (Harvard, 1997).

[42] Abraham ibn Duad, THE BOOK OF TRADITION, cited and translated by Halbertal, *supra* at 55–56.

alongside it. An alternative theory, which Halbertal labels the "constitutive view,"[43] emerges from the mystical and kabbalistic tradition,
obtainings its most famous articulation by the sixteenth century Polish
halakhist, R. Solomon Luria. In his introduction to his commentary of
the Talmud, R. Luria explains the genesis of halakhic debate as
follows:[44]

> You should not be surprised about [the Talmudic] disputes and the great
> divergence in their views: that one declares impure and another pure; one
> prohibits and one permits; one finds liability and the other exempts. So
> long as their opinions are for the sake of heaven. . . .they are all the words
> of a living God, and it is *as if* each scholar received the revelation from the
> Almighty and from Moses. To be sure, Moses himself never said two
> opposing views on the same matter. But even so, the Sages made this
> analogy due to the validity and strength of the positions expressed. . .
>
> And the mystics gave the following reason. Since all souls were present at
> Sinai, and they accepted the revelation through 49 channels. . . there are
> differences due to reception via different channels. Each person experi-
> enced the revelation based on his ability, and based on the on strength of his
> soul, each one a different message, until one can reach the opposite
> conclusion from the other; one declaring pure and the other impure, and
> a third in a middle position, and it is all true, and must be understood.
>
> Therefore you should ask yourself: Why Moses did not write from the
> Almighty a clear and lucid explanation of the Torah so that there would
> be no doubt. . . For there is no end to [the Torah's] depth. For if the entire
> heavens were parchment and all the oceans ink, it would not even suffice
> to cover but one paragraph of the Torah's richness, given all the questions
> that arise from it, and all the inferences that the Sages of Israel can deduce
> from it though in-depth analysis; constantly, deepening, broadening and
> expanding the Torah.

The mystical conception offers a counter-narrative to the legalistic
image of Divine Revelation introduced at the outset. According to
R. Luria, the debates within Jewish law are not the tragic consequences
of poor scholarship, nor concessions to the vicissitudes of history. Rather,
they are hard-wired into the nature of halakhah itself. For whereas the
jurist thinks of law as determinate legal rules, the mystic understands
halakhah as a conversation between finite Man and the infinite God. As
mankind is limited, it grasps only a sliver of the Divine spectrum. To
understand God, is to understand that the dialogue between God and
Man necessarily produces variation and multivalence.

---

[43] Ibid. at 63.   [44] Solomon Luria, YAM SHEL SHLOMO TO BAVA KAMMA, *Introduction*.

5   Conclusion

The question of multivalence in Jewish law and thought is connected to the theological question of how Man is understood to hear the Divine call. The bivalent view sees God as commanding clear-cut rules that leave Man with only two choices: obey and obtain reward; or disobey and suffer the consequences. The alternative view likewise calls on Man to obey God, but maintains that communication between the Infinite and finite is necessarily multivalent. As per its multivalent tendencies, both ideals are embodies in the halakhic tradition.

PART II

New Logics in the Relations of Legal Orders

4

Logical Tools for Legal Pluralism

JAAP HAGE

1 Introduction

Legal rules often conflict with each other. For our present purposes rules may be said to conflict if they are all applicable to one and the same case, while the legal consequences that would result from their application are incompatible.[1] This happens within one legal system, as when theft is punished with at most four years' incarceration, while theft during the nighttime is punished with at most six years,[2] or when a municipality locally prohibits pubs to be open on Sundays, while that is allowed nationally. It also happens when the norms of a national legal system deviate from those created by an international organization, as when a Member State of the European Union taxes what is not taxable according to EU Law.[3] It happens when a contract violates rules of mandatory law, and also when state law collides with rules belonging to a particular religion such as the Shari'a or Jewish law.[4]

With legal rules stemming from diverse sources, law has perhaps always been pluralist, with rule conflicts as a consequence. However, even if legal pluralism is an old phenomenon, it has gained in importance during the last decades of globalization. The resulting rule conflicts have also gained in prevalence, and it is important to pay special attention to the ways in which law can deal with them. The central question of this contribution is whether logic can be helpful in this connection. In his famous book LEGAL TRADITIONS OF THE WORLD, Patrick Glenn (2014)

---

[1] In the following I will write about the incompatibility of legal consequences, and about the inconsistency of conclusions of rule applying arguments. The reason for this difference in terminology is that (in)consistency is a characteristic of linguistic entities such as descriptive sentences or propositions, while (in)compatibility is a relation between facts.

[2] Dutch Penal Code (*Wetboek van Strafrecht*), Art. 310 and 311.

[3] CJEU case 26/62 [1963] (Van Gend & Loos).

[4] A more elaborate overview of kinds of conflicts between legal rules can be found in Berman 2012, pp. 23–57.

already raised this question. After having described the main legal traditions, he addressed in the tenth chapter of his book the question how the different traditions could be reconciled, and in this connection he pointed to modern developments in logic which might make it possible to leave the traditional laws of consistency and of the excluded middle behind. This contribution is an attempt to explore these possibilities in a mainly informal way. The emphasis will in this connection be on the use of logical tools that are usually associated with the technical notion of non-monotonicity (Hage 2005, p. 24).

At first sight, the logic of rule application is nothing else than an ordinary syllogistic argument (Alexy 1983, pp. 273–283; MacCormick 1978, pp. 19–53). The facts of a case are subsumed under a general rule, and the conclusion that describes the legal consequence of the case follows deductively. For example, a rule reads that the major of a city has the power to issue emergency regulations. Boris is the mayor of Kropotkingrad. By subsuming this fact under the rule, the conclusion can be deduced that Boris is competent to issue emergency regulations.

An argument can only be deductively valid if it is logically impossible that all the premises of the argument are true, while the conclusion of the argument is false (e.g. Weinberger 1989, p. 91). Because a conclusion of a rule-applying argument is deduced from the two premises, it can only be false if either one of the two premises is false. The falsity of the conclusion would imply that either the used rule is not valid, or the facts are different from what the second premise said.

Given this definition of deductive validity, a conflict of rules may lead to inconsistent legal consequences. Suppose that there is a rule that emergency regulations can only be issued in case of an emergency. If Boris issues an emergency regulation although there is no emergency, the power-conferring rule leads to the conclusion that the emergency regulation that Boris created is valid. The rule specifying the circumstances under which an emergency regulation can be issued, however, makes invalid the regulation by Boris. Going by deductive logic alone, the regulation is both valid and invalid, an unattractive outcome.

It will be obvious to most lawyers that the two rules should be combined. An emergency regulation can only be created in case of an emergency, and then the mayor of the city is empowered to do so. Obvious as this outcome may be, it can only be reached if the logic of rule application is not ordinary deductive logic. Lawyers often say that they handle such cases by means of 'interpretation', but that does not clarify much. We would like to have a more precise account of what goes

on when legal subjects or legal decision makers must cope with conflicting rules. In the last few decades major developments have taken place
with regard to the logic that can be used to model rule application
(Schauer 1991; Gordon 1995; Verheij 1996; Hage 1997, 2005; Prakken
1997; Lodder 1999; Sartor 2005). The question that will be addressed in
this paper is in what manner these modern logical theories can help
lawyers to deal with conflicting rules.

2 The Roles of Logic

Before the real argument starts it is important to make clear what can be
the role of logic in law. Lawyers sometimes have been a bit suspicious
about this role. The suspicion can be recognized in the resistance of
lawyers against 'formalism' (Hart 2012, pp. 124–154) and '*Begriffsjuris-
prudenz*' (Kaufmann and Hassemer 1977, pp. 92–95). Characteristic in
this connection is the famous quotation from Oliver Wendell Holmes
that '[t]he life of law has not been logic: it has been experience . . .'.[5]

Most likely, this resistance can be traced to the fear that logic would
dictate solutions for legal cases that are not desirable, but which are
nevertheless taken because logic would 'require' them. Such a fear would
be misgiven, because in the first instance, logic does nothing else than to
indicate which conclusions follow from which premises. It cannot indicate that particular conclusions should be drawn; the most it can do is
to show that a particular conclusion follows from certain premises.
Moreover, deductive logic is as 'empty' as possible. Logical rules are
formulated in such a way that the task of determining the outcome of
an argument is as much as possible assigned to the premises of the
argument. Deductive logic aims to do no more than to make explicit
what was already implicit in the premises. This means that a legal decision
maker who, for whatever reason, does not want to draw a particular
conclusion that follows from his premises, can always decide to drop
one or more of the premises rather than to draw the conclusion. Logic, in
the first instance, informs us what follows from what, but it cannot force
us to draw a specific substantial conclusion. Therefore, the fear of some
that logic may require that legal decision makers take the 'wrong' decisions is not justified.

---

[5] Quoted after http://en.wikiquote.org/wiki/Oliver_Wendell_Holmes,_Jr. (last visited on
May 1, 2015).

The limited role of logic also means that the hopes of some others, that logic may assist the legal decision maker in cutting difficult knots, is also misgiven. This still holds if the blunt instrument of deductive logic is replaced by the sharper edged instruments of modern logic. It is the task of logic – and this is more a programmatic starting point than an empirical observation – to be as 'empty' as possible. Logic should study which conclusions follow from which premises, but it should at the same time attempt to leave as much as possible of the factors contributing to some conclusion to be determined by premises that deal with the content of a domain. To phrase it by means of a slogan: *if it can be a premise, do not turn it into logic.*

However, there is also an additional function for logic, a function that has little to do with making inferences. Logic can help us in making analytical distinctions that are useful in formulating precise theories about law. We have already seen an example of this function of logic when we noticed that if the logic of rule application would be deductive logic, the application of conflicting rules to a set of cases may lead to incompatible legal consequences. Logic does not force us to adopt these incompatible consequences; it only makes clear that if we want to avoid them we had better look out for a different logic of rule application. Moreover, it can also help us to find alternatives for deduction that do more justice to good legal reasoning as it actually takes place. If the logic of rule application is treated as if it were a branch of deductive logic, it is likely that conflicting rules will lead to inconsistent conclusions for concrete cases. Through adoption of a non-deductive logic, which allows for exceptions to rules, the inconsistencies that seemingly result from conflicting rules can be avoided (see Sections 4.4 and 4.5). However, let me repeat the warning: do not expect from logic that it tell us how immanent conflicts of rules should be handled. The law determines which rule prevails if there is a conflict; logic can only show how a higher-level rule can solve the conflict. The content of this higher-level rule is still a legal matter.

3   Kinds of Conflicts

There are two ways in which rules conflict with each other. It is possible that one rule provides that something is the case, while another rule provides that something else is the case. For instance according to one rule, Blackacre is owned by Geraldine, while according to some other rule John has title to this ranch. Because rules impose facts upon the world – they make it the case that these facts obtain – such conflicts will be called *conflicts of imposition*. The conflicting rules impose incompatible facts upon the world, facts that cannot co-exist. On the assumption that the ranch Blackacre cannot have two owners, the fact that Geraldine owns the ranch is incompatible with the fact that John owns it.[6]

The second kind of conflict has to do with rules which prescribe incompatible forms of behavior. Such a conflict occurs if a farmer is obligated to combat thistles, but is at the same time not permitted to destroy plants. Another example would be that a journalist is obligated to reveal the sources on which he based a controversial publication, while she promised her informant not to reveal his identity. Such conflicts may be called *compliance conflicts*.

Rules conflict with each other if their conditions for application allow a case to which the rules attach to involve incompatible legal consequences. Which legal consequences are incompatible may depend on other rules. Examples of conflicting rules are:

- the rules that a bona fide buyer becomes the owner of a good that was transferred to him, and the rule that the transfer of a good by a non-owner does not pass ownership;
- the rule that prescribes house owners to clean away the snow from the pavement before their houses and the rule that prohibits the use of snow blowers, if somebody can only clean the pavement with the use of a snow blower.

4   Rule Conflicts within a Legal System

To discover which logical tools are available to deal with conflicting rules that stem from different legal systems, it is useful to study first how rule conflicts are dealt with within single legal systems, because conflicts within a single system are the most frequent manifestation of rule conflicts. This immediately raises the question what a single legal system is.

4.1   *The Definition of a Legal System*

One way to answer this question is to look at the sources of law. A simple theory is that a legal system consists of all the rules that stem from one

---

[6] The phenomenon that the conflict of rules is also determined by constraints that determine which facts can go together plays a central role in Hage 2005, pp. 142–144.

'highest' rule which points out what the sources of the legal system are. An example of such a highest rule would be that law consists of those rules that were created by agents (legislators, judges) who were made competent by rules belonging to the system. This rule has a ring of circularity because it defines the content of a legal system in terms of the content of the system (the rules belonging to the system). However, this circularity can be circumvented by pointing out one rule that certainly belongs to the system even if it was not created on the basis of some other rule of the system. Kelsen (1960, pp. 204–209) called such a rule the '*Grundnorm*' of the system; Hart (2012, pp. 105–110) called it the 'Ultimate Rule of Recognition'. It is questionable whether such a highest rule that is the source of the rest of the legal system actually exists in all legal systems. Kelsen (1960) actually denied that the *Grundnorm* exists as a matter of social fact, and merely claimed that its existence is a necessary presupposition of the validity of the norms belonging to the system.

For my present purposes I will take a pragmatic approach and start from the perspective of an agent who has to apply the law to a concrete case, a judge for instance. Such an agent wants to have an unambiguous outcome for the case, and will therefore work on the assumption that the law, if it applies to the case, attaches a single legal consequence to it. The law is therefore assumed to be consistent. However, it does not follow from this assumption of consistency of the law as a whole that there are no conflicting legal rules within the system. The assumption of consistency 'merely' boils down to requiring that the rules of the system, whether they are consistent or not, somehow contribute to the content of the law, and that the result of the combined relevant rules of the system is somehow consistent.

We have already seen an example of how the combination of rules works in the case of Boris who made an emergency regulation for Kropotkingrad even though there was no emergency. The two inconsistent rules were combined into a single 'rule' that leads to a single consistent result. The word 'rule' was placed within quotes because it differs from the two rules that were used to construct it. Let us assume that both the rule that the mayor is competent to make emergency regulations and the rule that these regulations can only be made in case of an emergency can be traced back to an official legal source such as a statutory provision. The constructed 'rule' cannot be traced back directly to such a source but is the result of combining the two original rules in the light of what is their apparent purpose.

The example that theft is punished with at most four years of incarceration, while theft at night gives up to six years, is dealt with in a similar fashion. The general rule about theft is (restrictively) interpreted as dealing with 'ordinary' theft, while the second rule is interpreted as dealing with theft during the nighttime. The resulting constructed 'rules' are that theft during daytime is punished with at most four years' incarceration, and theft during nighttime with at most six years. These reconstructed rules do not conflict.

In an earlier publication (Hage 2005, p. 17) I introduced the expression 'case-legal consequence pair' (CLCP) for these constructed 'rules'. It is possible to describe a legal system as defined by an exhaustive set of such CLCP's: for every kind of case that has legal consequences there exists a CLCP that gives the characteristics of the kind of case and the legal consequences attached to it. These CLCP's are the outcome of the original rules (including rights and legal principles) of the system, interpretation and solutions of eventual rule conflicts by means of priority rules (such as *Lex Superior*) or whatever other techniques the system in question employs to resolve rule conflicts. The CLCP's are constructed in such a way that no particular case can fall under two different case descriptions to which incompatible consequences are attached. For example, there will be a case description for 'theft during daytime' and one for 'theft during nighttime', but not one for theft in general because the latter might give a different legal consequence in a concrete case of theft during nighttime. The legal system, as I will define it for my present purposes, consists of such an exhaustive set of CLCP's and all the other materials (rules, rights, principles; the 'underlying materials' of the system) that were used to construct this set.[7] Given the way in which CLCP's have been defined, it is not possible that a case has inconsistent legal consequences according to a single legal system. Immanent inconsistencies are filtered out in the step from the original rules to the CLCP's.

4.2   The Scope of Rules

The idea of a legal system that does not lead to inconsistent legal consequences is a theoretical construction, and the question is still open how to arrive at such a system if the actual rules within a system do

---

[7] This makes a legal system agent-relative. It consists of the CLCP's and the underlying materials as used by this agent (Hage 2013, 2015). A 'real' legal system can only exist if many agents ('officials') use the same materials to construct their CLCP-set.

conflict.[8] Here is where the logical tools come into play. One of them has to do with the scope of rules. Most legal rules identify by means of their conditions the kind of cases to which they are applicable. However, even rules without conditions, such as the prohibition on committing murder, do not apply to everything. There are limitations on the cases to which a rule applies that are not mentioned in the conditions of the rule. These are scope conditions, which combine with the rule conditions in the narrow sense to determine to which cases and/or persons rules should be applied.

The rules about the applicability of Dutch criminal law (articles 1–8d Penal Code) provide a nice illustration of the operation of scope conditions. The first condition is that only those acts can be punished that are punishable on the basis of a rule that existed at the time of the act. This condition is a limitation of the scope of the Penal Code in time. More generally, all legal rules have a *scope in time* in the sense that they can only apply to cases that occur during a particular time span. This time span will often coincide more or less with the time that the rule exists, but that is not necessary. An exception that occurs quite often is that of retroactive effect which is, as we saw, excluded for Dutch penal law. If two rules have non-overlapping time scopes, they cannot apply to the same case, and that excludes the possibility of a rule conflict.

Dutch criminal law can be applied to everybody who commits a crime in the Netherlands. *E contrario* this means that in principle it cannot be applied to crimes not committed in the Netherlands. There are several exceptions to this latter principle, but that does not detract from the starting point that Dutch criminal law deals with crimes committed in the Netherlands. Dutch criminal laws tend to have a *territorial scope*. Since the criminal laws of other countries in principle have a similar territorial scope, the possibility that criminal laws from different countries lead to conflicting outcomes for a single case is limited to transterritorial cases.[9] The same effect also holds within the Dutch legal system, because municipalities have the power to define criminal offences for, by and large, their territories. Those definitions will seldom conflict because the territories of the municipalities do not overlap.

---

[8] To facilitate my exposition, I ignore the possibilities of conflicts between legal principles, between principles and rules, between rights and rules, and more in general all conflicts that are not conflicts between rules. My hope is that these other conflicts can be handled along more or less the same lines as rule conflicts.

[9] One of the effects of the rise of the internet and of globalization is that such 'transterritorial cases' have become quite frequent.

Dutch criminal law can also be applied to persons with Dutch nationality for some kinds of crimes outside the Netherlands. This is an example of *personal scope* which functions as an exception to the territorial scope of Dutch criminal law. Personal scope can also be the starting point of criminal liability. This will particularly be the case if the legal system in question is not defined by a territory but, for instance, by membership of a community defined by religion. In that case, personal scope can function as a tool to avoid rule conflicts, as when the Shari'a only applies to Muslims, while Jewish law only applies to members of the Jewish people.

4.3   Limitation of Power

A common way to avoid inconsistencies within a single legal system is to avoid rule conflicts. We have seen in the previous section that rule conflicts can be avoided by limiting the applicability of rules through their conditions and scope. They can also be avoided by making it hard for conflicting rules to enter into existence at all. If, for instance, the national legislator has made an exception to the general right of free speech for cases of hate speech, it will not allow a local legislator to make an exception to the exception for hate speech against people of a particular origin, say French-speaking people from Walloon. If a local legislator nevertheless attempts to do so, its rules will simply not be recognized as valid law. The local legislator does not have the power to make rules that conflict with the 'higher' rules of the national legislator. This limitation of power avoids conflicting rules and therefore also inconsistencies arising from rule conflicts.

A different example of the same idea would be that contract partners cannot validly contract to do something that is prohibited by legislation or, in some systems, that is immoral. As this last example illustrates, the technique of 'disempowerment' can be used not only within a single normative system, but also in the relation between parallel normative systems such as national law and morality.

4.4   Applicability and Application

There are two fundamentally different ways to look at the operation of legal rules, each with its own merits. One view sees legal rules as operating 'automatically'. If a case falls under a rule, that is if the conditions of the rule itself and the scope conditions are satisfied, then the rule is applicable to this case. On this 'automatic' view, an applicable rule will always attach its consequences to the case. Theoretically this might even happen if nobody were aware of it (Hage 2012). For example, if somebody violates a duty of care and causes damage, he automatically becomes liable for damages.

The other view sees rules as tools, used by legal decision makers, to attach consequences to cases. It is up to the decision makers to apply the rule or not. A rule is applied to a case when somebody attaches the consequences of the rule to the case. For example, a decision maker may decide to apply a rule by analogy to a case. Then the rule is applied, even though not all of its conditions were satisfied. Or the decision maker decides to make an exception to the rule and does not apply it, even though all the rule conditions are met. On this second view the issue whether a rule is to be applied to a particular case is not completely determined by the rule's applicability. Other factors may also play a role, such as the purpose of the rule, and also a possible conflict between the rule and some other rule. In particular this last possibility is relevant for us here.

4.5   Exceptions to Rules

Normally a rule is applied if it is applicable, but it is possible to apply a non-applicable rule and not to apply a rule that is applicable (Hage 1997, pp. 86–124; 2005, pp. 87–95). If a rule that is applicable in a case is nevertheless not applied to that case, we say that in that case an *exception* was made to the rule. The existence of an exception is the reason that an applicable rule is not applied, and for the existence of this reason there must be other reasons. It is, for instance, not possible to say that Günther committed theft, but should not be punished because there is an exception to the rule that thieves should be punished, even though there are no reasons for making such an exception.

The 'logic' of exceptions to rules works as follows.

- If a rule is applicable to a case, this is a contributory reason to apply the rule and to attach its conclusion as legal consequence to this case.
- Normally there are no reasons against applying an applicable rule, and then the applicability of the rule suffices as the reason to actually apply the rule and make it attach its consequences to the case.
- Sometimes there are contributory reasons against applying an applicable rule. It is not a matter of logic what such reasons might be.

- If there are both contributory reasons for and against applying a rule to a case, these reasons must be 'balanced'. This 'balancing' is little more than taking a decision which reasons outweigh the other reasons.
- If the balance of reasons leads to the conclusion that an applicable rule should not be applied, we say that there is an exception to the rule. This exception is nothing else than the outcome of balancing the reasons for and against application.
- If in a particular case there is an exception to a rule that is applicable to that case, this rule should not be applied, and its consequences are not attached to the case.

It should be noted that this logic of exceptions to rules only provides a tool to deal with exceptional circumstances. It does not indicate what such exceptional circumstances might be, nor does it tell us how the exceptional circumstances should be balanced against the applicability of the rule.

4.6   Prevalence between Rules

There may be many reasons to make an exception to a rule. For instance, in a particular case application of an applicable rule would be against the purpose of the rule. Or the person invoking a rule may have acted in such a way that invocation would be against good faith. For the present purposes the most important reason to make an exception to a rule is that the rule belongs of a set of conflicting rules which are applicable to the same case.

Since it is not desirable that the rules of a legal system attach incompatible legal consequences to a case, the possibility that this might occur is a reason not to apply one of two rules that are in conflict.[10] The question then becomes which rule to apply and which rule to disregard, or – in other words – which rules prevails over the other rule. Logic is not suited to answer this question by itself, but it can provide the tools to deal with prevalence between rules and the implication this has for avoiding actual rule conflicts. The argument that is relevant in this connection would be along the following lines:

---

[10] Some might argue that it is even impossible that two rules attach inconsistent legal consequences to a case. However, it is not immediately clear that the reality that is constructed through rule application must be consistent. It may be worth the effort to investigate the possibility that institutional reality can be inconsistent, but this is not the place to undertake that enterprise.

- If two rules are applicable to a case, and their application would result in inconsistent legal consequences, this is a contributory reason against application of one of the two rules.
- The fact that application of both rules would lead to an inconsistency is a stronger reason against application than the applicability of the rules as a reason for application.
- The intermediate conclusion is that one of the two conflicting rules should not be applied. But which one?

That is a matter of prevalence: the rule that prevails over the other rule should be applied. Logic cannot answer the question which rule prevails (under which circumstances). This is a substantive legal issue. As a matter of fact several contributory reasons can play a role in this connection:[11]

- The rule that better fits in the overall legal system prevails over the less fitting rule (Coherence)
- The rule that was made by the 'higher' authority prevails over the rule with the rule made by the lower authority (Lex Superior).
- The more specific rule prevails over the more general rule (Lex Specialis).
- The rule that was more recently made prevails over the older rule (Lex Posterior).

4.7   More Is Less

In deductive logic, the inconsistency of a set of propositions is the result of too much information. A simple example can illustrate this. Take a set of propositions that contains only one proposition, for instance the proposition that Boris has the power to create emergency regulations. This set is consistent. If we add to this set the proposition that Boris does *not* have the power to create emergency regulations, the result is inconsistent. The inconsistency can be taken away again by removing either one of the two sentences from the set. The more propositions are added to a set of propositions, the more opportunities arise for an inconsistency between two or more of the propositions. Moreover, if a set of propositions is inconsistent, the addition of more propositions cannot make it consistent. Only the removal of one or more propositions can make an

---

[11] This list is not exhaustive.

inconsistent set consistent. To state it in a maxim: more is less. The more propositions a set contains, the less chance that the set is still consistent.

In a non-deductive logic, such as the logic for rule application that was above sketched in outline, this 'more is less'-maxim can be turned around: more propositions can bring about that conflicting rules do not lead to inconsistencies. In this connection, 'more is less' stands for 'more propositions lead to fewer inconsistencies'. Let me illustrate this at the hand of the example of theft during nighttime. Suppose we have two rules, the rule that theft can be punished with four years of incarceration and the rule that theft at night theft can be punished with six years of incarceration. Add to these rules the case of Judy, who stole a bracelet during nighttime. If this is all, both rules are applicable and will be applied, leading to the inconsistent conclusions that Judy is both punishable with maximally four and six years of incarceration. By adding the rule that if two rules conflict in a particular case there is an exception to the more general rule, it becomes possible to make an exception to the general rule about theft. The inconsistency is then avoided, because this more general rule, although applicable, is not applied anymore, and only the conclusion that Judy is punishable with six years of incarceration can be drawn. As this example illustrates, the addition of the 'conflict rule' (and the information that the rule about theft during nighttime is the more specific one) prevented the rule conflict from leading to an actual inconsistency.

4.8   Intermediate Summary

A legal system was defined as an exhaustive set of CLCP's, in combination with its underlying materials. Such a system is consistent in the sense that it does not attach incompatible legal consequences to a case. Logical tools can be helpful in constructing such a consistent system from the potentially conflicting underlying materials. One technique in this connection is the avoidance of conflicts within the underlying materials by limiting their applicability. In this connection both the ordinary and the scope conditions of rules play a role. A second technique is to allow exceptions to rules, because exceptions make it possible that an applicable rule that is involved in a rule conflict is not applied to a case. Logic cannot detail how exceptions will be used to this purpose, but it can make clear which possibilities are available to legal decision-makers. The maxim 'more is less' plays a role in this connection. It indicates that the addition of more rules to a conflicting rule set can avoid that the conflicts lead to incompatible legal consequences.

5   Rule Conflicts between Distinct Normative Systems

Rule conflicts can exist between distinct legal systems and between legal and non-legal systems (Glenn 2014). Examples of conflicts between distinct legal systems would be conflicts between:

- the national law of two countries, such as France and Argentina;
- national law of a country and a personal (religion-based) legal system, such as a conflict between German and Canon law;
- national and international law, as when a Polish rule violates the freedom of religion as protected by the European Convention on Human Rights.

The typical case of a conflict between law and a non-legal system is a conflict between law and morality.

The question that needs to be addressed in this section is how logic can help us in dealing with conflicting rules from separate normative systems.

5.1   Separation

According to Raz (1979, pp. 28–33), law claims authority, and this claim involves two things. First, law provides us with reasons for action, and second, these reasons exclude other reasons. With this last point, Raz means that according to the law, reasons for deviating from what the law prescribes should in principle be ignored. It is true that law makes exceptions to this principle, for instance by sometimes allowing conscientious objection, but the starting point is that the law not only provides reasons for action itself, but also takes away the reason-giving force of norms from other systems. *From the legal point of view* it is in principle irrelevant if what the law prescribes conflicts with morality, or with some other legal system In this way, a legal system separates itself from those other systems.

The separation becomes visible in the necessity to add subscripts to legal judgments. For instance, it is not the case anymore that Giovanni ought not steal *tout court*. If normative systems become separated, the judgment must be that morally, or legally, Giovanni ought not steal. In this example the subscripts distinguish between the legal and a non-legal (the moral) point of view. However, it becomes also possible to distinguish between different legal points of view. For instance, according to Dutch law the creditor of a contract can claim specific performance from her debtor, but according to English law she cannot. According to the law of Spain it is allowed to charge an interest for a money loan, but according to the Shari'a it is not.

If the legal and other judgments are subscripted, seemingly conflicting judgments are logically not inconsistent. If a debtor is, according to Dutch law, obligated to provide specific performance, while according to English law he only has to pay damages, there is no incompatibility or inconsistency involved.

5.2 Fusion through Practical Reason

Legal norms have as their aim to guide human conduct. If a debtor must, according to applicable Dutch law, perform his contract, this is normally a reason for this debtor to specifically perform his contract. If this same debtor can, according to equally applicable English law, restrict himself to paying damages, this takes away the reason which the debtor had to perform the contract. Logically there is no incompatibility between the Dutch law obligation to perform specifically, and the English law permission not to perform specifically. From the standpoint of the agent who must decide whether to perform, there is a dilemma however.

The norms from the two legal systems, which are from a logical point of view separated because of their being subscripted, nevertheless cause a dilemma for the agent who sees reasons for action in the norms of both legal systems. Practical reason – the reasoning involved in deciding what to do – joins again that which the legal systems separated. Although from a logical point of view it is not necessary, legal systems nevertheless try to avoid the dilemmas resulting from intersystematic rule conflicts.

5.3 Avoidance of Conflicts

The easiest ways to avoid the dilemmas from intersystematic rule conflicts is to make sure that such conflicts do not occur. Scope conditions have as their main function to do just that. If the criminal law of countries only applies to cases that occurred within the territories of these countries and if multiterritory cases are rare, there will be few situations in which rules from more than one territorially defined legal system conflict. However, nowadays multiterritory cases are not rare anymore.

Scope conditions influence the applicability of rules. However, it seems to remain possible that rules from different systems are applicable to one and the same case and would, if applied, lead to legal consequences that pose a dilemma for the agent who wants to comply with her legal duties. Private international law (PIL) is there to prevent the dilemmas that might result from intersystematic rule conflicts. It does so by indicating which legal system provides the rules that a legal decision-maker should use to deal with a case. PIL is part of the various legal systems and it may therefore be different from one system to another. If it were, there would be little gained by the existence of PIL. If Dutch PIL says that a contract case is governed by Dutch law, while English PIL says that it is governed by English law, the dilemma of the contract party who wonders whether to perform specifically is not taken away. However, large parts of PIL have been created through international conventions, with the result that the PIL of legal systems is harmonized in the sense that the PIL of different systems identifies the same rules as those governing a case (see also Section 5.4 on incorporation). For example, Article 3 of the Convention on the law governing transfer of title in international sales of goods would, if it were in force, make local law decisive for the correct procedure for the transfer of title in sold goods.

It is not easy to determine what goes on logically when PIL determines that the rules of a 'foreign' legal system govern a case. The ordinary conditions of local rules, for instance the Dutch rules for the transfer of real estate, do not mention cases in, for example, Belgium. If a Dutch judge were to apply Belgian law to determine whether the buyer of a house has become the owner through transfer of title, it cannot well be said that this judge is making an exception to the Dutch rules. Therefore the most likely candidate for giving a logical account of what goes on in PIL are the scope conditions. The rules of PIL can be seen as giving scope conditions for local rules: the local rules are only applicable if rules from another legal system are not declared applicable instead.

5.4   Reference and Incorporation

The choice of applicable law through PIL involves more than merely a limitation of the scope of the 'own' rules, usually called the *lex fori* or the law of the forum. It is also necessary to assign applicability to the 'foreign' rules that do not belong to the forum law. Somehow these foreign rules should be made applicable without making them part of the law of the forum. This can be done by means of a technique that will be called reference. A second technique, that avoids conflicts altogether, is to *incorporate* 'foreign' rules into the forum law.

Foreign rules can be used in the forum law through a technique which may be called 'reference'. The foreign rules are not incorporated in the forum law, but their existence and content is considered by the forum law as matters of fact that are relevant from the point of view of the forum law. For example, Dutch family law may treat the fact that Islamic family law has a particular content as a fact that is legally relevant for Dutch family law. Rules from Islamic law are then applied to cases that involve Muslims because the rules of Dutch family law refer to the rules of Islamic family law. Formally the case is governed by Dutch family law, but it is Islamic family law that determines the content of the Dutch law.

The ubiquitous references to good faith in regulations of contract law are also an example of reference, in this case from a legal system to a non-legal norm. By stating that contract parties ought to deal with each other in good faith, a legal rule makes non-legal standards for proper behavior legally relevant. More generally, the so-called open norms are examples of reference.

Another example would be that a personal legal system declares territorial law relevant for dealing with cases where legal subjects that fall under the system of personal law live in a particular country. The Talmudic concept of the 'law of the land' would be an example of this construction.

And, finally, a plausible interpretation of how *soft law* operates is that the valid law of a system refers to soft law which is treated as a factual phenomenon that is legally relevant.

Reference avoids conflicts between the rules of the referring system and the rules of the system to which reference is made, because the content of the referring system is adapted to the content of the referred system.

In case of reference, the content of a foreign system is treated by the forum law as a matter of fact that co-determines the content of the forum law. In case of *incorporation*, foreign law becomes part of the forum law. The typical example of this phenomenon is the incorporation of international law in a national legal system in so-called monist legal systems. The Dutch legal system nicely illustrates incorporation. Provisions from international treaties ratified by the Netherlands and rules created by international organizations in which the Netherlands participates (in particular the European Union) automatically become part of the Dutch legal system (Art. 93 *Grondwet*). The foreign rules are not foreign anymore, except in the sense that they were not created by native Dutch legislative bodies. However, they are part of the Dutch legal system to the same extent as home-made rules.

Strictly speaking, incorporation is not a technique to deal with conflicts between rules of different systems, but a way to ensure that only one legal system is relevant. If EU regulations become automatically part of the Dutch national law, there is no need any more to pay attention to EU law, because the relevant rules are already part of Dutch national law. In the case of the EU one may even ask whether there exists such a thing as the EU legal system. It may be argued that the EU only provides organs which can create (uniform) law that becomes part of the national legal system of the Member States. The same may be said about the provisions of human rights treaties: they create uniform human rights in different legal systems and it may be argued that there is no separate international human rights system. However, it is imaginable that some legal systems incorporate part of a foreign legal system, while that foreign system has independent existence. This might be the correct understanding of the relationship between domestic law and international law in so-called dualist systems, in which international law does not automatically become part of the domestic law until it is specifically incorporated by a law of the domestic system. The situation is comparable to one country that uses the national currency of some other country.

6   Conclusion

The development of the internet, the rise of transnational law, the co-existence of different legal traditions and subtraditions, and globalization, all increase opportunities for conflicts between rules of different legal systems. One of the tasks of legal science is to deal with these possible conflicts and, as Glenn pointed out, the insights of modern logic are one place to look for assistance. Logic neither can nor should dictate a particular way of dealing with rule conflicts, but it can be of help by providing a conceptual framework that clearly defines when a rule conflict occurs and which tools are available to avoid these conflicts or to deal with them.

A conflict of rules occurs when it is possible that two or more rules attach incompatible legal consequences to a case. Within a single legal system, the possibility of rule conflicts is limited by adding scope conditions to the ordinary rule conditions. Mechanisms such as PIL extend this role of scope conditions to the relation between rules from different systems. Another limitation of the possibility for rule conflicts consists in the limitation of the powers of rule creating agents. Often it is impossible to create rules that conflict with already existing rules.

If there are actually conflicting rules, it becomes necessary to handle the conflict. By adopting a non-deductive logic for rule application it becomes possible to account for exceptions to rules. An exception to a rule leads to the result that a rule which is applicable in a case should nevertheless not be applied. Then the rule does not attach its legal consequences to the case. One reason for making an exception to a rule is that application of the rule would lead to legal consequences which are incompatible with the legal consequences of another applicable rule. An important insight in this connection is that inconsistencies because of conflicting rules are prevented, not by removing information, but by adding more information in order to handle the rule conflict (more is less).

If a conflict occurs between rules of different legal systems, there is logically speaking no need to deal with the conflict. It is logically well possible that an agent ought to do X from the point of view of one legal system, and ought to refrain from doing X from the point of view of another legal system. However, an agent who is subject to incompatible prescriptions from different legal systems is burdened with a dilemma. Legal system often come to the assistance of such individuals by referring to the rules of other systems, or by incorporating 'foreign' law.

References

Alexy, R., THEORIE DER JURISTISCHEN ARGUMENTATION, 7th edn Auflage, Frankfurt a/M: Suhrkamp, 1983.

Berman, Paul Schiff, GLOBAL LEGAL PLURALISM: A JURISPRUDENCE OF LAW BEYOND BORDERS, Cambridge: Cambridge University Press, 2012.

Glenn, Patrick, LEGAL TRADITIONS OF THE WORLD: SUSTAINABLE DIVERSITY IN LAW, 5th edn (1st edn 2000), Oxford: Oxford University Press. 2014.

Gordon, Th. F., THE PLEADINGS GAME. AN ARTIFICIAL INTELLIGENCE MODEL OF PROCEDURAL JUSTICE, Dordrecht: Kluwer 1995.

Hage, Jaap C., REASONING WITH RULES, Dordrecht: Kluwer 1997.

STUDIES IN LEGAL LOGIC, Dordrecht: Springer 2005.

Hage, Jaap, Construction or reconstruction? On the function of argumentation in the law, in C. Dahlman and E. Feteris (eds.), LEGAL ARGUMENTATION THEORY: CROSS-DISCIPLINARY PERSPECTIVES, Dordrecht: Springer 2012, 125–144.

Three kinds of coherentism in Michal Araszkiewicz and Jaromir Šavelka (eds.), COHERENCE: INSIGHTS FROM PHILOSOPHY, JURISPRUDENCE AND ARTIFICIAL INTELLIGENCE, Dordrecht: Springer 2013, 1–32.

The justification of value judgments. Theoretical foundations for arguments about the best level to regulate European Private Law, in Bram Akkermans, Jaap Hage, Nicole Kornet and Jan Smits (eds.), WHO DOES WHAT? ON THE ALLOCATION OF REGULATORY COMPETENCES IN EUROPEAN PRIVATE LAW, Cambridge: Intersentia 2015, 15–56.

Hart, Herbert L. A., THE CONCEPT OF LAW, 3rd edn, (1st edn 1961). Oxford: Oxford University Press 2012.

Kaufmann, A. and W. Hassemer (eds.), EINFÜHRUNG IN RECHTSFILOSOPHIE UND RECHTSTHEORIE DER GEGENWART, 1st edn, Heidelberg: Müller 1977.

Kelsen, Hans, REINE RECHTSLEHRE, 2nd edn, Wien: Franz Deuticke 1960.

Lodder, Arno, DIALAW: ON LEGAL JUSTIFICATION AND DIALOGICAL MODELS OF ARGUMENTATION, Dordrecht: Kluwer 1999.

MacCormick, Neil, LEGAL REASONING AND LEGAL THEORY, Oxford: University Press 1978.

Prakken, Henry, LOGICAL TOOLS FOR MODELLING LEGAL ARGUMENT. A STUDY OF DEFEASIBLE REASONING IN LAW, Dordrecht: Kluwer 1997.

Raz, Joseph, THE AUTHORITY OF LAW, Oxford: Clarendon Press 1979

Sartor, G., LEGAL REASONING, A COGNITIVE APPROACH TO THE LAW, Dordrecht: Springer 2005.

Schauer, F., PLAYING BY THE RULES, Oxford: Clarendon Press 1991.

Verheij, Bart, Rules, Reasons, Arguments. Formal Studies of Argumentation and Defeat, Dissertation, University of Maastricht 1996.

Weinberger, O., RECHTSLOGIK, 2nd edn, Berlin: Duncker & Humblot 1989.

5

Legal Inconsistency and the Emergence of States

NICHOLAS W. BARBER[1]

Should contractions within legal orders always be regretted? Most of the time they are clearly undesirable. The conflicting demands that they make runs against the rule of law – they impair the capacity of the law to guide conduct, and, worse still, may sometimes compel individuals to choose a law to break. Normally, institutions within the legal order should strive to avoid creating contradictions and, where such contradictions exist, should work towards their elimination. Sometimes, though, there are countervailing benefits, especially in the area of constitutional law. Here, contradiction between legal rules may reflect political disagreement about the balance of power within the state or, even more profoundly, disagreement about where the boundaries of the state should be drawn. Allowing a legal contradiction to persist may permit those with profoundly different understandings of the constitution to work within the existing institutional structure. This may sometimes be a temporary fix, merely postponing a constitutional crisis to a future date, but sometimes the problem resolves itself: one side of the argument is a clear winner, and the legal order can adjust itself to reflect this victory. By delaying the resolution of the dispute, the legal contradiction may have helped avoid a constitutional crisis.

This chapter will begin by outlining a version of legal pluralism that turns on contradictions within legal orders. As this account of legal pluralism turns on the possibility of legal contradiction, and, indeed, argues that there is sometimes a utility to be found in these contradictions, the paper sits comfortably alongside Patrick Glenn's account of legal orders.[2] It is not claimed that this is the only possible meaning that could

---

[1] Some paragraphs of this paper draw heavily on N. W. Barber, *Legal Pluralism and the European Union* (2006) 12 EUROPEAN LAW JOURNAL 306, and I am grateful to the editor of that journal for permission to make use of that article. Thanks are also due to Cora Chan, Ewan Smith, Lionel Smith, and Greg Weeks for their helpful comments on an earlier draft of this paper.
[2] See especially, P. Glenn, LEGAL TRADITIONS OF THE WORLD, 5th edn. (Oxford: Oxford University Press, 2014), chapter 10.

be ascribed to legal pluralism, but it is an interpretation that fits with some of the older writings on pluralism and, more importantly, picks out a significant constitutional phenomenon that merits consideration. Having set out this model, it will be argued pluralism can be identified within a number of emerging political orders, and is sometimes used to accommodate political disagreement about the boundaries of the state.

1 A Model of Legal Pluralism

Legal pluralism emerged as a collection of approaches to understanding legal orders during the 1970s and 1980s.[3] There were two broad groups of ideas that marched under the pluralist banner. First, some writers developed a pluralist model through reflection on the ways in which different normative orders can interact. These accounts of pluralism started in the analysis of imperial legal systems, examining the ways these systems had accommodated, incorporated, and limited religious and local law.[4] Other scholars challenged the divide between 'legal' and 'non-legal' rules by drawing attention to the totality of rules that govern people's lives: state law was not the only normative system that impacted on members of the state.[5] For these scholars, legal pluralism embodied the recognition that people were governed by different normative systems, systems which the legal orders of states often tried to accommodate or shape in some way. The second strand of legal pluralism – and one which is more directly relevant to the focus of this book – considered the potential for inconsistency, or contradiction, between rules, claiming that there can be contradictory 'legal mechanisms' applying to single factual situations.[6] These two strands sometimes come together: on occasion, it

---

[3] See generally, J. Griffiths, *What is Legal Pluralism?* (1986) 24 JOURNAL OF LEGAL PLURALISM 1 and D. J. Galligan, LAW IN MODERN SOCIETY (Oxford: Oxford University Press, 2006), chapters 9 and 10.

[4] For instance, M. B. Hooker, LEGAL PLURALISM: AN INTRODUCTION TO COLONIAL AND NEO-COLONIAL LAWS (Oxford: Oxford University Press, 1975).

[5] S. Moore, *Law and Social Change: The Semi-Autonomous Social Field as an Appropriate Subject of Study* (1973) 7 LAW AND SOCIETY REVIEW 719; Griffith, note 3, 38–39; see also E. Ehrlich, FUNDAMENTAL PRINCIPLES OF THE SOCIOLOGY OF LAW, transl. W. L. Moll (New York: Russell and Russell, 1936).

[6] J. Vanderlinden, *Le Pluralisme Juridique: Essai de Synthèse* in J. Gilissen, ed., LE PLURALISME JURIDIQUE (Brussels: Université de Bruxelles, 1971), 19. See also: S. Merry, *Legal Pluralism* (1988) 22 LAW AND SOCIETY 869, 870; R. de Lange, *Divergence, Fragmentation and Pluralism* in H. Petersen and H. Zahle, eds., LEGAL POLYCENTRICITY: CONSEQUENCES OF PLURALISM IN LAW (Aldershot: Dartmouth Publishing, 1994); A. Arnaud, *Legal Pluralism and the Building of Europe* in the same volume; N. MacCormick, *Juridical*

is the interaction of two normative systems that has generated the inconsistency in the rules that apply to individuals.

A significant challenge to the would-be pluralist is to show that their accounts of legal orders are distinctive. If it is the recognition that there can be interaction between different normative orders that is at the heart of pluralism, pluralism, as a distinct way of conceiving law, would appear unremarkable. Legal orders commonly recognise and even apply the rules of other systems,[7] and even the staunchest of legal positivists would acknowledge that other normative systems can bear on an individual and can have a practical impact as great as, or greater than, law.[8] Whilst the consequences of interaction between normative orders can be fascinating,[9] the recognition that they do interact is unexceptional. Similarly, the assertion that rules *can* place contradictory demands on those they address would be very widely endorsed. There is very broad, perhaps even universal, acceptance that the rules of different normative orders can impose contradictory demands on individuals. And, with the exceptions of Hans Kelsen[10] and, perhaps, Ronald Dworkin,[11] most would recognise that it is possible that rules within a single normative order can conflict; indeed, normally, it is one of the core tasks of the judge to bring such conflicts to an end.

Indeed, the challenge to those who want to talk of 'contradiction' or 'inconsistency' in the context of legal rules may be even more profound. Others in this volume debate the question, but the logical principle of

---

Pluralism and the Risk of Constitutional Conflict in N. MacCormick, QUESTIONING SOVEREIGNTY (Oxford: Oxford University Press, 1999).

[7] H. Kelsen, GENERAL THEORY OF LAW AND THE STATE, transl. A. Wedberg (Cambridge, MA: Harvard University Press, 1945), 243–248.

[8] Ibid., 24–28, discussing Ehrlich, note 5.

[9] P. Glenn, THE COSMOPOLITAN STATE (Oxford: Oxford University Press, 2013).

[10] Kelsen, note 7, 407–408; H. Kelsen, THE PURE THEORY OF LAW, transl. M. Knight (California: University of California Press, 1967), 205–208. Kelsen abandoned this claims, though he never fully explained the reasons for his change of mind: J. Harris, *Kelsen and Normative Consistency* in R. Tur and W. Twining, eds., ESSAYS ON KELSEN (Oxford: Oxford University Press, 1986); S. Munzer, *Validity and Legal Conflicts* (1973) 82 YALE LAW JOURNAL 1140, 1164. I engage with Kelsen's claim that legal rules cannot be set in contradiction in N. W. Barber, THE CONSTITUTIONAL STATE (Oxford: Oxford University Press, 2010), chapter 9.

[11] R. Dworkin, *On Gaps in the Law* in P. Amselek and N. MacCormick, eds., CONTROVERSIES ABOUT LAW'S ONTOLOGY (Edinburgh: Edinburgh University Press, 1991); R. Dworkin, 'No Right Answer?' in P. M. S. Hacker and J. Raz, eds., LAW, MORALITY AND SOCIETY (Oxford: Oxford University Press, 1978); Munzer, note 10, 1156–1162. I engage with Ronald Dworkin's objection to pluralism in N. W. Barber, *Legal Realism, Pluralism, and their Challengers* in U. Neegaard and R. Nielsen, eds., EUROPEAN LEGAL METHOD – TOWARDS A NEW EUROPEAN LEGAL REALISM? (Copenhagen: DJOEF Publishing, 2013).

contradiction is often taken to be confined only to propositions of fact; normative systems are commonly excluded from its reach.[12] The factual claim that A exists and A does not exist violates the logical principle of non-contradiction; most people would think that one or other of these claims must be false. But on some understandings of morality, a person can find that they are subject to moral obligations that conflict; morality may require both action and inaction.[13] More strongly still, law is an artificial normative structure, a structure within which legislatures and courts can craft and impose obligations. Even if it is the case that the principle of non-contradiction applies in systems of ethics it does not follow from this that it necessarily applies in systems of law. Indeed, one of the foremost advocates of deontic logic, G. A. von Wright expressly excluded legal systems from its reach.[14] Though it may be desirable that rules within a legal order not contradict each other, this, according to von Wright, is not a logical truth about such orders.[15] Legal systems are artificial normative structures, and, as such, are not constrained to comply with all the dictates of logic – and the examples given in the remainder of this chapter will show how the institutions of law can, sometimes generate opposing rules. The challenge to those who talk of contradiction within and between legal orders is, then, to explain what this means in the context of law.

Bernard Williams tackled this problem by shifting normative statements into their descriptive equivalents, which might be termed compliance statements.[16] So, the normative statement 'Albert must not kill Alberta' is transposed to 'Albert did not kill Alberta', which is contrary to the rule 'Albert must kill Alberta' transposed to 'Albert did

---

[12] See the discussion in J. Jørgensen, *Imperatives and Logic* (1937–1938) 7 ERKENNTNIS 288 and S. Coyle, *The Possibility of Deontic Logic* (2002) 15 RATIO JURIS 294.

[13] P. Foot, *Moral Realism and Moral Dilemma* (1983) 80 JOURNAL OF PHILOSOPHY 379. See also T. Nagel, *The Fragmentation of Value* in T. Nagel, MORTAL QUESTIONS (Cambridge: Cambridge University Press, 1979) and B. Williams, *Ethical Consistency* in B. Williams, PROBLEMS OF THE SELF (Cambridge: Cambridge University Press, 1973).

[14] G. A. von Wright, *Deontic Logic* (1999) 12 RATIO JURIS 26, 32–33.

[15] Note that a distinction can be drawn between a proposition about a norm (there is a rule you must do x) and the obligation imposed by the norm (you must do x). The logical principle of non-contradiction may well apply to propositions about norms (such a rule either does or does not exist). It is harder to see that it applies to the obligations imposed by the norm, as there may be other norms that require the opposite action.

[16] B. Williams, *Consistency and Realism* in B. Williams, PROBLEMS OF THE SELF (Cambridge: Cambridge University Press, 1973) and H. L. A. Hart, *Kelsen's Doctrine of the Unity of Law* in H. L. A. Hart, ESSAYS IN JURISPRUDENCE AND PHILOSOPHY (Oxford: Oxford University Press, 1983), 324–327.

kill Alberta.' This device allows us to talk of contradictory rules without assuming the logical conception of non-contradiction can be directly applied to normative statements. The transposition also makes clear that the contradiction between rules lies not in their inherent truth or falsity, but in their subjects' inability to fully comply with the rules: a claim that both had been fully complied with would necessarily be untrue. Whilst it is appropriate to judge assertions of the possibility of joint compliance as being true or false, it is not necessary to assume that the obligations themselves that generate these compliance statements are susceptible to attributions of truth-value. Consequently, the claim that contradiction can be found within and between legal orders is, or should be, less controversial than a general rejection of the logical principle of non-contradiction found in classical logic.[17]

On both of these grounds – the possibility of multiple normative orders and the potential for inconsistency within a normative order – legal pluralism faces the challenge that its central theses might prove to be trite: if its central claims are very widely endorsed, it might not be all that valuable as a distinct way to look at legal orders.

In earlier work, I have argued that contradiction between legal rules becomes particularly interesting when it is found at the foundational level of legal orders. Sometimes, this inconsistency concerns the hierarchy of sources of law within a system and, as a consequence of this, the system may lack an institution that is legally empowered to resolve the inconsistency. There are multiple, inconsistent, rules of recognition that give priority to rival sources of law, and there are rival institutions that purport to have the final say about the content of the legal order. Consequently, pluralist legal orders contain a risk, which need not be realised, of constitutional crisis; of officials being compelled to choose between their loyalties to different public institutions.

The claim that legal orders can exist with multiple, unranked, rules of recognition is controversial. The rule of recognition is a central part of Herbert Hart's account of law and – if it is to achieve the ends Hart set for it – such inconsistency must be rare. For Hart, the rule of recognition served to unite the rules of a legal system, providing a test by which other

---

[17] I discuss the significance of the logical principle of non-contradiction for normative systems – and the complexities of Bernard Williams' notion of 'compliance statements' – at far greater length in N. W. Barber, THE CONSTITUTIONAL STATE (Oxford: Oxford University Press, 2010), chapter 9.

rules could be shown to form part of the legal order.[18] Each legal system therefore possessed its own unique rule of recognition,[19] and all the rules that could be identified through the application of the rule of recognition constituted a single legal system. The rule of recognition also provided an answer to the question of the continuity of legal systems, the means by which we can show that two different sets of legal rules are manifestations of the same legal system at different points in time.[20] These sets of rules are aspects of a continuing legal system when the changes that occurred between the two sets of rules occurred in conformity to the rules of change identified by the rule of recognition. The existence of a single rule of recognition was necessary for the success of Hart's answer to these central jurisprudential questions: it sought to explain how the boundaries of a momentary legal order could be drawn, and how a series of momentary legal orders can be identified as constituting a single legal order stretched over time.

Hart was not unaware of the problems that disputes over the rule of recognition caused his theory. In the context of revolutions and invasion he acknowledged the possibility of such a state of affairs: it was conceivable that two rival rules of recognition might operate within a territory, and yet only one legal system was in operation.[21] This was, though, a 'substandard, abnormal case containing with it the threat that the legal system will dissolve.'[22] For Hart, such cases needed to be marginalised because if they were a common occurrence they would throw doubt on the success of the rule of recognition as the answer to the identity questions posed earlier.

Hart's account of a legal system was non-pluralist, in the sense invoked in this chapter. The central case of a legal system contained a single rule

[18] H. L. A. Hart, The Concept of Law, 2nd edn. (Oxford: Oxford University Press, 1994), 113–115.
[19] H. L. A. Hart, *Legal Duty and Obligation* in H. L. A. Hart, Essays on Bentham (Oxford: Oxford University Press, 1982), 155, ftn. 77. See also: N. MacCormick, *The Concept of Law and 'The Concept of Law'* (1994) 14 Oxford Journal of Legal Studies 1, 13–15; N. MacCormick, *A Very British Revolution* in N. MacCormick, Questioning Sovereignty (Oxford: Oxford University Press, 1999).
[20] Though Hart does not make this point explicitly: see J. Finnis, *Revolutions and Continuity of Law* in A. Simpson, ed., Oxford Essays in Jurisprudence (Second Series) (Oxford: Oxford University Press, 1973), 54–57.
[21] As in Rhodesia: G. Marshall, Constitutional Theory (Oxford: Oxford University Press, 1971), 64–72; J. Eekelaar, 'Splitting the Grundnorm' (1967) 30 Modern Law Review 156.
[22] Hart, note 18, 123.

of recognition, directing the law-applying institutions to the sources of law. Whilst Hart envisaged the possibility of pluralist systems, where there were inconsistent rules of recognition, he understood these as deviant cases. They constituted legal systems because of their similarity to the central case he presented, and were inherently unstable. If pluralist systems are more common, or more lasting, than Hart believed, the centrality of his non-pluralist account would have to be reassessed. Reflection on these, and other, problems with the rule of recognition has led Hart's students away from the rule of recognition as the answer to the questions of the identity of legal systems: both Joseph Raz and John Finnis have advanced more flexible understandings of legal systems, which moved away from Hart's rule-focused account and have made room for the possibility of pluralist legal orders.[23]

2   Examples of Pluralist Legal Orders

There are a number of reasons why it is valuable to identify pluralist legal orders. First, and building on arguments made in the previous paragraphs, such an exercise may help us answer general questions about the nature of law, questions of the type Hart sought to answer. If it can be shown that pluralist legal orders are comparatively common and, at least sometimes, are stable, it suggests that the general account of law provided by Hart requires modification.[24] Second, the exercise may be of interest to those who study constitutions and the operation of states. A pluralist legal order may provide a distinctive form of constitutional ordering that might mitigate the corrosiveness of some profound political disagreements. Thirdly, it may prove of interest to those interested in the particular legal orders examined: comparing these systems with others experiences similar challenges may illuminate shared and significant features. The present chapter focuses on the second of these three tasks.

Three examples of potentially pluralist legal orders, or groups of legal orders, will be given in this section: the legal orders of the European Union, the legal order of Australia before 1986, and the current legal order of Hong Kong. As we shall see, in all of these cases the legal

---

[23] Finnis, note 20; J. Raz, *The Identity of Legal Systems* in J. Raz, THE AUTHORITY OF LAW (Oxford: Oxford University Press, 1979).

[24] I explore the jurisprudential implications of pluralism at far greater length in Barber, note 17, chapters 9 and 10.

inconsistency that is characteristic of legal pluralism has, at its root, a political disagreement over the boundaries of the state. Here, legal pluralism is a consequence of the disputed relationship between a region – the Member States, Australia, and Hong Kong – and a larger constitutional entity – a putative European state, the British Empire, and China. This political disagreement then entails disagreement over the authority of the institutions of that larger entity over the region.

2.1   The European Legal Order

I have discussed the implications of legal pluralism for Europe's legal orders at length elsewhere, but, in brief, the interaction of the Court of Justice of the European Union and some national supreme courts has created the possibility that pluralist legal orders may emerge at both the European and national levels.

The Court of Justice of the European Union makes three, interconnected, claims of supremacy:[25] first, that the Court of Justice is entitled to definitively answer all questions of European Law;[26] secondly, that the Court of Justice is entitled to determine what constitutes an issue of European law;[27] and thirdly, that European law has supremacy over all conflicting rules of national law.[28] Set against this, many national constitutional courts have adopted a very different view of the force and nature of European law. Perhaps the most widely discussed set of judgments is found in the German legal system.[29] In *Solange I*[30] the German Constitutional Court rejected the supremacy of European Law: rules of Community Law that conflicted with fundamental constitutional rights would not be applied in the German order. This was a challenge to the third of

---

[25] K. Alter, ESTABLISHING THE SUPREMACY OF EUROPEAN LAW (Oxford: Oxford University Press, 2001), chapter 1; J. Weiler, *The Autonomy of the Community Legal Order* in J. Weiler, THE CONSTITUTION OF EUROPE (Cambridge: Cambridge University Press, 1999).

[26] Art. 234 (formally Art. 177).

[27] J. Weiler, *The Transformation of Europe* in J. Weiler, THE CONSTITUTION OF EUROPE (Cambridge: Cambridge University Press, 1999), 21. Case 314/85, *Foto-Frost* v. *Hauptzollamt Lübeck-Ost* [1987] ECR 4199.

[28] Case 6/64 *Costa* v. *ENEL* [1964] ECR 585.

[29] For recent tensions produced by the European Arrest Warrant, see M. Fichera, *The European Arrest Warrant and the Sovereign State: A Marriage of Convenience?* (2009) 15 EUROPEAN LAW JOURNAL 70.

[30] *Internationale Handelsgesellschaft mbH* v. *Einfuhr- und Vorratsstelle für Getreide und Futtermittel*, [1974] CMLR 540.

the three assertions of supremacy. In the *Maastricht*[31] decision, the Court rejected the Court of Justice's claim to have the final say as to the meaning and scope of European Law. The German Court stated that it would not accept surprising readings of the Treaty that had the effect of extending the Union's powers.[32] The recent decision on the Lisbon Treaty follows this jurisprudence: European law takes effect through and because of the German Constitution, and that Constitution limits what can be done in the name of European Law.[33] These two accounts of the force of European law present us with a pair of inconsistent rules.

First, there is a pair of rules that ascribe precedence to different sources of law. According to the German Constitutional Court the German Constitution is the highest source of law within Germany. European Law takes effect through the German Constitution, and, consequently, can be constrained by constitutional rules. This supremacy doctrine is presented as implicit within the framework of the German Constitution. In contrast, the Court of Justice regards European Law as the highest source of law within the European Union, which, of course, encompasses Germany. This supremacy doctrine is presented as a consequence of the signing of the Treaties establishing the Union, and does not depend on the validation of the German Constitution. Each supremacy claim contains an implicit negation of the other. In both cases these rules are presented as duties resting on the courts: each court claims that it is compelled to give precedence to the different sources of law.

Secondly, there is a pair of inconsistent rules relating to the hierarchy of courts within Germany. Again, this inconsistency takes the form of a combination of duties and powers. In some situations both courts regard themselves as under a duty to make the final determination about the content of law in Germany. The rules are asymmetrical: whilst the German Constitutional Court regards itself as under a duty to have the final say about the content of all the laws operative in Germany, the Court of Justice only claims to be obliged to have the final say about those laws with a European element that are operative in Germany. These duties could be acquitted by merely endorsing the decision of the other body – but the

---

[31] *Brunner v. The European Treaty* [1994] CMLR 57. See M. Zuleeg, *The European Constitution Under Constitutional Constraints: The German Scenario* (1997) 22 EUROPEAN LAW REVIEW 19 for energetic criticism of the decision, and M. Kumm, *Who is the Final Arbiter of Constitutionality in Europe?* (1999) 36 COMMON MARKET LAW REVIEW 351.

[32] *Brunner*, note 31, paragraphs 33, 48–49.

[33] See C. Wohlfahrt, *The* Lisbon *Case: A Critical Summary* (2009) 10 GERMAN LAW JOURNAL 1277.

duties prohibit the acceptance of the other body's claim to authority. A simple pair of duties to express a view about the law within a territory would not be inconsistent – what makes these rival claims to adjudicative supremacy inconsistent is their assertion of finality: a duty to state authoritatively for those affected by the law what the law requires of them. Adjudicative supremacy is a duty coupled with a power to bind people, courts and other institutions. It is these powers, inextricably mixed with the duties, which create the potential for inconsistency. This inconsistency need not be realised – perhaps the rival bodies will agree – but there is the unavoidable potential for actual inconsistency; that individuals will be placed in a position where they cannot fully comply with the directives produced by each court.

This type of conflict can generate a form of legal pluralism that is both novel and interesting. It can lead to multiple unranked rules of recognition, each according priority to a different source of law and different adjudicative institution. The jurisprudence of the German Constitutional Court is far from unique, and other national courts have adopted similar positions.[34] This conflict – between the Court of Justice and national constitutional courts – has the potential to create a form of legal pluralism at two levels.

First, the European legal order may, itself, be pluralist. The European legal order consists of courts at the European level and, also, courts at the national level. If we take the courts of Europe to comprise parts of a single legal order, this legal order will include multiple rules of recognition. Different judges in different courts would have different views about the hierarchy of legal sources within the Union – even if they accepted that this disagreement existed within a legal order.

Secondly, the legal orders of the Member State are, or, more likely, may become, pluralist. Over time, judges within the Member States may disagree over the rule of recognition – with some judges following their national constitutional courts and others following the Court of Justice. It is possible that this disagreement might arise in a time of crisis, with all the parties compelled to find a solution quickly,[35] but it might also arise

---

[34] See, among others: Italy: *Frontini* v. *Ministero delle Finanze* [1974] 2 CMLR 372; France: *Nicolo* [1990] 1 CMLR 173; United Kingdom: *R (HS2 Action Alliance Ltd)* v. *Secretary of State for Transport* [2014] UKSC 3. See also W. Sadurski, *Solange, Chapter 3: Constitutional Courts in Central Europe – Democracy – European Union* (2008) 14 EUROPEAN LAW JOURNAL 1.

[35] As with Rhodesia, see note 21.

over a long period of time, without any single moment of conflict. Indeed, it is possible that such a situation could be stable, with the judges agreeing on the substantive law that needs to be applied to cases before them, but disagreeing on whether this is because their national constitution requires it, or because of their country's membership of the European Union.

2.2   The Pre-1986 Australian Legal Order

Within Europe, legal inconsistency is the product of political disagreement; the inconsistencies in law are, in part, motivated by rival visions of the future of the Union. Australia may provide an example of legal inconsistency arising as a result of a contrasting process, where a developing political consensus triggered a shift in the law.

The Australian legal order started life as an off-shoot of the imperial legal order, with the Imperial Parliament – Westminster – being the highest law-making body in the system, and the Privy Council standing as the final court of appeal. As Australia's distinct constitutional identity emerged during the twentieth century, this legal position appeared increasingly anachronistic. Well before the Australia Acts, passed in 1986 by the Australian and United Kingdom Parliaments,[36] settled the issue, the fundamental base of Australian law was disputable. Even before the formal severance of Australia's link with the Imperial legal order, Australian judges had started to create constitutional space between Australia and the old imperial institutions.

First, the role of the imperial courts was steadily reduced.[37] Initially, this was as a result of legislation – in 1968 and 1975 the Australian Parliament limited the range of cases in which a litigant could appeal to the Privy Council[38] – but these legislative limitations were supported and reinforced by the judges. The High Court confirmed that the Australian Parliament did, indeed, possess the capacity to constrict access to the imperial court,[39] and it was the High Court, rather than the Parliament, that finally ended the capacity of the Australian states to appeal through

---

[36] Australia Act 1986 (Cth); Australia Act 1986 (UK).
[37] G. Williams, S. Brennan and A. Lynch, AUSTRALIAN CONSTITUTIONAL LAW AND THEORY, 6th ed. (Sydney: Federation Press, 2014), 118–121.
[38] Privy Council (Limitation of Appeals) Act 1968 (Cth); Privy Council (Appeals from the High Court) Act 1975 (Cth).
[39] *Attorney-General (Cth)* v. *T & G Mutual Life Society Ltd* (1978) CLR 161.

it to the Privy Council.[40] As the possibility of appeal to the Privy Council was steadily restricted, the High Court also sought to limit the significance of the rulings of that body. In *Viro* v. *The Queen* it was no longer bound by decisions of the Privy Council,[41] and a majority of the judges in that case asserted that state courts should treat decisions of the High Court as taking precedence over decisions of the imperial body. For a time, then, the High Court and the Privy Council both presented themselves as the apex court within the Australian system. A pair of inconsistent rules existed in the Australian legal order. The first identified the High Court as the final court of appeal, and imposed a duty on others within the Australian system to accept its decisions as taking precedence over the decisions of other courts. The second identified the Privy Council as the final court of appeal, and, similarly, imposed a duty on others within the system to accept its rulings, and accord them precedence over the decisions of other judicial bodies.

Secondly, alongside the marginalisation of the Privy Council, a number of Australian judges indicated that they would no longer accept the authority of the Westminster Parliament over Australia.[42] Justice Murphy, in *Bistricic* v. *Rokov*, argued that the United Kingdom Parliament had lost the power to pass statutes that were effective in the Australian legal order in 1901 after the enactment of Commonwealth of Australia Constitution Act 1900 (Imp).[43] According to Murphy, the constitutional basis of the Australian system was the acceptance by the Australian people of this statute, rather than its enactment by Westminster; Westminster's law-making power over Australia had expired. In a later case Justice Deane expressed a similar view, albeit in more cautious language, indicating that, in future, the judges might endorse the view that Australia was a sovereign state, and, like Murphy, identifying the Australian people as the source of its constitutional authority.[44] These opinions were far from uncontroversial, and as late as 1979 there were

---

[40] *Kirmani* v. *Captain Cook Cruises Pty Ltd (No. 2)* (1985) 159 CLR 461. Though the capacity of the State courts to allow appeals remained until 1986: *Southern Centre of Theosophy Inc* v. *South Australia* (1979) 145 CLR 246.

[41] *Viro* v. *The Queen* (1978) 141 CLR 88.

[42] P. Oliver, THE CONSTITUTION OF INDEPENDENCE: THE DEVELOPMENT OF CONSTITUTIONAL THEORY IN AUSTRALIA, CANADA AND NEW ZEALAND (Oxford: Oxford University Press, 2005), 233–239.

[43] *Bistricic* v. *Rokov* (1976) 135 CLR 552, 565–567. See also *Robinson* v. *Western Australia Museum* (1978) 138 CLR 283.

[44] *Kirmani* v. *Captain Cook Cruises Pty Ltd (No.1)* (1985) 159 CLR 351, 442.

judges who were prepared to argue that Westminster retained a power to legislate for Australia.[45] Consequently, in the period before the 1986 statutes, there was both explicit and deep disagreement about the basis of Australian law.[46] This inconsistency between rival rules of recognition is even starker than that relating to courts, discussed in the previous paragraph. On the one hand, some judges identified the Westminster Parliament as the highest source of law in the Australian system. If Westminster chose to legislate for Australia, the Australian judges would be under a duty to apply these laws – no matter with what Australian law they conflicted. On the other hand, some judges regarded Westminster as standing outside of the Australian legal order. If Westminster chose to legislate for Australia this legislation would be ineffective – Australian judges lacked the power to give it legal force and, indeed, under the Australian system, would be under an obligation apply the Australian law on the topic.

The inconsistencies relating to Australia's highest court and to its highest law-making body did not generate practical problems for litigants. Whilst the disagreements were profound, they did not affect the substantive, lower-level, laws that applied to individuals. The costs of the disagreement were potential rather than actual: these inconsistencies could have generated a constitutional crisis but, in the event, did not. Weighing against these risks, though, were benefits: the inconsistent rules stood as a warning, as an opportunity, and as threads that could later be woven into the constitutional story of an independent Australia. As warnings, these inconsistencies raised the potential costs for the Westminster Parliament in the – highly unlikely – event that it might be tempted to legislate for Australia. There was a chance that such legislation would be ignored by the Australian courts and – as in the Rhodesian incident[47] some twenty years earlier – the attempt to exercise the remnants of imperial power would lead to the extinction of that power. As an opportunity, the inconsistencies indicated that a portion, at least, of the judiciary would be willing to support Australian constitutional independence, even without the consent of the Westminster Parliament. The eventual mechanism used to secure independence – legislation enacted in both the Australian and Westminster Parliaments simultaneously – was

---

[45] See J. Stephen, in *China Ocean Shipping Co.* v. *South Australia* (1979) 145 CLR 172.

[46] See A. Dillon, *A Turtle By Any Other Name: The Legal Basis of the Australian Constitution* (2001) 29 FEDERAL LAW REVIEW 241.

[47] See note 21.

effective, but was, perhaps, not the only way in which this end could have been achieved.[48] Finally, these inconsistent rules form part of the ideology that now animates the Australian constitution. When, after 1986, in *Leeth* the Australian High Court identified the Australian people as the source of the constitutional order, the judges were building on the ideas expressed in these earlier decisions.[49]

2.3   The Contemporary Hong Kong Legal Order

In Australia the rise of legal inconsistency tracked a developing political consensus about the appropriateness of Australian constitutional autonomy: an emerging consensus shared by Australia and Westminster. In Hong Kong, in contrast, it is arguable that a form of pluralism has emerged because of a lack of consensus: uncertainty about Hong Kong's political relationship with China has been reflected in legal uncertainty over the basis of Hong Kong's legal order. Whilst there is agreement within Hong Kong that the historic origin of the Basic Law – Hong Kong's constitution – is found in the Chinese Constitution,[50] there is uncertainty over the on-going constitutional status of these instruments and their relationship. On one understanding, the Basic Law is contained within the Chinese Constitution; empowered by it, and subject to its provisions and institutions. The Chinese Constitution, on this account, is, ultimately, the highest source of law in Hong Kong. On an alternative understanding, the Basic Law is autonomous from the Chinese Constitution and it is the Basic Law, rather than the Chinese Constitution, that is the highest legal source within the territory of Hong Kong. If this alternative interpretation of the relationship between China and Hong Kong were adopted, the power of Mainland institutions over Hong Kong – and the import of the Chinese Constitution more generally – would be mediated through, and constrained by, the Basic Law.

In one of the first cases in Hong Kong decided after the return of the island to China, *Ma Wai-kwan*,[51] the Hong Kong Court of Appeal considered the continuing applicability of common law rules to Hong Kong.

---

[48] Compare the experience of Ireland: K. Wheare, THE CONSTITUTIONAL STRUCTURE OF THE COMMONWEALTH (Oxford: Oxford University Press, 1960), 90–92. Dillon, note 46, 262–264.

[49] (1992) 174 CLR 455. See also *Nationwide News Pty Ltd* v. *Wills* (1992) 177 CLR 1. See Dillion, note 46 above, 246–253 for a sceptical consideration of the claims about popular sovereignty.

[50] See Constitution of the People's Republic of China, Article 31.   [51] [1997] 2 HKC 315.

It decided that these rules remained part of that legal order, but only because the Basic Law incorporated them into the system. The foundation of the legal order had shifted from English law[52] to the Basic Law, which was, itself, grounded in the Chinese constitutional order: even though the vast bulk of the laws of Hong Kong remained constant, their constitutional foundation had changed. Albert Chen described this as amounting to a replacement of the *grundnorm*:[53] the changing loyalties of the judges, motivated by the actions of the British and Chinese states, altered the fundamental rule of the Hong Kong legal order.

Ma Wai-kwan provided an account of the Hong Kong system that presented it as a subset of the Chinese constitutional order. If this were the case, the Chinese legislature, the National People's Congress,[54] would enjoy the same capacity to legislate over Hong Kong that it possessed over the rest of China; a capacity unfettered by any form of judicial control.[55] Under *Ma Wai-kwan's* model of the new constitutional order, Hong Kong had fully reunited with China, with the highest Chinese institutions accorded the same constitutional status they possessed within the rest of the Chinese system. In *Ng Ka-Ling*,[56] decided shortly after, the judges of the Court of Final Appeal took a different view. They presented Hong Kong's Basic Law as constraining the capacity of the Mainland's institutions to act within Hong Kong's constitutional order: Hong Kong's courts could review legislation of the National People's Congress and the interpretive decisions of the Standing Committee that extended to Hong Kong. Where those decisions went against the Basic Law the Hong Kong courts could find them invalid or ineffective. This ruling proved to be the high-water mark of judicial separatism in Hong Kong. Following pressure from the Mainland, the Court glossed its decision, making clear that decisions of the Standing Committee of the National People's Congress bound the courts,[57] and in

---

[52] The pre-1997 Hong Kong legal order rested on the exercise of a prerogative power: see A. Chen, 'The Interpretation of the Basic Law: Common Law and Mainland Chinese Perspectives' (2000) 30 HONG KONG LAW JOURNAL 380, 417–420.

[53] Ibid., 418.

[54] It is worth noting that the National People's Congress is of limited effectiveness: it consists of about 3000 representatives who meet for about 10 days a year, and is controlled by the Chinese Communist Party. See Q. Zhang, THE CONSTITUTION OF CHINA (Hart: Oxford, 2012), chapter 4.

[55] Ibid., 95–96.

[56] *Ng Ka-Ling & Others* v. *Director of Immigration* [1999] 1 H.K.L.R.D. 315.

[57] Ibid., 577. See A. Chen, *The Rule of Law Under 'One Country Two Systems' The Case of Hong Kong 1997–2010* (2011) 6 NATIONAL TAIWAN UNIVERSITY LAW REVIEW 269, 271–276.

Lau Kong Yung,[58] decided later that year, the Court revisited the question of the relationship between the legal institutions of Hong Kong and those of the Mainland. It accepted that the Standing Committee of the National People's Congress had the power to issue binding interpretations of the Basic Law – even if there had been no judicial request for a ruling by that body. However, the case left open the question of whether this power was grounded in a provision of the Basic Law[59] or in the Chinese Constitution[60] – as each instrument included such an interpretative power, the Hong Kong Court probably saw no need to choose between them. *Lau Kong Yung* consequently steers a middle course between *Mai Wai-kwan* and *Ng Ka-Ling*: the question of the fundamental basis of Hong Kong law is left open, and the possibility remains that a future court could hold that the Standing Committee's jurisdiction is confined within the bounds set by the Basic Law, as determined by Hong Kong institutions.

The power asserted in the first *Ng Ka-Ling* decision has never been invoked by the Hong Kong courts.[61] If the National People's Congress's power to amend the Basic Law is limited by the Basic Law,[62] it could be argued that the case places the Basic Law above the Chinese Constitution in the context of the Hong Kong system: Hong Kong judges will only recognise as effective those amendments that are permitted by the Basic Law, after all, on this account, it is the Basic Law and not the Chinese Constitution that empowers the National People's Congress to act in Hong Kong. It is safe to assume that were this question put to the Standing Committee of the National People's Congress, this institution would side with the account of Hong Kong's legal order given in *Ma Wai-kwan* and reject that articulated in the original *Ng Ka-Ling* ruling.

Like the Australian cases, discussed above, the decision in *Ng Ka-Ling* creates ambiguity over the fundamental base of the Hong Kong order, an ambiguity that persists after *Lau Kong Yung* – and it is, perhaps, significant that one of the judges in *Ng Ka-Ling* was Sir Anthony Mason who had sat on a number of the key Australian cases discussed earlier.[63] As with the pre-1986 Australian dicta, the judgment in *Ng Ka-Ling* should be

---

[58] *Lau Kong Yung v. Director of Immigration* [1999] 3 H.K.L.R.D. 778.
[59] Article 158 of the Basic Law.   [60] Article 67 of the Chinese Constitution.
[61] Though see *HKSAR* v. *Ng Kung Siu* [1999] 1 H.K.L.R.D. 783 in which the Court of Final Appeal did review a decision of the Standing Committee to insert a Chinese law on flag desecration into the Basic Law, but, in the event, found it compatible with the Basic Law.
[62] Article 159 of the Basic Law precludes amendments that 'contravene the established basic policies of the People's Republic of China regarding Hong Kong'.
[63] Mason sat in *Bistricic* and *Kirmani*, and the post-1986 case of *Leeth*.

seen as one that creates constitutional space rather than as an assertion of a power that the courts can utilise: as a matter of raw politics, it is hard, in present circumstances, to imagine a Hong Kong judge declaring a decision of the National People's Congress contrary to Hong Kong law. But the decision does create the possibility that, at some point in the future, Hong Kong's judges could use *Ng Ka-Ling* to distance Hong Kong's legal order from that of the Mainland. There is the potential that – in changed times – Hong Kong's courts could set aside attempts by China's institutions to determine the laws of Hong Kong – a potential that might, in itself, help restrain Beijing. And if there were a political will in Hong Kong to push towards constitutional independence, the Hong Kong courts, like their Australian cousins, would have introduced the flexibility into the constitutional order needed to accommodate these aspirations.

3   Conclusion

Ordinarily, inconsistency in law is a bad thing. Lon Fuller rightly claimed that the presence of inconsistent rules amounts to a standing criticism of the order that contains them, a blow against the rule of law.[64] But there may be some situations where inconsistency is desirable; a way through which the law can accommodate competing political visions that are, on the surface, irreconcilable. This may be especially useful when the competing visions relate to the identity of the state. The three examples given in the last section show the different ways in which this model of legal pluralism may moderate the political problems raised by the emergence of new states by accommodating different visions of their constitutional futures.

In Europe, legal pluralism permits the Member States and the European Union to present themselves as states.[65] The legal model favoured by the Court of Justice of the European Union is very similar to that of a federal state, with the treaties effectively dividing power between the European and national levels, and the Court of Justice acting as constitutional court, resolving questions over this division. The model favoured by many national courts, in contrast, is confederal, with the European Union enjoying a limited law-making power that is dependent on the agreement of, and support of, Member States.

---

[64] L. Fuller, THE MORALITY OF LAW, rev. ed. (New Haven: Yale University Press, 1969), 65–70.
[65] See Barber, note 17, chapter 10.

In Australia, the shifting judicial view of the basis of the authority of the Australian constitutional tracked a shifting political consensus about Australia's relationship with the United Kingdom. Whilst the judges lacked the legal power to effect a split from the old imperial legal order – their legal authority was grounded in that system – their constitutional position enabled them to open the possibility of a split. The inconsistent rules within the legal order reflected the older view of the Australian legal order within the imperial system and a newer view, which accorded the Australian system autonomy. Had the United Kingdom resisted calls for Australian autonomy, or if it had sought to start legislating for the territory, this new view would have allowed the courts to counter such actions, presenting the possibility that the judges would side with Australian institutions against the old imperial power.

Unlike Australia, there is no clear political consensus about the future of Hong Kong. The legal relationship between Hong Kong and China resembles, in some respects, the old legal relationship between Australia and the United Kingdom, but the political connection between the two is far tighter. And whilst the gradual constitutional separation of Australia and the United Kingdom was both anticipated and broadly accepted, Hong Kong's constitutional future is far less clear. The inconsistency in Hong Kong's legal order stands as a potential vision of the future of that territory, a future in which Hong Kong would enjoy practically full constitutional independence from China, an autonomy that would virtually amount to statehood. Whilst such a development is politically inconceivable today, it may become viable in the future – or, perhaps, presenting it as a possibility may help guard the more limited autonomy Hong Kong presently enjoys.

There are, then, at least three reasons why legal inconsistency of this type may sometimes be valuable.

First, this sort of inconsistency described here may amount to a political compromise; a tacit agreement to disagree.[66] It allows supporters of European supremacy and supporters of national supremacy to both claim victory; conversely, and perhaps even more importantly, it avoids either constituency having to admit defeat. These inconsistent laws need not

---

[66] C. Richmond, *Preserving the Identity Crisis: Autonomy, System and Sovereignty in European Law* (1997) 16 LAW AND PHILOSOPHY 377; M. Maduro, *Europe and the Constitution: What If This Is as Good as It Gets?* in J. Weiler and M. Wind, eds., EUROPEAN CONSTITUTIONALISM BEYOND THE STATE (Cambridge: Cambridge University Press, 2003). See also N. Krisch, *The Open Architecture of European Human Rights Law* (2008) 71 MODERN LAW REVIEW 183.

demand inconsistent action; the constitutional dilemma can remain unresolved, provided that each side exercises restraint. The emergence of
pluralist legal systems with the European Union may provide a desirable
compromise between the old models of sovereignty and constitutional
supremacy, and the new claims to supremacy made by Europe. Similarly,
in Australia the relationship between Australian law and imperial law was
widely debated, whilst a split was inevitable the speed with which this
occurred was debated: the judicial disagreement over the fundamental
base of the Australian legal order tracked this political debate. Whilst the
political debates in the European and Australian examples turn on finality,
and cannot reach a compromise through the adoption of an agreed middle
course, the pluralist model provides a compromise framework within
which these inconsistent claims can co-exist in law. Provided that the
practical conflict within this model remains potential, and actual disputes
are avoided, this can provide a stable, even a long-lasting, form of settlement. The advantage of such a settlement is that it avoids unnecessary and
potentially destructive conflict, and allows the protagonists to work
together on beneficial projects where agreement exists.[67]

Secondly, the pluralist model can create flexibility in the law that may
facilitate the emergence of a new constitutional settlement. The inconsistency in the European legal order may prove long-lasting, but it could be,
over time, that the federal model wins out. The existence of inconsistency
presents this model as a possibility within the constitutional order, an
option that the system can move towards. This facilitative role for
inconsistency can be seen even more clearly in the Australian example,
where the beginnings of constitutional autonomy pre-date the legislative
provisions that brought about this end.

Thirdly, these inconsistent rules, embodying competing supremacy
claims, could provide a form of 'constitutional self-defence'.[68] A rule of
constitutional self-defence empowers an institution to protect itself against

---

[67] Compare the long-standing debate in English constitutional law over which institution
has the final say over the extent of parliamentary privilege: C. Wittke, THE HISTORY OF
ENGLISH PARLIAMENTARY PRIVILEGE (Ohio: Ohio University Press, 1921); J. Chaftez,
DEMOCRACY'S PRIVILEGED FEW (New Haven: Yale University Press, 2007), chapter 3; and
J. Dean, HATRED, RIDICULE OR CONTEMPT (London: Constable, 1953), chapter 19.

[68] See N. W. Barber, Self-Defence for Institutions (2013) 72 CAMBRIDGE LAW JOURNAL 558 and
N. W. Barber and A. L. Young, Prospective Henry VIII Clauses and Their Implications for
Sovereignty [2003] Public Law 112. Similar points are discussed by Weiler and by Walker: see
J. Weiler, The Reformation of European Constitutionalism (1997) 35 JOURNAL OF COMMON
MARKET STUDIES 97 and N. Walker, Sovereignty and Differentiated Integration in the
European Union (1998) 4 EUROPEAN LAW JOURNAL 355, 375–379.

other constitutional bodies. For instance, legislatures are given judicial powers in the area of privilege to stop the encroachment of the courts, and judges often run the administrative side of the court process. Sometimes these measures are more aggressive, giving one institution a weapon it can use against another: for instance, giving one legislature the power to strike down the acts of another legislative body. Competing claims to supremacy arm national and European courts with weapons that may help ensure mutual respect and restraint. If the potential conflicts caused by inconsistent rules of recognition were realised, with inconsistent rules addressed to individuals, all sides in the dispute would pay a price. Further, in the event of actual conflict, one side will, probably, emerge from the crisis as a victor: whilst it is unclear who will win, each side has an interest in avoiding the contest. The risks of actual conflict provide incentives on each party to strive towards harmonious interpretation of the law. It encourages the Court of Justice to interpret European law in a manner that will be palatable to national courts,[69] and, at the same time, discourages national courts from blindly insisting on the primacy of national rules. In short, the competing supremacy claims may serve to create an atmosphere of co-operation between the courts, where each side has an incentive to strive to respect the position and tradition of the other. Similarly, in Hong Kong the possibility that the Hong Kong courts might reject a purported ruling of the Standing Committee of the National People's Congress on the interpretation of the Basic Law might encourage this body to exercise restraint when engaging with Hong Kong.

---

[69] As evidence of this see, perhaps, J. Coppel and A. O'Neill, *The European Court of Justice: Taking Rights Seriously?* (1992) 12 LEGAL STUDIES 227, though their claims are challenged in J. Weiler and N. Lockhart, *"Taking Rights Seriously": The European Court and its Fundamental Rights Jurisprudence* (1995) 32 COMMON MARKET LAW REVIEW 51 and 579.

6

Political Settlement and the New Logic of Hybrid Self-determination

CHRISTINE BELL[1]

This chapter examines how a form of 'fuzzy logic' is assisting in managing and even resolving self-determination disputes, by enabling parties to break away from a binary logic of 'unity versus secession' so as to reach a new political settlement. The chapter contributes to understandings developed by Patrick Glenn in his book the COSMOPOLITAN STATE (2013) that lie at the heart of this collection, by showing how more multivalent understandings of the binaries at the heart of the self-determination norm, are providing a resource from which to create a zone of compromise in which fundamental differences at to the nature and legitimacy of the state can continue to be worked out. I suggest that these new approaches to self-determination are possible because they tap into the multivalence inherent in the formulation of a norm that itself responds to competing values that are necessary to stable statehood.

To set out my argument in summary, I suggest that a new law of 'hybrid self-determination' is emerging as a legalised technique of conflict resolution. Self-determination law appears to hold out binary either/or options of unity or secession which create an 'excluded middle' – that is, a middle that is impossible because each option logically precludes the other. In contrast, the more 'multivalent' approach of the new law of hybrid self-determination conceives of the 'excluded middle' as a required space of conflict resolution. In contrast to binary logic's exclusion of this middle, the idea of re-inventing or creating space for the excluded middle speaks to a project of deliberately creating a conceptual space and a real-world political and legal institutions which can at once

[1] Christine Bell is Director of the Political Settlement Research Programme (PSRP) (www.politicalsettlements.org). This chapter is an output from the PSRP supported by the Department of International Development UK (DFID), although DFID has had no input into the chapter and the views expressed herein do not represent DFID.

be both (and therefore neither) of the binary opposites in a new form of fuzzy statehood.

The idea of re-introducing 'the excluded middle' attempts to capture, both as metaphor and as a practical political project, efforts to create political and legal spaces of transition from conflict that enable parties to move towards peaceful co-existence while fundamentally disagreeing as to the nature of the state in ways that were hitherto understood to be so irreconcilable as to prompt violence. The attempt to create a formerly 'excluded middle' is an attempt to square a circle or engage in 'fuzzy logic' by moving from a discourse of impossible polarised binary choices, to a discourse of accommodation.

However, I suggest that the space of the excluded middle is not a static space, but one which will continue to have to be created and defended to resist the on-going pull of binary logic as the parties to conflict attempt to return to their preferred binary 'default' position. Often a range of internal and external interveners have to be relied on to continue to broker the space of the excluded middle. However, external interveners too often intervene from a position of binary logic and misunderstand and fail to see the newly created excluded middle or understand the challenges of sustaining it. To engage effectively they need to engage with the excluded middle's reality of hybrid political and legal orders. Otherwise they too engage in a binary logic that stands to undo the excluded middle's potential for conflict resolution because undoing the space risks falling into one party's preferred default position.

While the language and analogy of logic can sound very theoretical, understanding and engaging with the excluded middle carries immense practical policy implications, and I explore how other metaphors, notably that of 'hybridity', are being used to grapple with these implications. In my concluding section I make general recommendations for those who seek to intervene more effectively to promote inclusive peace settlements.

1   Binary Logic and International Law of Self-determination

International self-determination law has long been acknowledged to be unhelpful to resolving secessionist disputes. It has become a truism to state that the law on self-determination is unclear, unhelpfully promising different things to states and to peoples. Emerging in the de-colonisation period as a legal norm to underwrite a move to colonial independence (somewhat after-the-fact), its post-colonial significance has been unclear. A set of binary oppositions underwrite this clash.[2]

On one hand, the norm appears to promise self-government and nations, and on the other hand to promise to existing states that their territorial integrity will be preserved. Self-determination conflicts typically therefore see both sides to a conflict appeal to the norm whose application remains disputed. Outside the de-colonisation context the norm's two pillars, respect for territorial integrity and a commitment to representative government for peoples, appear to clash. Rather than resolving violent self-determination disputes the norm stands accused of fuelling them.[3]

In another binary distinction self-determination law rests on a notion of absolute indivisible sovereignty. This indivisible sovereignty is the prize for both the state and its non-state contenders in a tussle over whether the sovereignty of the unified status quo state, or the sought sovereignty of the secessionist people and entity will prevail. It appears that no zone of compromise is possible between two logically incompatible positions over the appropriate and legitimate demos, polis and territory of the state. Over the years, attempts to square the circle and render the norm's two poles internally consistent has led to other binaries being reached for. For example, a binary division between a 'people' and a 'national minority' tries to distinguish between those who are entitled to 'independent statehood' and those who are not. The idea that there can only be one constituent people, and one 'nation' in the nation state, forces the logic that only the 'whole' peoples of a state are entitled to statehood, while non-majority 'nations or nationalities' are relegated to a status of 'national minority' and entitled to something less.

2   Multivalent Logic and Real Life

Even if these legal binaries were ever so absolute, increasingly none of them match up with reality in our contemporary world. Any idea that states contain only one 'nation' is difficult to maintain: states in which self-determination disputes exist are now often acknowledged to be plurinational with different nationalities co-existing, and in cases where there are more than two nationalities, no one group may be in the overall majority.[4] We also increasingly accept the complexity of relationships

---

[2] Koskenniemi (1994).   [3] Weller (2009).   [4] Tierney (2007).

among political, ethnic, racial and national identities. Attempts to distinguish between 'peoples' entitled to statehood and 'nationalities' entitled to something less – as something that can be determined by water-tight definitions – quickly run aground. It is almost impossible to create mutually delimited categories which draw a clear distinctions between these categories sufficient to deciding the different national entitlements that apply as a consequence. Indeed international law has had to bend to deal with indigenous identities by acknowledging indigenous peoples as 'peoples' even though they are not the majority within the state's borders. Moreover, as Anderson so famously observed, all these identities involve a measure of self-identification and are 'imagined' as much as real.[5] We could go further and argue that in fact such identities fuse the binary of 'imagined' and 'real', as to imagine and act on is to make real – as those in former Yugoslavia found out in 1990 when the former socialist republic began dissolving (or its bits seceding – another of self-determination law's binary choices) under the pressure of resurgent national rhetoric.

In summary, law's binaries inadequately map onto more messy realities of identity claims that underlie secessionist disputes. These claims both appear absolute and exclusionary, but are also made complicated by people who understand themselves as neither and all of the identities on offer, and – even more complicated – who understand identity as having a fluid and relational dimension depending on what is being discussed or who it is being discussed with. The difficulty appears to be one of law not being able to adequately capture and appropriately frame categories which can map in a targeted way, to appropriate forms of participation in public decisions.[6]

Law's binaries, in particular its sovereign/not sovereign binary, also seem inapposite to our globalised world which places ever more limits on territorially-based sovereignty. Sovereignty no longer means what it did; even the most stable and monolithic of Western states accept that governance can take place out-with and across state borders. Regional and international organisations limit traditional state sovereignty in all sorts of ways. Post-conflict these organisations can even create explicit forms of 'shared sovereignty' post conflict, with interim international administrations.[7]

[5] Anderson (1983).
[6] See Kymlicka's analysis (2007) and (2008) in which he points to a retreat from 'targetted norms' which treat different types of minorities differently, discussed later nn 13–14.
[7] See further Wheatley (2015) (arguing that complexity theory helps to explain 'degrees of recognition' afforded secessionist states such as Kosovo).

Territorial borders can be understood as not necessarily territorially defined but conceptually movable depending on context (see US immigration desks in Shannon Ireland, or US military use of Guantanamo Bay in Cuba). Or borders can be conceptually made fuzzy in novel forms of alliance and cross-border arrangements, for example by giving state-like powers, including treaty-making powers, to sub-state entities. Border delimitation can be indefinitely postponed by providing for staged processes as the attempts to provide for arbitration in the Abeyi region on the border between Sudan and South Sudan, or the Brcko district of Bosnia Herzegovina illustrate – these last two borders having been left open by respective peace settlements.[8]

Therefore, the contemporary legal world appears to hold out all sorts of institutional and territorial innovations, including 'degrees' of sovereignty, and porous borders, that are capable of breaking free from law's binary logic because they enable breaking free from an 'all-or-nothing' form of territorially-based nation-state sovereignty.[9]

3 The Move to Multivalent Logic in Self-determination Law

Law, of course, is traditionally taught in terms of binary logic that has only two values – yes and no (or true and false). Traditional logic traces its foundations back to Aristotelean reasoning that is bivalent. To some extent law's commitment to bivalent logic is driven by its function as a tool of decision-making through legal adjudication. Legal adjudication has to come up with binary answers to legally framed questions. This pushes the art of effective advocacy into manoeuvring with respect to how the relevant question is decided on, framed and so answered.

However, the logic of statecraft and conflict-resolution is not binary but involves the tricky business of how to move parties from irreconcilable positions to exploring their mutual interests and finding some

---

[8] See THE GENERAL FRAMEWORK AGREEMENT FOR PEACE IN BOSNIA AND HERZEGOVINA, 14 December 1995, available at www.ohr.int/dpa/default.asp?content_id=380; THE COMPREHENSIVE PEACE AGREEMENT BETWEEN THE GOVERNMENT OF THE REPUBLIC OF THE SUDAN AND THE SUDAN PEOPLE'S LIBERATION MOVEMENT/SUDAN PEOPLE'S LIBERATION ARMY, 9 January 2015, available at www.unmis.unmissions.org/Portals/UNMIS/Documents/General/cpa-en.pdf.

[9] See Walker (2015); and Wheatley (2015) who both argue for the complexity of the new arrangements, Walker noting that the idea of degrees of sovereignty not only raises the possibility of new post-sovereign arrangements, but new forms of resistance to them, because states are understood as now able to reach creative containment solutions.

creative way of meeting them, by re-framing binary clashes over state identity, territory and sovereignty so as to address violent conflict that resolves around attempted 'winner-takes-all' sovereign solutions. The logic of conflict resolution must seek to attempt to find middle ground where there appears to be none.

There is, of course, a model of logic which speaks to this project, as centrally addressed by Glenn and this collection – multivalent logic, or 'fuzzy logic'. Often attributed to Bart Kosko, fuzzy logic is the idea that instead of the Aristotelian A or not-A mode of thinking some things can be defined mathematically as including statements that are true to some degree and therefore having a value between 0 and 1. This more multi-valent logic deals with the imprecision of language and the difficulty of capturing in words, concepts that are themselves relational and mutable. Multivalent logic also attempts to confront and negotiate between apparently incommensurate claims which in a sense pass each other by, because they speak to different truths or realities. As Patrick Glenn argued in one of the last pieces he wrote on law and logic, multivalent logic underlies and even underpins diverse legal and constitutional traditions, despite law's ostensible commitment to bivalent logic, because it is necessary to holding different world and national views together:

> All of these complex, major [legal] traditions because of their proven ability to hold together, to sustain, mutually inconsistent sub-traditions. . . It is a way of thinking which has been described as multi-valent, as opposed to bi-valent, because sub-traditions are not either right or wrong, but may be right in different, multiple (inconsistent) ways. The traditions are hence multivalued.[10]

In part because of our contemporary reconceptualisation of both identities and state sovereignty, our new world appears to hold possibilities for a more multivalent approach to self-determination law. In recent years, the more fluid concepts of sovereignty and a burgeoning peacebuilding architecture and technology have been argued to have produced a new approach to self-determination law that tries to move beyond polarised binary choices, and work more as a background facilitative norm.

A number of writers, drawing on slightly different data, illustrate the ways in which self-determination norm's internal contradictions are now being understood to be being transcended in approaches which point to a more multivalent understanding of international law's capabilities. To

---

[10] Glenn (2013: 367).

quickly review the key accounts: Klabbers, for example, reviewing post-colonisation decisions of the International Court of Justice in 2006, argued that the then scant jurisprudence illustrated a tendency to avoid direct pronouncements on self-determination or grants of secession in favour of endorsing a 'right to take part' or a right to negotiations.[11] In essence, he saw a norm which was moving from a substantive outcome-focused norm, to a process oriented norm. He argued that the procedural right he saw evidence of, was bolstered by analogy to procedural theories of rights more generally. However, the extent of the normative shift he identified was unclear: it was unclear who had the right to be heard, and what that right entitled them to – that is, whether there was any requirement on the state to act differently as a result. In a sense, Klabbers' account of the norm's new trajectory could not fully evade questions of substance by being framed as a procedural norm.

Weller in 2009 similarly argued that new ways of resolving self-determination claims were being developed in practice in ways which were 'dissolving' the traditional distinction between internal and external self-determination.[12] Analysing forty settlements he set out nine techniques by which self-determination disputes have been resolved through techniques such as constitutional recognition and accommodation. He too faced difficulties in his account of the norm's shift, most notably while he notes that a sharp distinction between external and internal self-determination appear to be in the process of being dissolved, he viewed the developments as in essence a shift from external self-determination (for example secession), to internal self-determination (a right to more representative and inclusive government), and a political rather than a legal development.

A third perspective was provided in Kymlicka's *Multicultural Odysseys* of 2007. Famous for having saved liberalism from incapacity to accommodate group rights with a concept of 'multicultural liberalism',[13] more than ten years on Kymlicka argued that the world had broken out in a rash of 'multicultural liberal' activity.[14] For Kymlicka, international law, international legal institutions and a wide variety of states in conflict had all turned to a practice of multicultural liberalism, as in liberal institutions reworked to enable group accommodation necessary to resolving identity conflicts. However, many of his examples embraced neither liberalism nor cultural diversity but could more easily be analysed as rather flimsy conflict resolution devices between highly illiberal intolerant groups,

---

[11] Klabbers (2006).   [12] Weller (2009).   [13] Kymlicka (2007).   [14] Ibid.

coerced by international organisations and third party states into uneasy power-sharing arrangements and a commitment to elections. Kymlicka argued that both a practice and a legal requirement of multicultural liberalism was emerging. However, he found the international legal norms promoting multicultural liberalism were 'ad hoc and unstable' and diffi-cult to roll out beyond the European context. He viewed international law in this area as at a cross-roads between general anti-discrimination law standards and more specific norms targeted at specific types of minority group – national minorities, indigenous peoples, racial minorities.

More recently, Tourme-Jouannet has argued that these types of development comprise a new 'international law of recognition' in which minority groups get forms of recognition through international legal provision for cultural identities, human rights, and reparations.[15] How-ever, she too points to a potential 'dark side' of the new law of self-determination and unresolved questions of how international law will satisfy demands for recognition, or resolve questions of whose identities will be recognised, and how recognition of cultures and identities will be reconciled with other branches of law – notably human rights law.

All these writers, on their own and taken cumulatively, usefully set out the ways in which the practice and law of self-determination appears to be moving away from absolutist notions of peoples versus territory that fuelled rather than resolved violent conflict, to a creative 'something else'. They agree that something new is going on in self-determination prac-tice. They also agree that the ingredients of this something new in general terms include a move towards giving space to political negotiation aimed at group accommodation and new ways of achieving group accommoda-tion through new power-maps for the state. They agree that this some-thing new has implications for the law of self-determination and the international legal system more generally.

However, while each of the above accounts usefully attempts to re-frame the traditional binary logic of self-determination law, rather than moving beyond such logic, each commentator suggests merely an alternative binary logic that should prevail. For Weller, this new logic is one that moves from external to internal self-determination: new conceptions of self-determination work within notions of state sovereignty, by push-ing forms of self-government that can be delivered within the framework of the new globalised state. For Klabbers the new logic is one that moves

---

[15] Tourme-Jouannet (2013).

from substance to process: self-determination is reconceived as a process-oriented, rather than an outcome oriented norm. Similarly, for Tourme-Jouannet the new logic involves a move from international law as concerned only with state recognition to recognition also of sub-state groups. For Kymlicka the move is from forms of majoritarian liberalism to multicultural liberalism as enabling better accommodation of groups within state formations.

4   How to Be Both: Re-claiming the Excluded Middle

In contrast, I suggest that the new legalised practice is better understood as a normative shift towards a more multivalent approach to what the norm requires. The new normative approach, rather than involving a shift from one type of binary to another, involves an attempt to combine the different poles pointed to by the norm, and use creative institutional-isation to deliver elements of both. Rather than a new process right, a set of techniques of internal self-determination, or a right to multicultural liberalism, or recognition, I suggest that the phenomena described by Klabbers, Weller, Kymlicka and Tourme-Jouannet can best be understood as evidence of a new form of 'hybrid self-determination'. This hybrid self-determination incorporates and addresses both internal and external self-determination claims in identity conflicts, but also operates to fashion a form of self-determination that is ambiguous as to whether processes of constitutional negotiation or substantive change in the nature and territory of the state, or a corporatist or liberal democratic state is on offer. In fact, I suggest that this understanding of current developments helps explain why these writers are all right in their quite different accounts of what is going on, and also helps explain why they all see the same 'something new' but understand it in quite different terms. A little like the story of the three blind men who each grasp a different part of the elephant – the tail, the leg and the trunk and believe its nature to be rope – like, tree – like or snake – like, when in fact an elephant combines all these attributes, so with the new self-determination each commentator looking from a different angle recognisably 'sees' the same thing, but grasps different bits of a norm which is best understood more holistically in terms of a new reach to multivalence rooted in an apparently impossible fuzzy logic.

The substance of the practice from this holistic point of view can be understood as four elements.

A procedural 'right to be heard'. The first element of the new norm is indeed a procedural 'right to be heard' as identified by Klabbers and Tourme-Jouannet. The new practice of self-determination has involved states being prepared to negotiate with peoples or non-state actors. Increasingly, states have negotiated with their most fundamental dissenters – minorities, armed opposition groups, terrorists, or their representatives. Since 1990 negotiated settlements between states and non-state armed actors or political groupings have come to form one of the main ways of ending intra-state conflict. Leaving aside for now the legal status of a 'right to be heard', who have states negotiated with in practice? The answer appears to be: groups with long-standing connections to the territory who can coherently argue that they are structurally excluded from a state that has been defined in terms of just one of its pluri-national groups. The key question with regard to how to constitute the group that is to be heard, is to ask whether it has a coherent claim of being historical excluded ofrom the state's foundation, in ways that traditional majoritarian democracy cannot remedy. The on-going group exclusion may happen because of ethnic voting patterns, the lack of a vote, or because of state 'capture' by powerful and elite groups.

The new practice of self-determination while responding to identity claims, is therefore not dependent on finding a globally agreed definition of what defines and unites the group in identity terms. The troubled question of who are the 'people's or 'minorities' is bypassed in favour of an approach that accepts the group's self-definition, and responds to their capacity to destabilise the state and its constitutional order, politically, morally, and even militarily, by withdrawing their consent from any social contract.

The move to direct negotiations between state and sub-state groups has both a political and a legal basis. Politically, negotiations tend to emerge as a response to 'mutually perceived hurting stalemates' where both parties stand to gain more at the negotiating table than they can on the battlefield. Legally, in addition to the law cited by Klabbers, emerging international legal standards dealing with marginalised groups have begun to involve the participation of those groups in international law-making, so as to produce standards which then require effective participation as a substantive legal requirement of domestic constitutional processes.[16]

---

[16] See generally Boyle & Chinkin (2007: 41–97).

The involvement of the marginalised in international law-making can in part be viewed as a response to the legitimacy deficits of international law-making as a purely interstate process. Those with an interest as beneficiaries of international instruments have been asserted to have a necessary place at the table of their negotiation: women in instruments affecting women[17]; victims in international criminal law[18]; indigenous peoples with regards to law on indigenous peoples[19]; minorities with regard to minorities.[20] The resulting international legal instruments then require participation of the relevant group in relevant processes, including domestic processes as one of their key elements.[21] Indeed, the twinning of participation in international standard-setting to required participation of the excluded in domestic political decision-making is less an example of international regulation of the domestic constitution, and more an example of marginalised groups needing to impact on both international and domestic constitutional spheres together to impact on either.[22] Interestingly, in addition to standards addressing groups on the basis of their identity a number of legal standards now also address the need for inclusion and participation in peace processes and agreements and the institutions they establish, most notably UN Security Council Resolution 1325 (2000) requiring the involvement of women in peace negotiations.[23]

---

[17] For an overview, see Bell & O'Rourke (2007: 30–35); Bell (2015).

[18] For example, the significant involvement of NGOs in formulating the Rome Statute of the International Criminal Court, see Boyle & Chinkin (2007: 71–74)

[19] For discussion, see Eide (2006).

[20] For example, the UN Sub-Commission on the Promotion and Protection of Human Rights established a subsidiary organ, the Working Group on Minorities, to provide a framework within which members of minority groups can participate in the development of relevant international standards, UNITED NATIONS GUIDE FOR MINORITIES, *Pamphlet No. 2: The UN Working Group on Minorities* at www.ohchr.org/english/about/publications/docs/pam2.doc.

[21] BEIJING PLATFORM FOR ACTION, FOURTH WORLD CONFERENCE ON WOMEN, G.1 'WOMEN IN POWER AND DECISION-MAKING', UN/DOC.A/CONF.177/20 1995; ROME STATUTE OF THE INTERNATIONAL CRIMINAL COURT, 17 JULY 1998, 2187 UNTS 3 [hereafter ROME STATUTE], article 68 (participation of victims); DECLARATION ON RIGHTS OF INDIGENOUS PEOPLES, articles 18, 19 and 20; UN DECLARATION ON MINORITIES, articles 2(3) and 5.

[22] See generally Keck & Sikkink (1998) (on processes of transnational mobilisation).

[23] New standards on impunity also provide for the participation of women, minorities, and victims in the design of transitional justice mechanisms, and associated rule of law reform, see UPDATED SET OF PRINCIPLES FOR THE PROTECTION AND PROMOTION OF HUMAN RIGHTS THROUGH ACTION TO COMBAT IMPUNITY [hereinafter UPDATED PRINCIPLES ON IMPUNITY], 7(c) & 35. See also United Nations Secretary-General (2004: para

These participation standards point to the need for the exercise of international and domestic public power to be inclusive of marginalised groups who stand to permanently lose out in majoritarian systems. The standards operate to underwrite a right to participate as requiring creative revisions of representative democracy at the domestic level.

A right to elections. The second element of the new multivalent law of self-determination, is the commitment to a substantive right to elections understood in individual rights terms. Self-determination settlement terms invariably mention elections and aim for some form of liberal democracy, although they vary on matters of timing and transition. Again, the move to elections has an international legal basis: international standards now promote and enforce electoral representation.[24] There are two distinct sources of law. The first is international human rights treaty provision for a right to free and fair elections along with the jurisprudence that has emanated from those treaty provisions. The second is the common standards found in the mandates of UN election monitoring missions.[25] Fox argues that these two strands, as a matter of practice, abre converging to produce a new regime that goes some way towards a 'right to democratic governance' by providing detailed requirements for conducting representative democracy through periodic elections.[26]

A right to state redefinition and accommodation through fair participation in public institutions. The third element is a substantive right to mechanisms of fair participation through state redefinition. At the level of symbolism and rhetoric, self-determination settlements aim to provide a fundamental redefinition of the state, to enable the inclusion of the

64(f)) providing that participation of 'groups most affected by conflict and a breakdown of the rule of law, among them children, women, minorities, prisoners and displaced persons'. New standards on a right to return of refugees and displaced persons, similarly note their right to 'participate in the return and restitution process and in the development of the procedures and mechanisms put in place to protect these rights', see, for example, the RIGHT TO RETURN OF REFUGEES AND INTERNALLY DISPLACED PERSONS, SUB-COMMISSION ON THE PROMOTION AND PROTECTION OF HUMAN RIGHTS, E/CN.4/ SUB.2/RES/2002/30, 15 August 2002, para 6.

[24] See, for example, Fox (1992), Fox & Roth (2000). On right to democratic government more generally, see Franck (1992).

[25] Fox ibid and Fox and Roth ibid.

[26] Ibid. (Fox argues that the first strand has developed to provide four elements: universal and equal suffrage, a secret ballot, elections at reasonable periodic intervals, and an absence of discrimination against voters, candidates or parties. The second sub-strand has developed a set of matters that should be verified as part of any assessment of whether elections were 'free and fair').

state's dissenters and so respond to their allegations of state illegitimacy. The redefinition of the state's nature and purpose is reflected both in constitutional language claiming that the state has changed, and in the articulation of new principles that will guide its new formation, such as inclusiveness or democratic renewal. These re-definitions defy any binary logic – they work in the sphere of the excluded middle. See, for example, the Belfast Agreement's provision of a referendum both North and South of Ireland – across two jurisdictions subject to the consent of the Northern vote – as an exercise in constructive ambiguity between self-determination claims to united Ireland and claims to unity with the UK.[27]

'Constructive ambiguity' enables opposed sides to live with a common language. However, in reaching for this new language for how the state is to be understood, the apparently symbolic redefinition of the state does not remain symbolic. The very articulation of state redefinition has a performative power changing the nature of the state, as one which has a multivalent character as newly inclusive of even those who reject the state's legitimacy and foundational narrative. To return to the Northern Irish example, the new Northern Irish state which is created is in some fundamental sense 'bi-national'.

A right to a disaggregated states. Fourthly, at the level of institutional detail, self-determination settlements disaggregate power by re-conceptualising state governance and jurisdiction as being capable of being disaggregated into a wide variety of territorial, functional, and identity-based mechanisms and institutions, so that competing group demands for power can be accommodated. Territorial sub-division of government, consociational government, forms of personal jurisdiction, robust human rights machinery, and power-sharing in justice and security apparatus – used separately or even cumulatively – are some of the vehicles through which power can be disaggregated. The disaggregation of power addresses the state's internal sovereignty. While state redefinition re-configures the conceptualisation of the relationship between state and people, disaggregating power involves re-configuring the state's institutional formations, so as to give effect to the redefinition.

As with the first prongs of the new self-determination, this fourth prong is underwritten by international legal standards. A series of legal developments largely initiated as a response to intrastate conflicts, now underwrite a requirement for states to work to accommodate minorities that lose out in majoritarian conceptions of democracy, most notably

---

[27] The Agreement Reached in the Multi-party Negotiations 10 April 1998, available at www.cain.ulst.ac.uk/events/peace/docs/agreement.htm.

convention and declaration.[28] Minority rights standards were also promulgated as discrete responses to the dissolution of the USSR and former
Yugoslavia, in an attempt to address the prospect of escalating intrastate
conflicts in the states and entities that emerged from these dissolutions,
in the form of Guidelines on recognition.[29] These minority rights standards contemplate pro-active policies of recognition and accommodation
as opposed to assimilation, emphasising throughout the 'right to participate effectively', with a positive duty on the state to facilitate this throughout public decision-making; similarly indigenous people's rights standards
talk of the need for free and informed prior consent to decisions affecting
them.[30] The standards, as discussed in detail in Kymlicka's work, have
indeed begun to suggest that states should move beyond representative
democracy towards fair participation in accommodating national minorities and indigenous peoples.[31]

    A right to fuzzy sovereignty. The fifth element of the new self-
determination is fuzzy sovereignty. While so far the elements of the new
law appear to be consistent with a concept of 'internal self-determination',
many new self-determination settlements tend to add elements of external

---

[28] The standards most notably include the Declaration on the Rights of Persons
    Belonging to National or Ethnic, Religious or Linguistic Minorities, UNGA
    Res 47/135, annex, 47 UN GAOR Supp. (No. 49) at 210, UN Doc A/47/49 (1993)
    [hereafter UN Declaration on Minorities], and the Council of Europe's Framework
    Convention on the Protection of National Minorities, ETS No 148, 1994, *entry into force*
    1 February 1998 [hereafter Framework Convention], that draws on the Conference on
    Security and Cooperation in European (later OSCE) documents that preceded it (see, for
    example, *Report of the CSCE Committee of Experts on National Minorities*, Geneva,
    19 July 1991, in 30 ILM 1692 (1991)). The Convention concerning Indigenous and Tribal
    Peoples in Independent Countries (ILO No. 169), 72 ILO Official Bulletin 59,
    adopted on 27 June 1989 by the General Conference of the International Labour
    Organisation at its seventy-sixth session, *entry into force* 5 September 1991, similarly
    emphasises recognition and the need to move beyond representative democracy to ensure
    participation: article 2(1) provides that 'Governments shall have the responsibility for
    developing, with the participation of the peoples concerned, co-ordinated and systematic
    action to protect the rights of these peoples and to guarantee respect for their integrity';
    article 6(1)(b) provides that Governments are to 'Establish means by which these peoples
    can freely participate, to at least the same extent as other sectors of the population, at all
    levels of decision-making in elective institutions and administrative and other bodies
    responsible for policies and programmes which concern them'.
[29] See *European Community: Declaration on Yugoslavia and on the Guidelines on the
    Recognition of New States*, 16 December 1991, 31 ILM (1992) 1485.
[30] UN Declaration on Minorities, *supra* note 12, article 1(1); Framework Convention,
    supra note 12, article 5(2).
[31] See generally Kymlicka (2007: 3–55, *passim*) (arguing that these are a key part of the
    're-internationalization' of state-minority relations).

self-determination to the settlement mix. Settlement terms often operate to dislocate power from the pre-existing *demos* of the territorially-defined state by making concepts of sovereignty 'fuzzy'. Dislocated power addresses the state's external sovereignty by attenuating it. In practice dislocating power involves 'fuzzying-up' the concept of sovereignty through two devices used separately or together: bi or pluri-nationalism – typically used in cases of ethnic conflict and secessionist demand, and international supervision – used in a range of conflicts.

A form of institutionalised pluri-nationalism can be achieved by acknowledging competing nationalisms as equally legitimate and creating institutional vehicles for governance that move beyond a traditional understanding of the state's territorial limits. Mechanisms for achieving pluri-nationalism include: cross border governance; devolution of all powers and trappings of statehood to a sub-state entity; dual citizenship and provisions providing for 'parity of esteem' of different national groupings; and postponed referenda on secession which reconstitute the state as requiring on-going consent. These mechanisms can be combined in various matrices to produce arrangements that unravel the conventional links between sovereignty, territory and national citizenry, so as to produce a new set of relationships capable of accommodating national identities not just within but also across borders.

Again, international legal standards relating to minorities and indigenous peoples have moved in the direction of underwriting fuzzy sovereignty. As well as underwriting inter-group contacts within the territory, these standards refer to the right of ethnic groups to maintain cross-border contacts with ethnic counterparts in other jurisdictions, and even provide for states to sign bilateral agreements to this effect.[32] This provision parallels and underwrites self-determination settlement attempts to sever notions of 'nationhood' from territorially-based notions of 'statehood'. Soft law standards have gone further and attempted to suggest a right to specific institutional arrangements to ensure 'effective participation' – such as informal and formal types of power-sharing, or autonomy regime.[33]

---

[32] UN DECLARATION ON MINORITIES, ibid. articles 2(5), 5(2) and 6; FRAMEWORK CONVENTION, ibid., articles 17 and 18.

[33] The Lund Recommendations on the Effective Participation of National Minorities in Public Life & Explanatory Note, September 1999, at www.osce.org/documents/hcnm/1999/09/2698_en.pdf. UNITED NATIONS DECLARATION ON THE RIGHTS OF INDIGENOUS PEOPLES, adopted by the UN General Assembly on 7 September 2007, UN Doc. A/61/L.67, provides in article 18 for a right to self-determination and effective participation as including the right to participate 'in decision-making in matters which would affect their

A second quite different way to dislocate power is through the concept of international supervision. International supervision conditions full sovereignty on the building of political and legal institutions that will disaggregate power, to ensure that all groups are accommodated. In the interim period (often left indefinite) international actors are given extensive roles in domestic political and legal institutions, with a view to enforcing and developing these institutions and with them, the peace agreement. International involvement can range from full international territorial administration (Bosnia), to international actors playing roles on peace agreement implementation bodies (e.g. South African Brian Currin implementing prisoner release provisions in Northern Ireland).

Again, normative revision has underwritten these novel forms of international-domestic hybridity. Full forms of international supervision can be authorised by UN Security Council, but the internal constitutions of international organisations also permit diverse mechanisms of intervention. There are moves to articulate at the international constitutional level a more fundamental revision of state sovereignty in the concept of 'responsibility to protect' which attempts to link sovereignty to a duty to protect citizenry, endorsing international intervention when that duty is breached.[34] Again, these legal developments have been produced in response to situations of conflict, and underwrite the types of settlement terms understood to be required to end these conflicts.

5   How Hybrid Self-determination's Multivalent Approach Works

Under binary logic, the excluded middle cannot exist; it is logically excluded by framing the only possibilities as being '1' or '0'. In contrast, these new self-determination approaches attempt to find a middle way, in an attempt to transcend very real conflict impasses. The descriptions of Klabbers, Kymlicka, Tourme-Jouannet, and Weller are useful in reconceptualising the current directions of international self-determination law and capture that indeed 'something new is going on'. However, as suggested earlier, they each point to a new (and different) way of

---

rights, through representatives chosen by themselves in accordance with their own procedures, as well as to maintain and develop their own indigenous decision-making institutions.' Article 19 provides for the right of indigenous peoples to participate fully by requiring that states 'obtain their free, prior and informed consent before adopting and implementing legislative or administrative measures that may affect them'.

[34] On responsibility to protect, see www.un.org/en/preventgenocide/adviser/responsibility .shtml.

understanding the binary in question which prompts moving to a different poll: from external to internal self-determination, from substance to process; or from majoritarianism to more group-oriented approach.

In contrast, I suggest that we better understand the 'something new' of self-determination law as incorporating all of these binaries rather than shifting between them, involving a move to a more ambiguous multivalent formulation. Indeed, understanding the multilayered approach to how self-determination is being reworked helps explain why each of the commentators discussed sees something new and similar at play, and yet see it in such different ways. This multivalent perspective understands the norm to function not as an imperative-requiring norm, but as a shaping-programmatic norm, which attempts to enable the re-creation of the excluded middle capable of transcend ing the binary division. The re-creation of the formerly excluded middle enables both a conceptual space and a functioning real political space in which the only possibility for reconstructing polities and relationships can be attempted.

In other words: this is a shift from binary logic altogether towards multivalent or fuzzy logic (to embrace that term as non-pejorative). The form of self-determination that results is multivalent across all of the binaries identified above. Interestingly, this multivalence can be argued not to be a new fashioning of the norm, but rather to be a new acknowledgement of the multivalence that generated a somewhat normatively incoherent and ambiguous norm in the first place. Legal articulations of the norm can be argued to capture a variety of different elements of what is understood to be important to sovereign statehood, when conceived of as itself a multivalent relational concept. The 'incompatible pillars' of self-determination law's legal formulation as hybrid between a commitment to territorial sovereignty and representative government which have underwritten so much conflict, when viewed from a more multivalent perspective can be understood as capturing the need for a unified demos, polis, and territory to be closely linked to representative government if the state is to be effective, rather than as incoherent. As Musgrave argues, the norm always been understood to underwrite different ideas as regards 'the self' protected by the self-determination norm among different regional blocks of states; often the key resolutions which have documented the norm have attempted to capture these quite different understandings in one definition.[35] Thus the norm can be understood to

---

[35] Musgrave (2000).

be multivalent in its foundation: a norm whose conceptions of legitimate statehood have different emphasis in different parts of the globe. Rather than a departure therefore, we can understand the new law of hybrid self-determination as in a sense embracing and creatively working with the norm's inherent multivalence to give it a clearer practical basis. How then does the law work as a multivalent norm?

Hybrid between internal and external self-determination. First, the new norm is multivalent between external and internal self-determination both of which historic legal and political statements of self-determination valorise.[36] Hybrid self-determination in a sense reconciles irreconcilable claims to internal and external self-determination, both of which were inherent in the norm's formulations. Traditionally, self-determination as a legal concept was viewed in terms of external self-determination – the right to change the status of the state from colonial to independent, or from one state to two or more.[37] Co-existing much more nebulously has been a concept of 'internal self-determination' – a concept that focuses on 'the relationship between a people and 'its own' state or government, rather than state formation itself.[38] The two concepts are arguably both present in legal articulations of the norm – and of course de-colonisation aimed to deliver both external and internal self-determination simultaneously.[39] From this view, the norm itself is hybrid claiming to link the state's external legitimacy to its internal legitimacy, as reinforced by the persistent idea that denial of internal self-determination in extreme cases involving wholesale and brutal denial of human rights, may give rise to a right to external self-determination.[40]

---

[36] While theories of hybridity can be found in other areas, post-colonisation studies, in particular with reference to identity, and in systems theory, the term here is taken from the gardening world and the construction of hybrid plants (and it is suggested that this organic metaphor is the origin of other uses of the word). Interestingly, gardeners note that with hybrid plants, each of the 'parent' elements will continually try to take over the plant, or make it 'revert' to one parent. Thus, in variegated hybrids, for example, any appearing all green or all white leaves will have to be trimmed back.

[37] See, for example, Cassese (2005: 60–62).   [38] Thornberry (1991: 101).

[39] Ibid. Roots can be found in legal articulations of self-determination, see further Bell (2000: 165–6).

[40] This is suggested in the so-called 'get out' clause of Friendly Relations Declaration providing that territorial integrity or political unity of states only applies to states 'conducting themselves in compliance with the principle of equal rights and self-determination of peoples as described above and thus possessed of a government representing the whole people belonging to the territory without distinction as to race, creed or colour'.

The difficulty with delivering on both dimensions of the norm has been that the two concepts are conceived of as leading to quite different remedies: statehood in the case of external self-determination, and 'more representative government' in the case of internal self-determination.

The new law and language of hybrid self-determination points to a deliberate incorporation of both internal and external self-determination language and mechanisms. This language aims to reconcile the twin pillars of self-determination law, namely the commitment to representative government and the commitment to existing territorial boundaries. The commitments to a unitary existing state and the possibility of explaining institutional arrangements as forms of federalism, devolution, regionalism and autonomy which are consistent with unitary sovereignty point to an 'internal' solution. However, settlement terms frequently establish an institutional fabric and language that dislocate power by deliberately blurring the question of where sovereignty lies. In transition at least, the arrangements cannot easily be analysed as consistent with statehood as exclusive control over a fixed territory and a people with a common understanding of their national allegiance.[41] Self-determination settlements point to a state which claims to leave its territorial and sovereign basis somewhat ambiguous. However, the arrangements are often also designed so that they can be analysed and presented as in conformance with the concept of territorial integrity. In remaining deliberately ambiguous as to whether internal or external self-determination is being delivered, hybrid self-determination simultaneously delivers both and therefore neither one alone. The old state both continues to exist and is replaced. Conflict resolution and legal norm are brought together.

Hybrid between offering process or substance. Hybrid self-determination is also hybrid as between notions of process and substance, or put another way – multivalent in not committing to either a purely procedural or a purely substantive norm, but rather to an approach in which process and substance are closely interweaved. In one sense it offers self-determination as pure process: a right to negotiate. Again there is a conflict resolution imperative: often the only common endeavour that can ground agreement is the agreement to disagree or to talk about talking. The only matter on which there is agreement is the concept of groups participating in decisions affecting them. The move to conceptualising self-determination as process appears to enable the difficulty of what self-determination remedy should

---

[41] Convention on Rights and Duties of States, Montevideo, 26 December 1933, 49 Stat. 3097.

pertain to be transcended. Rather than a move to a particular type of state configuration, what is on offer is negotiation.

Yet in its very articulation as process, hybrid self-determination becomes substantive; it requires the state to have a commitment to on-going negotiation of who it represents and includes. A substantive conception of the state is required that understands it as capable of leaving its relationship to questions of identity and participation open. In other words, the state is 're-founded' as more explicitly multivalent and pluri-national, and is understood to involve consent as to developing processes of on-going negotiation rather than consent to a particular static political settlement. The commitment to ongoing dialogue requires that there be something to conduct dialogue about – and this requires the state's internal configuration to remain up for grabs. Very tangibly, the commitment to process dictates a particular substance to institutional provision in the form of concepts such as power-sharing and future constitutional revision. These concepts are explicitly designed around the need to leave open fundamental contests as to the nature and ownership of the state.

Indeed, logically, a right to negotiate cannot end with the production of broad settlement terms, but by implication must continue into all future political decision-making. The democratic vehicle therefore becomes re-conceived as a set of institutionalised mechanisms for the effective participation in the totality of governance of previously excluded groups. Power-sharing governments, complicated federal and confederal arrangements, carefully balanced police, armies, judiciary, and civil service, postponed referenda on independence and autonomy, and even the machinery of domestic human rights protection together claim to offer the possibility of ongoing mechanisms of 'fair and effective participation'.[42]

Hybrid between individualist representation and corporate participation. More controversially, hybrid self-determination is hybrid as between notions of representative and participative democracy, or – more problematically – between democratic and corporate forms of power. Representative democracy refers to the concept of democracy through periodic free and fair elections. Participatory democracy is a concept, variously described, that attempts to 'reinvent', 'engender' or establish 'deep', 'new', 'strong', or 'cosmopolitan' democracy, premised on increased citizen participation, in particular through a 're-visioning' of

[42] *Cf.* Framework Convention, *supra* note 17, and Comprehensive Peace Agreement, Sudan, 9 January 2005, at www.c-r.org/our-work/accord/index.php.

the role of civil society in a renewed democratic polity. Finding examples in Eastern Europe and Central America, but also in contemporary Western democracies, political theorists have argued with increasing force that civil society should be conceptualised within a theory of democracy as having a role in Habermasian deliberation.[43] This role addresses a democratic deficit occurring in transitions to democracy, but also in Western Democratic states, where participation through periodic elections no longer seems to accurately account for how citizens actually seek to participate, or to provide an adequate theoretical account of how public decision-making should be connected to the citizenry.

Like self-determination the concept of democracy can in fact be analysed as itself 'hybrid' between concepts of representation and participation. 'Participative democracy' contemplates a relationship with representative democracy, while 'almost every advocate of majority decision is committed to *some* form of deliberative democracy'.[44] However, the concepts of representation and participation locate the legitimacy of political decision-making in different places: representative democracy views legitimacy as rooted in the fact of the decision-maker being elected, while participative democracy locates legitimacy in the quality of the deliberation, the inclusiveness of the participation, or both.

While self-determination settlements invariably point a direction to elections, as we have seen they couple this with an attempt to secure broader and deeper ongoing participation in governance. The move in identity conflicts from straightforward majoritarianism to consociationalism itself endorses representative electoral democracy while also responding to its limits by offering groups guarantees of participation as a group. Power-sharing, proportional representation, and mutual vetoes replace 'pure' representative democracy, and so respond to the idea that majoritarian voting systems do not work in situations of conflict, where they stand to exacerbate rather than channel political divisions. The popularity of consociational-type arrangements lies in their ability to give effect to both representative and participative democracy. Consociationalism, understood as 'responsible realism'[45] aims to retain a commitment to representative democracy while recognising the need for group accommodation. Consociationalism's power-sharing devices, often thought of as a tool for ethnic conflict, now feature heavily as a conflict resolution tool in all types of intra-state

[43] Habermas (1984).   [44] Waldron (1998: 293).
[45] McGarry & O'Leary (2004: 19–24).

conflict.[46] Principled and responsible – consociationalism recognises
the legitimacy of representative democracy and individual equality
rights. Realist it provides a mechanism that recognises that group
identities and allegiances impact decisively on voter preferences.
Rather than wishing this away, consociationalism offers a mechanism
that recognises the group, but in a framework requiring elections and
individual equality rights.[47] In the move from majoritarian voting
mechanisms, consociationalism requires a notion of 'effective participation' rather than numerical 'representation' as the better measure of
democratic legitimacy.

Yet, lurking between even the most liberal of consociational of formu-
lae, is a notion of power as linked to 'corporate' as in 'group' interests,
rather than as linked to rule-based individualism. This is the 'realist' part
of consociationalism. As with the other hybrid dimensions of the new
self-determination, this form of hybridity has a conflict resolution dividend. The revision of the concept of democratic legitimacy to include
group participation attempts to enable the renegotiation and transition of
politico-military elites from private to public exercise of power, by giving
groups the chance to buy-in to power structures. In short, it enables the
elite pact which is necessary to any resolution of the conflict. Sometimes
the group participation is little more than an illiberal corporate deal.
However, sometimes the corporatist dimension is broadened to a range
of actors, including civil society actors, articulated in terms of a concept
of participation as buying time for elections to be held, while responding
to the defects of representative democracy. With representative democracy impossible in the short-term, and the relationship between elections
to public decision-making potentially problematic even in the long term,
participative democracy becomes attractive as a way to legitimate governance that is otherwise free floating of a connection with the governed.

---

[46] See, for example, GLOBAL AND INCLUSIVE AGREEMENT ON TRANSITION IN THE DEMO-
CRATIC REPUBLIC OF CONGO, 16 December 2002, III.7; LINAS-MARCOUSSIS AGREEMENT,
Cote d'Ivoire, 24 January 2003, 3; COMPREHENSIVE PEACE AGREEMENT BETWEEN THE
GOVERNMENT OF LIBERIA AND THE LIBERIANS UNITED FOR RECONCILIATION AND
DEMOCRACY AND THE MOVEMENT FOR DEMOCRACY IN LIBERIA AND POLITICAL PARTIES,
Accra, 18 August 2003, article 21; AGREEMENT BETWEEN THE GOVERNMENT OF GUINEA
BISSAU AND THE SELF-PROCLAIMED MILITARY JUNTA, 1 November 1998, 38 ILM 28
(1999), 4. Full text of agreements available at www.usip.org/library/pa/.

[47] See McGarry & O'Leary (2004: 32–36) distinguishing between pluralist liberal consociationalism and other forms.

However, there is also a normative dividend. As elections and partici-pation vie with each other in terms of which will deliver legitimacy and stability, emphasising both can avoid the deficits of each one. The settlement's legitimacy itself can be rooted in a notion of 'will of the people' that at once acknowledges the primacy of elections while offering fair and effective participation for minority groups. This hybridity does not just create an on-going working polity but creates an ambiguous, multiple overlaid authorship for the constitutional foundations of the political settlement itself: another form of multivalence.

6   Maintaining the Excluded Middle: Multivalent between 'war and peace'?

As Glenn has pointed out, states have always been more cosmopolitan than international legal accounts of nation statehood, or constitutional law accounts of the state's foundation have credited (Glenn 2013). Indeed, in a sense his work 'reclaims' the multivalent nature of statehood itself. His perspective is useful because it helps to locate the new law of hybrid self-determination, and the fluid concept of statehood that it promotes, as less 'new' than it might otherwise seem. However, a critical question remains in contemporary efforts to construct or reconstruct states destabilised by violent political conflict, as to who and how the state is to be created and sustained as multivalent – and whether this is possible at all. Do binary narratives have such a powerful hold on the political imagination of state-craft, that any other way of doing business is almost impossible?

There is a logic of conflict resolution which pushes political ambigu-ities – actual or linguistic: it is often vital to achieving an elite pact to tell everyone that 'they have won' the war in order to create and sustain some sort of compromise political outcomes. However, in creating an ambigu-ous form of statehood and democratic polity, a fundamental question remains as to whether the excluded middle is a space of radical potential in which identities and binary 'truths' about the state can be re-fashioned; or disguises a dishonest victory in which one side really 'wins' its preferred default position but with the other side given some linguistic concessions. If neither victory nor transformation can be achieved, the excluded middle may still self-maintain as some sort of dead in-between détente space: a frozen conflict zone of 'no war, no peace', because while there is no common commitment to a shared state at all neither is there on-going capacity for victory in war.

As a response to this question I argue that it is only by understanding the multivalent logic of attempted new solutions that we are able to understand that all three outcomes are possible and that progressive improved outcomes are not inevitable but require ongoing commitment. The very construction of the excluded middle requires that the choice as to the future is left open, the only alternatives being reversion to one of the default binary positions of the conflict – but this leaves the possibility of reversions open and sometimes reversion to more exclusive conceptions of the state is achieved.

The critical project for intervention in support of the settlement therefore, rather than working to institute a vision of a more traditional state, is to work to build the radical transformative potential of the excluded middle by ensuring that its contours are shaped by a project of agency rather than the balance of power dynamic between those at the heart of the conflict. Often the only people with a commitment to using the space of the excluded middle in a progressive and transformative way are what Bouventuras de Sousa Santos calls sub-alterns – that is non-elite power-holders such as activists and international actors.[48] However, often these groups are relatively disempowered with respect to implementing transitions, vis-à-vis elites empowered by political settlements founded centrally on elite pacts. It is important to understand that the excluded middle involves a space of on-going contestation between those who continue to push that the new settlement defaults back to one of the conflict's binary political poles, and those who seek a transformative space at the centre. Unless the space of the excluded middle is valued and built as a space of transformation it is unlikely to sustain and evolve 'naturally'. If the balance of power holds, the space may sustain, but as a dead zone of détente. If it does not, conflict is likely to return.

However, the difficulty of valuing the space of the excluded middle – even for those most committed to it – is profound: the excluded middle's multivalent attributes make it difficult even for those who most fought for it, to love and support it. The difficulties can be understood in terms of the continuing power of binary logic of both law and politics.

As regards law: the space of the excluded middle remains under pressure from binary logic of international law and its organising concepts. Notably the concept of sovereignty retains a firm hold: despite globalisation states still exist with a considerable authority and the concept

---

[48] Sousa Santos (2002).

of sovereignty as a totalising rather than a relational concept remains powerful. The death of the sovereign state has often been greatly exaggerated and in moments of crises it shows remarkable capacity to reassert itself. Weak or insecure states often assert their own sovereignty in particularly monolithic ways internally and externally as a form of political posturing and elite protection. Also, the dead hand of Westphalia has a powerful grip because we have little other known way of doing things. How does one really create a state that is not committed to its own territorial boundaries and whose self-definition leaves its future existence open and contingent? The language of law can be used to create this texture to the political settlement as we have seen, for example in the bi-national language of the Belfast or Good Friday Agreement in Northern Ireland. However, what does this language mean for how we create and work out new political and legal institutions? For example, what does a commitment to equality of aspiration to statehood and bi-national citizenship mean for who can join the civil service, the police or other security agencies – how loyal do they need to be and what are the implications of bi-nationalism for the state's monopoly on the use of legitimate force? What does bi-nationalism mean – say for when the (British) Union flag is flown over buildings in Northern Ireland that are still jurisdictionally in the UK, and whether the Irish flag is ever to be so allowed? Or what does 'parity of esteem' between different national groupings with different perspectives on the conflict mean for how we understand who were victims and who were perpetrators when we talk of the past? All these issues have bedevilled the implementation of the agreement in Northern Ireland and remain on a peace agreement 'to-do' list and subject to on-going negotiation almost fifteen years later.

Law itself can also at times play an unconstructive role with regard to the space, notably where its commitment to binary logic is strongest: in courts. Legal adjudication persists and even abounds in post-conflict jurisdictions, and plays a heightened political role given the constructivist on-going reform of legal and political institutions. As a result, often courts find ways of adjudicating on peace agreements and hybrid self-determination itself. So courts, for example, have been asked to bring peace agreements to an end or gut their central power-sharing provisions by striking them down in terms of constitutions, legislation or international human rights law or international criminal law.[49] Asking binary-framed questions of courts invites

---

[49] See for example *Case of Sejdić and Finci v. Bosnia and Herzegovina*, Applications nos. 27996/06 and 34836/06, Eur. Ct. Hum. Rts. GC, Judgment of 22 December 2009;

them to give binary yes or no answers that de-construct the multi-valence at the heart of the agreement: does the new fuzzy sovereignty arrangement violate the Constitution's commitment to 'unity'; does the power-sharing mechanism violate individual electoral rights? So while the legal language of peace agreement often is perfectly able to create and hold the excluded middle, court decisions made according to binary logic risk unravelling this space by unwinding the bargains that created and sustain it.

The second difficulty of sustaining and using the excluded middle as a space of transformation of the political settlement is political. The political order of the excluded middle is not accepted as anything more than a transitional space by the main parties to the conflict. Most of these parties aim to transit back to their default 'win' position and tend to have entered peace negotiations in a hope of that getting them more than they want at the negotiating table, than the war trajectory they were on. Elites seldom enter negotiations because they have somehow 'converted' to the notion of peace. However, the excluded middle is also an uncomfortable space for normative actors – internal and external – who include those who most politically support a move from the binary certainties of conflict. The political orders created in the excluded middle are in a deep sense hybrid between normatively attractive and normatively unattractive actors and positions. These are indeed zones of 'no war, no peace', and often operate as hybrid political orders that are hybrid between normatively principled liberal democratic institutions and informal power arrangements between elites that often shape and limit how these institutions work and even bypass them.

Indeed, some of the most interesting work on post-conflict peacebuilding has independently of hybrid self-determination analysis, reached to a notion of hybridity in trying to understand the orders that emerge and the normative ambivalence that they create. So Boege, et al, and Mac Ginty, all point to 'hybrid political orders' rather than 'liberal political orders' as the almost inevitable outcome of trying to marry

Prosecutor v Morris Kallon, Brima Bazzy Kamara, Case No SCSL-2004-15-AR72E, Case No SCSL-2004-16-AR72E (13 March 2004); *Robinson v Secretary of State for Northern Ireland and others* [2002] UKHL 32; *The Governor of North Cortabato City v Government of the Republic of the Philippines Peace Panel on Ancestral Domain, Philippines Supreme Court*, GR 183591 available at www.sc.judiciary.gov.ph/jurisprudence/2008/october2008/183591.htm.

liberal democratic structures with forms of corporate accommodation of power blocks.[50]

Here a biological analogy rather than a mathematical one, has been reached to, to similarly capture both a creative innovative attempt to 'be both' a liberal solution and a corporate power accommodation, and therefore 'neither'. The metaphor of hybridity also speaks to the dual possibilities of a brave new way of being, and of reversion to either of the mutant parents. In essence the biological metaphor like that of the multivalent or fuzzy logic metaphor, attempts to capture the complexity of political orders that emerge from the attempt to 'be both' in a way that speaks both to the creative fluidity of the order, but also its darker unresolved nature which are generated by the inherent tensions that multivalent value systems incorporated into the heart of the new order.

I suggest that situating hybrid political order analysis in a larger theory of multivalent self-determination logic helps to explain how these hybrid orders emerge, not as accidental compromised by-product of liberal peacebuilding failures, but rather as a *part and parcel* of the new fuzzy logic of hybrid self-determination techniques. The difficulty is, that having understood fuzzy logic and the reconstruction of the excluded middle as an important project for stopping the war, internal and external interveners find the space very unsatisfactory in terms of the types of transformation they would like to see the space enabling. The structure of the settlements means that each group engaging with the new political settlement – including international actors – often engages in an attempt to return to the binary pole they are normatively committed to. For the parties, this will typically be their exclusive version of the future, and a move to a limited access order in which they are the dominant (and dominating) group. For international actors it will typically involve attempting to move to a majoritarian form of liberal democracy – or open access order - in which the corporate dimensions of the 'deal' and indeed its 'fuzzy statehood' are pushed to evolve into something more recognisable in terms of Western liberal statehood.

Peacebuilding is strewn with the dilemmas for international actors that ensue, most of them focused on the question of how to sequence and the transition from fuzzy deal to liberal statehood. When should international actors permit amnesty and when insist on accountability? The first appears essential to the elite pact, and the second to any long-term

---

[50] See Mac Ginty (2010); Boege et al. (2009, 2008).

rule of law. Should international peacebuilders insist on elections or implement an 'institution-building first' approach? Either choice risks stabilising an exclusive elite pact, without any real transformative agenda or possibilities, and either choice is controversial in terms of the normative commitments to human rights and democracy of international organisations. These dilemmas are profound because failing to sustain the elite pact means that the liberal peace will never be reached, while sustaining the elite pact also appears to institutionalise the very forms of exclusion and division which require to be transcended if a truly peaceful society is to be achieved.

Whether the peace process succeeds or fails in practice often depends on whether the space of the excluded middle can be sustained or not. However, with no-one particularly committed to it, the excluded middle becomes sustained not by the agency of any of the actors, but by the balance of power between them as they attempt to pull back to their preferred default poles. As noted, the excluded middle often self-sustains but less as creative space and more as a space of 'frozen conflict', because the balance of power coupled with war weariness may continue to promote it as a space of détente. Those committed to 'good enough governance', can perhaps contemplate this as a form of success, however the excluded middle as a space of frozen détente is not an easy one in which to peacebuild or deliver good government because it is characterised by instability and constant threat of a return to violence. As Barnett, Fang and Zürcher argue, in practice international peacebuilders often remain committed to their normative ideals which encourage them to undo the excluded middle of hybrid political and legal arrangements as they attempt to promote a more traditional vision of liberal peace, while recognising that they must 'trade' with local political actors operating within local power structures in ways that frustrate liberal peacemaking ambitions. Often this is the only space in which peacebuilding is possible.[51] As a result, peacebuilders tend to engage in 'compromised peace building' in which an implicit 'peacebuilders contract' sees peacebuilders in essence transacting with local actors to have norms articulated by local actors, in return for working with what are contrasting local structures and incentives that pull in quite different directions from international norms.

[51] (2014).

7   Understanding How to Assist Political Settlement in Divided Societies: From Theory to Practice

What then are the policy implications of hybrid self-determination for peacebuilding? Or is this merely an intense theoretical discussion as to the adequacy of mathematical and biological analogies? I suggest that the policy implications are profound, although clear policy 'take homes' remain elusive. At its heart, the appeal to understand the conflict resolution project of constructing and maintaining the excluded middle is an appeal to understand and grapple with the hybrid compromised space in which conflict transformation takes place, rather than wish it to be a space with some 'better nature' than it has.

At the outset, it is important to recognise that wars only end in three ways and that this is what produces the need for the excluded middle to be created. The first way to end a war is to let the parties fight to conclusion and hope that the balance of power outcome that sees one party prevailing sustains a stable future. The second way to end a war is for outside actors intervene militarily to change the balance of power by assisting one party to win in the hope that the best party wins and that this assists a more sustainable future. The third approach, is for the parties with or without international assistance, to negotiate a messy moral, political and legal compromise capable of ending the fighting by creating new political and legal institutions in which to share power and to attempt to work out their differences less violently. The first two options involve permitting, or assisting one of the poles of the binary logic of war to win out. Neither of these options have a good record with regard to liberal democratic outcomes or a just peace. Moreover, while 'giving war a chance' has advocates, the contemporary new 'global marketplace' of conflict and external intervention indicates that rather than bringing clean victories leaving wars to fester may risk more complex regional and even international conflicts.[52] From a normative point of view, the most powerful rather than the most just and democratic, tend to win, but in fact many of the conflicts in question prove intractable for both sides. The third approach involves trying to re-create the excluded middle. For all the mess and normative compromises of the excluded middle, this last solution is usually more acceptable

---

[52] On giving war a chance, see Luttwak (1999); on the new 'global marketplace' see Carothers & Samet-Marram (2015).

to those who believe in justice and peace, and has a better evidence-basis for success, than either of the two binary-focused alternatives.

However, sustaining the excluded middle is an immensely political project, which involves international interveners being much more self-conscious from the outset about the nature of the project and the political compromises (for themselves and others) that they are caught up in. There currently appears to be some appetite for a more self-consciously political approach among a varied range of international actors. International interveners, from aid agencies to peacebuilding institutions are all expressing a strong sense of disillusionment with post-1990 practices of assistance to fragile and conflict-affected states based on understanding that they have failed to adequately engage with both their own internal political constraints, and the local political power realities in the contexts in which they intervene. This disillusionment is often expressed as a sense of being 'outwitted' by local actors and politics that they have field to sufficiently understand or anticipate. The institutions of good government that international interveners work to create often turn into something quite different, even when models of good practice are followed. Worse still, their own analysis and political will appear inadequate to an effective response. Rather than a failure of 'lessons learned', policy documents exhibit a sense that the real problem is more fundamental: they do not know what lessons to take from past failures and are not convinced that doing more of the same a bit harder will do the trick, and so they search for new analysis that will enable them to find a new approach altogether.

I suggest that if new ways of engaging with context-specific political realities are to be found, it is important for policy-makers to understand both the potential and the limitations of the excluded middle as a space for transformation which is deeply compromised from the outset. From this perspective, practical projects of intervention would seek to:

(a) Understand the ways in which peace settlements establish an excluded middle involving compromised institutional provision, which will remain under pressure to revert to one of the conflict's binary poles and design strategies which anticipate how international intervention may be likely to tilt the deal in unhelpful ways

(b) Understand the ways in which political bargaining by the main contenders for power will involve the strategic use of normative arguments, for example appeals to elections, and human rights, and the institutions and language of democracy, to engage in forms of reversion to exclusive forms of governance. International actors need to consider how democracy promotion may play out in a world in which democratic change is not the key goal of elites nor what they understand to be at the heart of the deal they have signed up to

(c) Understand that sustaining the space also risks freezing the conflict rather than transforming it, and evaluate the types of process of development and re-negotiation that can assist in keeping the space for transformation open and forward moving

(d) Analyse and evaluate the mechanisms, institutions and constituencies which have transformative potential and ensure that they are supported post-settlement

(e) Analyse and evaluate the limitations on transformation, imposed by the need to keep powerful actors on board

(f) Build capacity to be flexible and opportunistic as regards opportunities with transformative potential

(g) Evaluate and be realistic as to how supporting transformation involves political will and be aware that interventions are themselves highly political. Interventions need to be made with sufficient political will and capacity to engage in forms of power reallocation that will be resisted

Admittedly how to do any of these things this needs further thought and differentiated policies by different interveners. But I suggest that moving forward requires the modalities of post-settlement engagement to be re-thought. The key shift required is to move from a project that is less goal-oriented in terms of particular political outcomes, to one that is understood more as a project of looking for and supporting open political spaces of deliberation by pushing back against any return to conflict default positions. Such an approach requires a more sophisticated analysis of the ways in which local elites use the very language and institutional apparatus of the peace settlement to achieve their old conflict goals.

As an alternative, it may of course also be possible to muddle through in the fog of détente with only a half belief in what one is doing – provided that the balance of power between warring factions sustains. As Barnett, Fang and Zürcher suggest, this may not be a completely bad solution: a very imperfect peace may still be eminently more desirable than a very perfect war. Sometimes muddling through is better than the alternatives. However, I suggest that even muddling through could benefit from increased self-awareness of international actors as to the nature and importance of the excluded middle space of conflict resolution and the imperative to understand both the importance of multivalent thinking, and its peculiar state-building dilemmas. At least such thinking would avoid navigating post-conflict terrains with a degree of bad faith rooted in the inability to reconcile normative desires to practical political possibilities. This is a useful second best approach, unsatisfactory as it sounds and much as I would prefer something a little more ambitious to be attempted.

Bibliography

Anderson, Benedict, IMAGINED COMMUNITIES: REFLECTIONS ON THE ORIGIN AND SPREAD OF NATIONALISM (1983).

Barnett, Michael, Songyin Fang & Christopher Zürcher, *Compromised Peacebuilding*, 58 INT'L ST. Q. 608 (2014).

Bell, Christine, PEACE AGREEMENTS AND HUMAN RIGHTS (2000).

ON THE LAW OF PEACE: PEACE AGREEMENTS AND THE LEX PACIFICATORIA (2008).

Text and Context: Evaluating Peace Agreements for their 'Gender Perspective'. Political Settlements Research Programme, Research Paper 1, 2015.

Bell, Christine & Catherine O'Rourke, *The People's Peace? Peace Agreements and Participatory Democracy*, 28 INT'L. POL. SCI REV 293 (2007).

Boyle, Alan & Christine Chinkin THE MAKING OF INTERNATIONAL LAW (2007).

Boege, Volker et al. *On Hybrid Political Orders and Failing States: What is Failing? States in the South or Research and Politics in the West?*, 8 BERGHOF HANDBOOK FOR CONFLICT TRANSFORMATION 15 (2008), www.berghof -handbook.net/dialogue-series/no.-8-building-peace-in-the-absence-of-states.

Boege, Volker, Anne Brown, Kevin Clements & Anna Nolan, *Building Peace and Political Community in Hybrid Political Orders*, 16 INT. PEACEKEEPING 599–615 (2009).

Carothers, Thomas & Oren Samet-Marram, THE NEW GLOBAL MARKETPLACE (2015).

Cassese, Antonio INTERNATIONAL LAW (2nd edn) (2005).

Eide, Asbjørn, *Rights of Indigenous Peoples: Acheivements in International Law During the Lawt Quarter of a Century*, 37 NETHERLANDS YEARBOOK OF INT'L LAW 155–212 (2006).

Franck, Thomas M. *The Emerging Right to Democratic Governance*, 86 AM.J. INT'L L. 46 (1992).

Fox, Gregory H. *The Right to Political Participation in International Law*, 17 Y.J. INT'L. L 539 (1992).

Fox, Gregory H. & Brad Roth, *Introduction: The Spread of Liberal Democracy and its Implications for International Law* in Gregory H. Fox & Brad Roth (eds). DEMOCRATIC GOVERNANCE AND INTERNATIONAL LAW (2000)

Glenn, H. Patrick, THE COSMOPOLITAN STATE (2013).

Habermas, Jürgen, THEORY OF COMMUNICATIVE ACTION (1984).

Keck, Margaret E., & Katherine Sikkink ACTIVISTS BEYOND BORDERS: ADVOCACY NETWORKS IN INTERNATIONAL POLITICS (1998).

Klabbers, Jan, *The Right to be Taken Seriously: Self-Determination in International Law*, 28 HUM. RTS. Q. 186 (2006).

Koskienniemi, Martti, *National Self-determination Today: Problems of Legal Theory and Practice*, 24 INT'L & COMP. L.Q. 241 (1994).

Kosko, Bart, *Fuzzy Logic*, 269 SCI AMERICAN 76 (1993)
FUZZY THINKING: THE NEW SCIENCE OF FUZZY LOGIC (1993)

Kymlicka, Will, MULTICUTURAL ODYSSEYS: NAVIGATING THE NEW INTERNATIONAL POLITICS OF DIVERSITY (2007).
The Internationalization of Minority Rights, 6 EUR. J. INT'L L. CONST. L., 1 (2008).

Luttwak, Edward N. *Give War a Chance*, 78 FOR. AFFS. 36 (1997).

Mac Ginty, Roger, *Hybrid Peace: The Interaction between Top Down and Bottom Up Peace*, 41 SEC. DIALOGUE 391 (2010).

McGarry, John & Brendan O'Leary, THE NORTHERN IRELAND CONFLICT: CONSOCIATIONAL ENGAGEMENTS (2004).

Musgrave, Thomas, SELF-DETERMINATION AND NATIONAL MINORITIES (2000).

de Sousa Santos, Boaventura, TOWARD A NEW LEGAL COMMON SENSE (2002).

Thornberry, Patrick, INTERNATIONAL LAW AND THE RIGHTS OF MINORITIES (1991).

Tierney, Stephen, *We the Peoples: Balancing Constituent Power and Constitutionalism in Plurinational States* in Neil Walker & Martin Loughlin (eds) THE PARADOX OF CONSTITUTIONALISM 229 (2007).

Tourme-Jouannet, Emanuelle, *The International Law of Recognition*, 24 EUR. INT'L J. CONST. L. 667 (2013).

Waldron, Jeremy, *Precommitment and Disagreement* in L. Alexander (ed) CONSTITUTIONALISM: PHILOSOPHICAL FOUNDATIONS 271 (1998).

Walker, Neil, *Beyond Secession? Law in the Framing of the National Polity* in Stephen Tierney (ed) NATIONALISM AND GLOBALISATION: NEW SETTINGS NEW CHALLENGES 155 (2015).

Weller, Marc, *Settling Self-determination Conflicts: Recent Developments*, 20 EUR. J. INT'L L. 112 (2009).

Wheatley, Steven, *Modelling Democratic Secession in International Law* in Stephen Tierney (ed) NATIONALISM AND GLOBALISATION: NEW SETTINGS NEW CHALLENGES 127 (2015).

7

Choice of Logic and Choice of Law

H. PATRICK GLENN*

Differing laws may or may not be seen as in conflict. In the twelfth edition of Dicey and Morris on *The Conflict of Laws,* it was stated that '...laws may differ but they do not conflict: the only possible conflict is in the mind of the judge...'.[1] The name of the treatise was retained, however, because of the 'obvious inconvenience' of changing a name that had been in use for centuries.[2] Why then are laws seen as in conflict, and what is the role of logic in the process of the definition of conflict, and of its resolution?

1 Legal Orders and Legal Differences

Through most of Western legal history, differing laws were not seen as in conflict. Medieval legal orders were harmonized in their diverse operations on the same territory through multiple interpretive devices.[3] The notion of a common law was vital to this process and the (multiple) common laws of Europe all functioned in the same manner, acting as

---

* 1940–2014; late Peter M. Laing Professor of Law, Faculty of Law, McGill University. This short text is an edited version of the notes for Professor Glenn's presentation at the workshop on Multi-Valued Law and Multivalent Logic, Netherlands Institute of Advanced Study, Wassenaar, Netherlands, 17–18 June 2011.

[1] L. Collins, ed., DICEY AND MORRIS ON THE CONFLICT OF LAWS, 12th edn. (London: Stevens, 1993), vol. 1, 33.

[2] Ibid., 33. The statement that laws do not conflict was not retained in later editions [14th (2000), 15th (2012)]. It appears in the 10th (1980, at 29) and 11th (1987, at 32) editions. Earlier editions did not include the statement either. However, with reference to an example in which two legal systems gave different answers as to the validity of a marriage, those editions said that any conflict was only in the mind of the judge. The first three editions (1st, 1896, at 12; 2nd, 1908, at 13; 3rd, 1922, at 13) said, with reference to the same example, that the defect of 'conflict of laws' as a name for the subject 'is that the supposed "conflict" is fictitious and never really takes place'.

[3] S. Vogenauer, DIE AUSLEGUNG VON GESETZEN IN ENGLAND UND AUF DEM KONTINENT (Tübingen: Mohr-Siebeck, 2001).

supplemental or relational laws, yielding to all manner of local laws and local particularities.[4] They were multivalent in contemplating the operation both of their own norms and those of particular, differing, laws within the same territory. The common laws, in yielding, were non-monotonic in character. With the expansion of European law overseas, this essential character of the European common laws (most notably English, French, Dutch and Spanish) was retained and magnified. Multivalence and non-monotonicity have therefore been the major logical devices of western legal traditions until approximately the nineteenth century.

In some cases, this multivalence continued to prevail even through the nineteenth century process of nationalisation of law. This was the case for Equity in England. The maxims of Equity ('Equity follows the law'; 'Equity supplements but does not contradict the common law') were multivalent, interpretive devices for assuring the ongoing co-existence of the common law and Equity as distinct legal orders. The same can be said today. The trust itself may be seen as a multivalent legal instrument: the binary choice between owner and non-owner, accepted by civil law, canon law and common law courts was rejected by English Chancery judges and the intermediate notion of equitable ownership thus developed.[5] This raises the interesting question as to what then happens once an included middle – a formerly inconceivable middle ground between some proposition and its negation – has been formalized.

Legal differences were the object of major efforts of elimination within national states over the course of the nineteenth and twentieth centuries. By mid-twentieth century, books on legal 'antinomies' in the philosophy of law found few actual examples in domestic law.[6] They were seen as resolved by well-established methods of application of superior norms (for example, constitutional norms), or choice of the law later in time, as general techniques of interpretation. Conflicts were recognized between national legal systems, however, and by mid-nineteenth century an entire, rule-based discipline of the 'conflict of laws' had emerged.

---

[4] H. P. Glenn, On Common Laws (Oxford: Oxford University Press, 2006), ch. 1.

[5] See the paper by Lionel Smith in this volume for a discussion of the relationship between the common law and Equity in terms of the non-classical logical structure of 'chunk and permeate'.

[6] C. Perelman, ed., Les antinomies en droit (Brussels: Bruylant, 1965); G. Gavazzi, Delle antinomie (G. Giappichelli, 1959).

2   Conflict of Laws as a Modern, Statist and Binary Construction

The expression 'conflict of laws' was invented in the Netherlands by Ulrich Huber in the late seventeenth century. Huber was also the father of the modern notion of the territorial application of state laws. State law thus in principle precluded the operation of other laws on state territory, and no law of another state could be applied within a given state. Huber was an important figure in the obtaining of Dutch independence from Spanish rule, and the assertion of the territorial supremacy of Dutch law on Dutch territory was an important feature of the political and military struggle for Dutch independence. Huber's teaching was accepted by Joseph Story in the United States, and Story in turn influenced Friedrich Carl von Savigny in Europe in the mid-nineteenth century. Foreign law could thus be applied only as a gesture of 'comity' by the state of application.

Differences between national laws were thus conceptualized as 'conflicts' as an important feature in the construction of modern states from the seventeenth century. The construction of a 'conflict of laws' followed recognizable laws of classical logic. The law of identity (A is A) reinforced the separate existence and autonomy of each state, defined as a corporate person operative within a geographically limited territory. The law of non-contradiction (not [A and not-A]) dictated both the internal consistency of national laws and the impossibility of application of two national laws to a single, transnational problem.[7] Binary choice was necessary between conflicting laws. The law of the excluded middle (A or [not-A]) prevented any included middle between the laws seen as in conflict. It was legally impossible to admit of any solution other than one or the other of the two conflicting state laws and legally impossible to admit of any compromise between the two.

A Savignian-inspired discipline of rule-based choice of law ('the conflict of laws') was thereby generated. The rules in question were those of 'conflicts justice' as opposed to 'material justice' and their sole function was to allocate given relations to particular national legal systems for their regulation. Tort liability was thus to be governed by the law of the

---

[7] Kelsen argued that a legal system was characterized by its internal consistency, relying on the laws of non-contradiction and of the excluded middle: H. Kelsen, PURE THEORY OF LAW, 2nd edn., trans. M. Knight (Gloucester, MA: Peter Smith, 1989), 206. But see his later position in H. Kelsen, ESSAYS IN LEGAL AND MORAL PHILOSOPHY, ed. O. Weinberger, trans. P. Heath (Dordrecht: D. Reidel, 1973), 235.

place of the tort; rights in real property by the law of the *situs* of the property; the form of marriage by the place of celebration of the marriage. All legal space was thereby nationalized, and the relations of national legal orders were defined as inherently conflictual in nature. The general conclusion was compatible with Hegelian notions of the ultimate destiny of the state being defined in terms of belligerent relations with other states. This position is the positive law of jurisdictions such as Germany, Switzerland and Italy, in which conflict is presumed, such that even in the absence of any allegation by the parties that there is any difference of national laws which affects the resolution of their case, the judge must on his or her own initiative apply choice of law rules and decide which law is applicable to the case.

Conflictual perspectives on the relations of legal orders are today, however, in decline, as different and potentially contradictory legal orders multiply. Many written constitutions contain rights seen as conflicting; many constitutions of deeply divided societies are unable to resolve differences, and leave their reconciliation to ongoing, casuistic techniques. The EU is characterized not by hierarchy but by 'related hierarchies'. Religious legal orders are recognized by many states that guarantee freedom of religion. Multivalent or paraconsistent forms of logic are therefore emerging.

3 Multivalent Logic and the Conciliation of Laws

The multiplicity of contemporary legal orders is derived from the irrefutable claims of legitimacy that they make. Legal unity is thought of no longer as that which prevails within a state, but that which justifies recognition of a particular legal regime. The legitimacy of the EU cannot be denied by a national judge. No constitutional guarantee of a given right can be rejected by a national judge because of its inconsistency with another right. The discipline of the conflict of laws is now becoming subject to multivalent forms of analysis. A good argument can be made, moreover, that this was the case even throughout the nineteenth and twentieth centuries, although bivalence largely prevailed.

The constant feature of multivalence in the conflict of laws is found in the notion of public order. No choice of law rule was to be automatically applied, since the law it pointed to could be found to be objectionable in terms of the public order of the forum. Conflicts rules were 'blind' and the public order reservation was therefore a hedge against material solutions that were highly incompatible with the law of the forum. The public order exception, however, is an indication of multivalence. Both the governing law and the law of the forum are potentially applicable. The rules are non-monotonic and some form of reasoning is necessary in order to decide on their application or not. An included middle is opened. The French Court of Cassation has recently decided that whether an Islamic *talaq* divorce (given exclusively by the husband) should be recognized depends not on its compatibility with the constitutional principle of the equality of the sexes, but on whether the divorce makes adequate financial provision for the spouse.[8] Material justice emerges in the process of deciding on the application of an exception to the rule.

Further exceptions to the application of choice of law rules are now being recognized, all indicative of a larger reasoning process and all tolerant of multiple legal orders and their solutions. Such reasoning is now codified in the Rome I Regulation on The Law Applicable to Contractual Obligations, providing that 'mandatory' rules of a third state, not the forum state or the state whose law is in principle the governing law, *may* be applied.[9] Three laws are potentially applicable. A further process has also become evident of material solutions justifying a particular choice of law. The law to be applied is thus, for example, not the most geographically proximate law, but the law which best assures the interests of a child, or maintains the validity of a marriage, or assures the legitimation of a child.

In all of these latter cases, an included middle is being found which controls the resolution of the case in one manner or another. The included middle is also recognizable when arbitrators decide as amiable *compositeurs* and apply non-state law to the resolution of contractual disputes. The possibility of choice of non-state law in contractual matters was debated seriously in recent reforms of EU law and is presently before the Hague Conference on Private International Law.[10]

The move away from formal rules of conflict of laws is most evident in the United States, where rules have been abandoned entirely in some states, in favour of an interpretive process which may involve examination of the policies of both of the interested states ('comparative impairment') or even involve choice of the 'better law'. Professor von Mehren of

---

[8] G. Canivet, *La convergence des systèmes juridiques du point de vue du droit privé français* [2003], REVUE INTERNATIONALE DE DROIT PRIVÉ 7, 19–22.

[9] Art. 9.

[10] See art. 3 of the Draft Hague Principles on Choice of Law in International Commercial Contracts, July 2014, available at www.hcch.net.

Harvard Law School has advanced the proposal that in a simple dog-bite case, where a dog crosses the border between a strict liability state and a 'one-bite allowed' state, and bites someone, that person should recover (though depending on the precise circumstances of the case) approximately half of the damages they would receive in the state of strict liability.[11] The contradictory laws of both states are both potentially controlling; neither is necessarily controlling and no binary choice between them is necessary; an included middle is opened which allows the appropriate solution according to the circumstances of the case. This type of solution was well known in the Middle Ages;[12] it appears likely to re-emerge again.

4 Conclusion

The decline of the notion of conflict of laws, as evidenced above, appears to indicate two things.

(i) Laws do not conflict, as the editors of *Dicey and Morris* once concluded. Multivalent or paraconsistent reasoning has the potential not only of resolving conflicts, but of eliminating them. It is a conciliatory form of legal reasoning.

(ii) Multivalent legal reasoning is not inconsistent with binary legal reasoning or, put differently, multivalent legal reasoning includes binary legal reasoning. Given the current state of the discipline of 'conflict of laws', it is possible but not always necessary to follow a choice of law rule, Multivalent logic does not require a binary choice between itself and binary logic.

---

[11] A. T. von Mehren, *Special Substantive Rules for Multistate Problems: Their Role and Significance in Contemporary Choice of Law Methodology* (1974) HARVARD L. REV. 347, 366–367.

[12] S. Thorne, *Sovereignty and the Conflict of Laws* in S. Thorne, ESSAYS IN ENGLISH LEGAL HISTORY (London: Hambledon Press, 1985) 171.

8

Where Laws Conflict

An Application of the Method of Chunk and Permeate

GRAHAM PRIEST*

1 Introduction: Law and Logic

In his classic *Legal Traditions of the World*,[1] Patrick Glenn documents and explores the fact that the world contains many different legal traditions, often inconsistent with each other; indeed, even a single tradition can contain different sub-traditions that may be inconsistent with each other. Moreover, these traditions may interact with and inform each other in complex ways. In chapter 10, he raises the question of how to view this matter from the perspective of formal logic. The point of this essay is to address the question.

2 Many-Valued and Modal Logic

In a section of chapter 10, *Bivalence and Multivalence*, Glenn suggests that many-valued logic, and particularly fuzzy logic, may provide what is required. I think that this is the wrong machinery for the job. Let me explain why, before I explain what I take to be the right machinery.

In standard logic, there are just two truth values, *true* and *false*. In many-valued logics, there are more than two. Thus, in fuzzy logics, there is a continuum of truth values, all the real numbers in the interval between 0 (completely false) and 1 (completely true). Moreover (and this is crucial), the truth value of a complex sentence, such as a conjunction ($\wedge$) or a negation ($\neg$), is determined completely by the truth values of its parts. Thus, for example, if we write the value of the

* Philosophy Programs, Graduate Center of the City University of New York, and the University of Melbourne
[1] Glenn (2014).

statement A as $|A|$, in standard fuzzy logic, $|\neg A| = 1 - |A|$, and $|A \wedge B| = Min(|A|, |B|)$.[2]

If this machinery is to be applied to the situation concerning different legal traditions, it must be explained what each of the plurality of truth values means in this context. Nothing seems to be appropriate. The only things that suggest themselves are to interpret some value as *both true and false*, or – perhaps Glenn's favourite – *half true/false* (0.5 in fuzzy logic). These understandings misdescribe the situation, however. Calling something *half true/false* – call this value i – is the wrong way to characterize a claim, A, over which different legal traditions disagree. A is, in fact, *wholly* true/false: it is wholly true according to one tradition, and wholly false according to another. Even to say that it is both true and false is to misdescribe the situation, because it is true *according to one tradition* and false *according to another*. The qualifications are important.

To see this, just consider the case of a conjunction, $A \wedge B$. In every standard many-valued logic, if $|A| = |B| = i$ then $|A \wedge B| = i$. Now suppose that A holds in one tradition, and $\neg A$ holds in another. Then they have the same status, and so truth value. If conjunction behaves in the way described, then $A \wedge \neg A$ will have the same truth value as A and $\neg A$. But characteristically, $A \wedge \neg A$ will not have the same status: it will be rejected by *both* traditions.[3]

To do justice to the phenomenon in question, we need to make sense of the thought that the status of a claim is relative to a tradition. The obvious machinery to apply here, to one trained in the contemporary techniques of non-classical logic, is not many-valued logic, but modal logic.

In a standard modal logic, an interpretation for the language is a collection, W, of things normally called "possible worlds."[4] Statements at each world are two-valued, the values being *true* and *false*. But the value of a sentence may change from world to world. To compute the value of a conjunction or negation at a world, the standard rules of classical logic apply. Thus, $A \wedge B$ is true at a world if both A and B are true at that world; and $\neg A$ is true at a world if A is false there.[5] And what

---

[2] See Priest (2008b), chs. 7, 11.

[3] Nor does it really help to suppose that conjunction works in some other way. The point is that the status of a conjunction will *not* be determined by the statuses of the conjuncts, as required by many-valued logic.

[4] See Priest (2008b), ch. 2.

[5] A very distinctive feature of modal logics is the appearance of modal operators, such as "□" ("it is necessarily the case that"). Typically, □A is true at a world if A is true at *all* worlds (of a certain kind). We do not need to go into details for present purposes. I note that in *The*

is true at a world will be closed under an appropriate notion of logical consequence (classical, in the standard case). In other words, if all of $A_1, ..., A_n$ hold at a world, and $\{A_1, ..., A_n\} \vdash B$ (B follows from $A_1, ..., A_n$), then B holds at the world. Indeed, the standard definition of validity normally given for modal logics is that an argument is valid *just if* it preserves truth at any possible world (in all interpretations).

Though possible worlds are usually given a metaphysical interpretation, they may be given many kinds of interpretation. It is common, for example, to think of them as bodies of information. In the present context, it is natural to think of the worlds as legal traditions. What holds (is true) at a world is what holds according to that tradition. A claim can then be true at one world, and false at another. And the fact that the content of each world is closed under the appropriate consequence relation, is just a way of representing the fact that reasoning plays an important role in legal traditions: given a tradition, people use things that hold in it to infer other things that hold. Thus, one can think of the content of each world as all the matters of law in some tradition, plus all the matters of fact, plus whatever follows from them by acceptable reasoning. The picture, then, is this, where the outer box contains all the "worlds," and the inner boxes are the different traditions (three in this case):

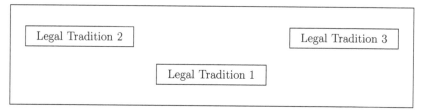

Let me make it clear that I am not denying the appropriateness of the use of many-valued logic in an analysis of legal reasoning. Indeed, in the next section I will argue that a paraconsistent logic may well be required; and some paraconsistent logics are many-valued logics.[6] My claim that

---

Applications of Bivalent Logic, and the Misapplication of Multivalent Logic to Law, pp. 208–35 of this volume, Andrew Halpin suggests using an operator, P, *it is determined that*. To a modern logician's eye, the most natural semantics for such an operator is a modal semantics, with P as some kind of necessity operator, the accessibility relation of which is at least reflexive (so that it is a logical truth that $PA \supset A$). See Priest (2008b), ch. 3.

[6] In his paper in this volume, pp. 236–72 *Fuzzy Law: a Theory of Quasi-Legal Systems*, Oren Perez argues that a fuzzy logic is required to deal with legal concepts that are vague; and in his paper in this volume, pp. 32–68 *Conjunction of Evidence and Multivalent Logic*, Kevin Clermont argues that a fuzzy logic is required to deal with conjunctions of legal conclusions.

a modal logic is required, rather than a many-valued one, is with respect to the situation in which one is required to deal with multiple traditions.

3   Paraconsistent Logic

So much for the basic idea. There is, of course, much more to be said. At this point, I need to introduce the notion of *paraconsistency*. Consider the logical principle that any contradiction implies anything: $\{A, \neg A\} \vdash B$ (for all A and B). This goes by the medieval name of *ex falso quodlibet*, and the more colourful contemporary name of *Explosion*. It says that once a body of information contains a contradiction, everything follows from it. The principle of inference is valid in standard logics, including standard modal logics (just because there is no world at which contradictory statements hold). Logics in which the inference fails are called *paraconsistent logics*. Explosion hardly looks plausible for many applications of logic. In particular, many legal traditions seem to contain contradictions, which do not "explode" them. It would appear, then, that legal reasoning should require a paraconsistent logic.

The matter is a sensitive one.[7] It is of course to be expected that the legal principles of any one tradition will contain *prima facie* contradictions. And usually, legal systems will have principles which resolve some of these. Thus, something enshrined in constitutional law will trump something inconsistent with it in statute law. And the principle of *lex posterior* tells us that a later law will trump something inconsistent with it in an earlier law.[8]

But all of this notwithstanding, there are going to be cases of genuine inconsistency. Actual cases at law are always going to be messy and contentious; so let me give a toy example. Suppose that a duly authorized statute contains the following clauses:

1. All property-holders shall have the right to vote.
2. No woman shall vote.

We may suppose that at the time when the statutes were authorized, the thought that a woman might hold property was just unthinkable; and

---

[7] The material in the next few paragraphs is taken from Priest (2006a), ch. 13.

[8] In his paper, *Fuzzy Law: a Theory of Quasi-Legal Systems*, pp. 236–72 of this volume, Oren Perez explores a different way in which conflicting laws may be reconciled, in a certain sense, when they are "soft," in a process he calls "deliberative coherence."

maybe that there are other clauses in the statute determining which male non-property-holders may vote.

In due course, we may also suppose, as enlightenment creeps over the society, women do come to hold property; and at some point, a woman – call her Jan – eventually fronts up at a polling booth demanding to vote. Jan may and may not vote.[9]

Of course, if and when this happened, the law would, in due course, be changed, either by a judge making a ruling, or by new legislation. The law is a guide for action, and contradictions frustrate this. But, until this is done, the law (plus the contingent circumstances) is inconsistent. And until the law is revised, there being no general principle of the kind just noted to resolve the contradiction in this case, *both* clauses are operative, as may be shown by the fact that each may be appealed to independently in other cases. However, no one would go into court and use this contradiction to argue that their cat has a right to vote. That would just be silly. In other words, Explosion is not a valid principle of legal argumentation in this context.

What this shows is that, in general, the logic operative in many, perhaps most, legal traditions, and under which the information in each of the "worlds" is closed, must be a paraconsistent one. Standard modal logic is not of this kind, but it is easy to construct modal logics where the logic is paraconsistent. The logic of each world may be a simple many-valued paraconsistent logic, for example.[10]

Paraconsistent logic is also relevant in another way. There is a standard mechanism for generating a paraconsistent logic out of a world-semantics. Given an interpretation, we simply define truth *simpliciter* (not truth at a world) as truth at *some* world. Explosion then fails for this logic (even if the logic of each world is explosive), since A may be true at one world, $\neg A$ at another, and B at no world. This procedure gives a *discussive* logic.[11] The main feature of a discussive logics is that the principle of Adjunction, $\{A, B\} \vdash A \wedge B$, fails (since A and B may hold at different worlds, and their conjunction at neither). This is a natural way of viewing the legal case. Truth (*simplicter*) is holding in some legal tradition or other; and one should not expect Adjunction to hold for truth *simpliciter*. The legal cosmos is just a complex, many-faceted, place.[12]

---

[9] The point is contested by J. C. Beall in his contribution to this volume. A discussion of his comments is too long for a footnote, so I defer it to an appendix of this essay.
[10] See, e.g., Priest (2008b), ch. 11a.   [11] See Priest (2002), pp. 299–302.
[12] This is essentially how things work in Jaina logic. See Priest (2008a).

4   Interactions between Legal Systems: Examples

So far so good. The problem is that it's not that simple. The only real problem on the horizon so far is determining which "world" – jurisdiction – we are in. There will doubtless be occasions when this is debatable, but usually it will be clear enough. The real trouble is that each world is not an island. The different systems and traditions interact, importing information from other traditions, even ideas that sometimes contradict the home tradition. Let me give three examples of this. I will then discuss how matters are to be handled logically.[13]

Example 1: A court can import a ruling from outside its jurisdiction. To take an historical example, the secular law might provide that inheritance go to the first "legitimate" offspring of a person. But, in certain cases, a civil court might allow what counts as legitimacy to be determined, not by civil law, but by canon law.[14]

Example 2: A court can import a precedent from another jurisdiction.[15] For example, in Australia, a Federal court may sometimes appeal to a precedent in State law (maybe not even the State where the case is being heard).

Example 3: In contract law, a court may choose to enforce the terms of a contract according to the laws of another jurisdiction.[16] For example, suppose that a and b, in countries A and B, make a contract concerning matters that will transpire in some other place, C, it being made clear that the laws of C shall govern their contract. a may then choose to sue b for breach of contract in A. The court may find against b on the ground that it was a breach of contract according to C's laws, even though it is not a breach of contract according to A's. Aspects of C's laws not relevant to laws of contract, such as laws of evidence, need not be accepted, though.

---

[13] The examples all concern reasoning to a judgment, which is our topic here. But one should note that importation can happen at other places as well. For example, in Australia, an Aboriginal may be punished for a crime by their community, under Aboriginal customary law. If they are then tried by a state court for the same crime, the judge may take into account the fact that some punishment has already been received in determining the appropriate sentencing. See Australian Law Reform Commission (1986), Section 507.

[14] See, e.g., Baker (2002), p. 489f.   [15] See, e.g., Adam and Pyke (1998), pp. 67, 122f.

[16] See, e.g., Davies, Bell, and Brererton (2014), pp. 441ff.

5   Chunk and Permeate: The General Framework

In this section I will explain a general logical framework for handling such matters. In the next, we will see how it may be applied to our three examples. The framework is called "Chunk and Permeate," and was originally developed for cases in science where mutually inconsistent information is appealed to in a single application.[17]

We suppose that our information is chunked. Information is then allowed to flow between chunks. Thus, information may permeate from a source chunk into a target chunk. The information that permeates may then be used as part of the information available for reasoning in the target chunk. It is crucial, however, that not all the information forth-coming in a source chunk be allowed to flow into the target chunk, or this may have untoward consequences; most notably, it may be inconsistent with something else already present in the target chunk. To prevent this, a filter is applied, letting through only information of a certain, predeter-mined, kind. A simple picture is something like this:

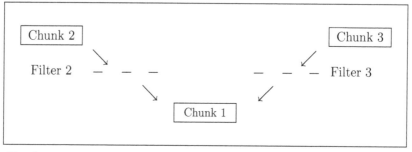

Chunk 1, we may suppose, is the "output chunk," that is, the place where we look for our final conclusions. The structure is called a *Chunk and Permeate structure*. The general mechanism of such a structure is more complex than I have so far explained, but the extra complexities are not relevant for our purposes.[18]

6   Application

Let us now turn to its application to our examples of Conflict of Law. In general, how to chunk information in an appropriate way is a non-trivial matter. But in the present case, it is straightforward. The chunking is

---

[17] The first application of the model came from considering the infinitesimal calculus of the seventeenth and eighteenth centuries, where inconsistent properties of infinitesimals were appealed to, systematically, at different points in a computation. The model is, however, a very versatile one. For other applications, see Brown and Priest (2015) and Priest (2014).

[18] Details of the general case can be found in Brown and Priest (2004).

already provided by the "worlds," that is, the different legal traditions. We need, in addition, an output chunk (let us call this "Chunk 1" in what follows), which we suppose to contain all matters of fact. Each of the other chunks contains the matters of law pertaining to a relevant legal tradition. In principle, there can be an arbitrary number of these, but for our examples, two will suffice (Chunks 2 and 3). Given the appropriate filters, legal information is allowed to flow into Chunk 1, where it is applied to the factual information already present there, to determine a final judgment. Let us see how this mechanism is applied in our three examples.[19]

Example 1: Here, Chunk 2 may be taken to contain all the legal information of the jurisdiction of the court. Filter 2 may let through everything except those laws relating to legitimacy. Chunk 3 may be taken to contain all the principles of Canon Law. Filter 3, however, lets through only matters pertinent to judgments of legitimacy. One would not want other things from Chunk 3 to flow into Chunk 1, simply because one would not want them to be operative. When, in Chunk 1, the judgments about inheritance from Chunk 2 and the principles of legitimacy from Chunk 3 are applied to the facts in Chunk 1, an appropriate judgment is drawn.

Example 2: Here, Chunk 2 may be taken to be the legal information relevant to Federal Law. Filter 2 may, this time, let everything through.[20] Chunk 3 may be taken to contain matters from the State law of the relevant state, including judgments based on precedent. Filter 3 lets through only the judgement of precedent relevant to the present case. Clearly, letting through other matters is very likely to conflict with matters of Federal law in this case. In Chunk 1, the judgment of precedent may then be appealed to in applying the Federal law to the matters of fact present.

Example 3: Here, Chunk 2 may be taken to contain the laws of jurisdiction A. In this case, the filter allows through *only* those things not relevant to the laws of contract (e.g. laws relating to permissible evidence). Chunk 3 may be taken to contain all the laws of jurisdiction C.

---

[19] I am assuming that each tradition is itself a unit; but in realistic cases, it may itself have a chunk and permeate structure. Structures can be nested in structures. I emphasise also that many of the features of my three examples (e.g., the number of chunks, where to put the "facts," etc.) are just artifacts of the way I have chosen to handle these cases. The chunk and permeate structure itself is much more general, and can be implemented in different ways – for example in the way that Lionel Smith does in his essay in this volume, "Law and Equity: Chunk and Permeate?," pp. 181–95. But there must always be an output chunk, where the ultimate judgment is to be found.

[20] We could then, if we wished just amalgamate Chunks 1 and 2 into a single chunk in this case.

Filter 3, however, lets through only those things relevant to laws of contract. When all the available information from Chunks 2 and 3 is then applied to information in Chunk 1, the appropriate judgment is forthcoming.

So much for the examples. There has to be a bit more to the general story than this. Something must determine what the relevant chunks and filters are. (The whole Chunk and Permeate structure which is operative must be determined by *something*.) Presumably, this is itself the jurisdiction we are actually in (Chunk 2, in our examples).[21]

7   Conclusion: Logic and Law

An important part of the law is reasoning.[22] It is the job of the discipline of logic to theorize reasoning. This does not mean that lawyers have to take notice of the discipline of logic (though occasionally this may help): they just have to know how to reason well. Similarly, it is the job of the discipline of linguistics to theorize language. People whose job it is to speak and write, do not, however, have to take notice of this (though occasionally this may help): they just have to know how to speak and write well.

---

[21] In the conclusion of *The Applications of Bivalent Logic, and the Misapplication of Multivalent Logic to Law,* pp. 208–35 of this volume, Andrew Halpin writes:

> As for the law, the conclusion of this chapter is that paraconsistent logic has nothing to offer; a conclusion in part supported by Graham Priest in his contribution to this volume, when he considers a move from the existence of contradictory norms within legal materials to their resolution at the point of judgment. At this point, Priest suggests a role for "chunk and permeate" logic, in tracking the influence of normative material from one normative order to another. But as he acknowledges, this only operates after the event, crucially, after the "chunks" and "filters" have been chosen, so transferring attention to the extra-legal factors at play in selecting the chunks and setting of the filters.

A couple of comments are in order here. The inference engine delivered by the model of chunk and permeate is paraconsistent in the following sense. The total amount of information available to be reasoned from (the union of all the chunks) may certainly be inconsistent. Yet not every conclusion is delivered. Next, though there is nothing in the model which requires the internal logic of each chunk to be paraconsistent, the material in Section 3 suggests that it may be. Third, I think it is too fast to say that the determination of the chunks and filters is determined by extra-legal factors. Clearly legal factors may be involved. Thus, in a federal system, where the jurisdiction lies (i.e., which chunk is terminal) may be determined by federal constitutional law.

[22] Of course, it is only one part: there is much more to the law than reasoning. For a discussion of some other aspects of law, see Haack (2007).

Logical theory in the history of Western philosophy has been dominated by the notion of deductive reasoning.[23] Most notably, in the last 100 years, it has been dominated by reasoning in mathematics. The tools of "Classical Logic" (or more aptly, "Frege-Russell Logic," after its inventors), were developed with this in mind. Though many have sought to impose a hegemony of classical logic, this is now coming to appear an unduly imperialistic attitude. In particular, the many different techniques of non-classical logic developed in the last 50 years, such as those of modal logic, many-valued (including fuzzy) logic, paraconsistent logic, can be seen as providing a more versatile and robust armoury of devices for analyzing reasoning in other areas (and maybe in some bits of mathematics too). The area that has been our concern in this essay is legal reasoning, especially in the context of the multitude of legal traditions and their interactions. This, it seems, is such an arena.[24]

Appendix: Beall and *Release*

In "Do Inconsistent Laws Deliver Gluts?" this volume, pp. 199–207, Jc Beall takes issue with my claim of Section 3, that the law can deliver genuine inconsistencies, that is, dialetheias, that is, true things of the form A and $\neg A$.

His point is essentially this. A claim of law, A, such as "one must drive on the left hand side of the road" or "people under 18 may not vote," is always relative to a jurisdiction. So, when properly understood, it is to be understood as of the form: *According to the law A*. Beall writes this as OA. Actually, it is better to make the jurisdiction explicit. So let JA be "According to jurisdiction j, A." So far so good. Next, Beall observes, J does "Release"; that is, one cannot infer A from JA; and such an inference

---

[23] Non-deductive reasoning, of course, plays an enormous part in ordinary and legal reasoning. The machinery explained in this essay concerns deductive reasoning. It can be generalised to machinery for non-deductive inference by applying the techniques of non-monotonicity. However, this complication is not necessary for present purposes. For a brief summary of the techniques of non-monotonicity, see Priest (2006b), 11.7.

[24] For advice on legal matters, thanks go to David Wood and Marcus Priest. For helpful comments on an earlier draft of the essay, I'm grateful to Kevin Clermont, Andrew Halpin, Owen Perez, and Lionel Smith. A first draft of this paper was given in June 2011, at the Workshop on Multi-Valued Law and Multivalent Logic, organized by Patrick Glenn in Wassennar, the Netherlands. I am very grateful for his invitation to engage with the subject, and his subsequent encouragement. It is sad that he did not live to see the present project to fruition. I dedicate this essay to him.

is required to deduce a contradiction. Again, so far so good. Dialetheias, infers Beall, do not arise.

Too fast. *J* certainly does not release in general. If I am driving in the US, and *j* is Australian jurisdiction, I cannot infer from *J* (I must drive on the left) to "I must drive on the left." But one *can* release if one is in the jurisdiction in question. Merely consider, for a moment, the following dialogue between a shopkeeper (*s*) and a customer (*c*).

- (*c*) A packet of cigarettes, please.
- (*s*) How old are you?
- (*c*) Sixteen.
- (*s*) I'm sorry, you can't have it.
- (*c*) Why not?
- (*s*) It's the law. The law says that if you are under eighteen, I'm not allowed to sell you cigarettes. So I can't give them to you.

The shopkeeper has exactly used "Release." He knows the legal jurisdiction he is in, and knows its law. He "releases" to the conclusion that if a person is under 18, a shopkeeper may not sell cigarettes to that person. He joins this to the premise the 16 is less than 18, to conclude that he is not allowed to sell to *c*.

In exactly, the same way, in the example of Section 3, let us suppose that the legal jurisdiction in which Jan finds herself is *j*. Then *J*(All property holders have the right to vote) and *J* (No women has the right to vote.) The person in control of the polling booth is, again, well aware that they are in jurisdiction *j*. They "release" to infer that all property holders have the right to vote, and that no women have the right to vote. A few more simple inferences shows them that they are in a bind.

It might be suggested that the *whole* inference process is under the scope of the *J* operator, so any ultimate conclusion is of the form *JA*, which is not a contradiction. Thus, to illustrate, consider the shop-keeper example again: *s* knows that *J* (one must not sell cigarettes to people under 18) and *J* (c is under 18) and concludes that *J* (I should not sell cigarettes to *c*). This is hardly a correct way to reconstruct the reasoning. The age of *c* is a matter of fact, not a matter of law. It is simply about the time elapsed since *c*'s birth. One cannot, therefore move from "*c* is under 18" to *J* (*c* is under 18).[25]

---

[25] Beall calls this inference *Capture*, and is clear that the inference is invalid. The truth predicate, he says, is unique in satisfying *Capture*. (See his note at the end of 4.2.)

And in any case, the move is of no avail. Even if the conclusion of the explicit reasoning is of the form JA, if one is in jurisdiction j, one must still apply "release." The law is action-guiding, and release needs to be applied to infer what to do. So imagine that s does, in fact, sell cigarettes to c, at which point a police woman, p, enters the shop. The following dialogue ensues:

- (p) Did you just sell cigarettes to this kid?
- (s) Yes.
- (p) You shouldn't have done that.
- (s) Why?
- (p) Because the kid is under 18, and the law forbids selling cigarettes to minors.
- (s) Yes, I know the law forbids selling cigarettes to minors.
- (p) So you shouldn't have done it.
- (s) That doesn't follow.

The police woman is not impressed

Beall buttresses his argument by an extra *ad hominem* argument. If the law delivers gluts (things that are both true and false), it also delivers gaps (things that are neither true nor false).

His example is where the law in jurisdiction, j, says that persons in category $C(x)$ must do such and such, $A(x)$; and some person, a, is such that whether or not $C(a)$ is indeterminate (maybe because the matter is vague). Then, says Beall, neither $A(a)$ nor $\neg A(a)$ is true. No. By Beall's own account, what holds is that $\neg JA(a)$ and $\neg J\neg A(a)$. This is compatible with $J(A(a) \vee \neg A(a))$, and so, given that we are in jurisdiction j, to $A(a) \vee \neg A(a)$.

References

Australian Law Reform Commission (1986), *Recognition of Customary Laws*, www.alrc.gov.au/publications/report-31.

Baker, J. H. (2002), *An Introduction to English Legal History*, 4th edition, London: Butterworths.

Brown, B., and Priest, G. (2004), *Chunk and Permeate I: The Infinitesimal Calculus*, Journal of Philosophical Logic 33: 379–388.

(2015), *Chunk and Permeate II: Bohr's Hydrogen Atom*, European Journal for the Philosophy of Science 5: 297–314.

Davis, M., Bell, A., and Brererton, P. (2014), *Nygh's Conflict of Laws in Australia*, 9th edn, Chatswood, NSW: LexisNexis Butterworths.

Glenn, H. P. (2014), *Legal Traditions of the World*, 5th edn, Oxford: Oxford University Press.

Haack, S. (2007), *On Logic in the Law: "Something, but not All"*, Ratio Juris 20: 1–31.

MacAdam, A., and Pyke, J. (1998), *Judicial Reasoning and the Doctrine of Precedent in Australia*, Sydney, NSW: Butterworths.

Priest, G. (2002), *Paraconsistent Logic*, pp. 287–393, Vol. 6, of D. Gabbay and F. Guenthner (eds.), *Handbook of Philosophical Logic*, 2nd edn, Dordrecht: Kluwer Academic Publishers.

(2006a), *In Contradiction*, 2nd edn, Oxford: Oxford University Press.

(2006b), *Doubt Truth to be a Liar*, Oxford: Oxford University Press.

(2008a), *Jaina Logic: a Contemporary Perspective*, History and Philosophy of Logic 29: 263–278.

(2008b), *Introduction to Non-Classical Logic: From If to Is*, 2nd edn, Cambridge: Cambridge University Press.

(2014), *Logical Pluralism: Another Application of Chunk and Permeate*, Erkenntnis 29: 331–338.

9

Law and Equity

Chunk and Permeate?

LIONEL D. SMITH*

1 Introduction

In arguing for the relevance of non-classical logics to legal analysis, Patrick Glenn often pointed out that until the rise of the nation-state, it was quite common to have multiple legal orders operating in the same territory.[1] This was certainly true in the early days of English law. To get a sense of the multiple overlapping and interlocking jurisdictions and systems of norms, it is only necessary to leaf through the pages of Sir John Baker's detailed study of the period 1483–1558.[2] Part III on 'The Courts' runs to over 200 pages. Almost half of this deals with the three royal courts of common law, and the Court of Chancery that administered English Equity; and it is the logical interaction between the common law and Equity that will be the focus of this study.[3] But there were many other courts and normative systems. There was the Star

* I am grateful to Graham Priest for helpful comments.

[1] See the essay by Patrick Glenn in this volume, at pp. 162.

[2] J. H. Baker, *1483–1558*, vol. VI in J. H. Baker (ed), THE OXFORD HISTORY OF THE LAWS OF ENGLAND (Oxford: OUP, 2003), 117–319.

[3] Here and elsewhere I say 'royal' courts of common law to mean the Court of Common Pleas, the Court of King's Bench, and the Exchequer Court (although the last did not *only* apply the common law). This is because some local courts also applied the common law, as a set of norms. Those local courts, some of which are described immediately below, were not royal because they did not act in the name of the King and their judges were not appointed by the Crown; as the expression goes, their 'writs did not run' throughout the realm. In general, however, the shorter phrase 'courts of common law' refers to these three royal courts of common law, rather than including local courts.

Of course, having three royal courts of common law also raised jurisdictional issues among them. In some matters jurisdiction was shared between these courts, while in others it was exclusive. Developments in what was formally procedural law (law about which claim could be used in which situation, and in which court) led indirectly to many important changes in the substance of the common law over the centuries.

Chamber and the Court of Requests, which like the Chancery derived
their authority from the King's Council. There was the High Court of
Admiralty and the Court of the Constable and Marshal, which applied
respectively the law of the sea and martial law. There were ecclesiastical
courts, which applied the law of the church to issues such as the proof of
wills, and to sinful conduct like adultery and simony. In London, there
was a Court of Hustings, a Mayor's Court, Sheriffs' Courts, and others.
Outside of London too, there were innumerable local courts, such as the
courts of the counties palatine of Chester and Durham, which were
outside the jurisdiction of the royal courts of common law, and county
courts in every county for local disputes. Many towns and cities had local
courts, including staple courts for merchants, which applied the law
merchant. Every fair and market had its own court of piepowder to
resolve issues arising within the fair or market, with cases often resolved
within hours.[4] And in principle every manor had its own local court; just
as the king was obliged to do justice between and among all of his
subjects, each lord was obliged to do justice between and among those
who owed him fealty. These courts applied the local law of the manor,
which might in principle differ from the law that was common to all the
realm – the common law.[5] Taking all these local courts together, one
author estimated that in the early seventeenth century, there were
12,000–15,000 courts in England and Wales.[6]

2   Common Law and Equity

It is not surprising that there were often difficulties about which court
had jurisdiction over a cause or an issue within a cause.[7] The principles

[4] See Baker (note 2) pp. 312–313 for a discussion of the speedy process in these courts:
'Steps which might have consumed a year or more in Westminster Hall [where the royal
courts sat] were thus compressed into a single day. Even more remarkably, when issues of
fact were triable by jury, a jury could be produced overnight.'
[5] For a discussion of manorial courts, and translation of selected records, see L. R. Poos and
L Bonfield (eds), SELECT CASES IN MANORIAL COURTS 1250–1550 (London: Selden Society,
1998).
[6] C. W. Brooks, PETTYFOGGERS AND VIPERS OF THE COMMONWEALTH (Cambridge:
Cambridge University Press, 1986), 305, note 21.
[7] Interactions between the courts of common law and the ecclesiastical courts, in roughly
the same period and in a range of different contexts, are discussed in R. H. Helmholz,
ROMAN CANON LAW IN REFORMATION ENGLAND (Cambridge: Cambridge University
Press, 1990), especially chapters 3 and 5. In relation to an earlier period, see D. Millon
(ed), SELECT ECCLESIASTICAL CASES FROM THE KING'S COURTS 1272–1307 (London: Selden
Society, 2009).

governing these questions could be complex, not least because they were subject to many exceptions.[8] If we consider the relationship between the royal courts of common law and the Court of Chancery, it must first be said that this relationship went through many phases over a long history. At its origin, English Equity was not understood by anyone to be a system of legal norms. It began in the twelfth or thirteenth century when petitioners sought the intervention of the Crown in cases of perceived individual injustice, and the Chancellor was delegated to hear these petitions. The decisions were individual and based on considerations of conscience. They were not law in the sense that they were understood to be particular interventions that did not reflect or create general norms; they bound no one but the parties. Over time, however, the Chancellor's rulings became more predictable and evolved into a system of rules that were clearly legal in nature; the Court of Chancery, which had been a court in the same sense that a king holds court, became a court administering a system of law. When precisely this change occurred is impossible to say, but it was during the Tudor period that the basis of the Chancellor's intervention shifted from 'conscience' to 'Equity'.[9]

In some ways, however, Equity never lost touch with its roots as an extraordinary corrective. It never became a complete system of law: for example, although Equity has its own remedies for breach of contract, it does not have its own rules as to how contracts are created.[10] Every rule of Equity originated in an attempt to correct a defect of the common law, but the converse was not true. A much-used example of the Chancellor's

---

[8] In this period, there was generally a monetary threshold of 40 shillings (£2) between manor courts and the royal courts of common law, with claims for more belonging to the royal courts and claims for less belonging to manor courts; but custom, or a grant from the Crown, could vary this in particular cases. See Baker (note 2) p. 316.

[9] A classic account of the origin of Equity is in F. W. Maitland, EQUITY; ALSO, THE FORMS OF ACTION AT COMMON LAW: TWO COURSES OF LECTURES, A. H. Chaytor and W. J. Whittaker (eds) (Cambridge: Cambridge University Press, 1929), Lectures I and II on Equity. See also CC Langdell, A SUMMARY OF EQUITY PLEADING, 2nd edn (Cambridge, MA: Charles W. Sever and Co., 1883), 27–42; J. H. Baker, AN INTRODUCTION TO ENGLISH LEGAL HISTORY, 4th edn (London: Butterworths, 2002), 99–111; W. H. Bryson (ed), CASES CONCERNING EQUITY AND THE COURTS OF EQUITY 1550–1660 (London: Selden Society, 2001), xviii–xxii. For discussion of the shift from conscience to Equity, see D. Ibbetson, *A House Built on Sand: Equity in Early Modern English Law* in E. Koops and W. J. Zwalve (eds), LAW & EQUITY: APPROACHES IN ROMAN LAW AND COMMON LAW (Leiden: Martinus Nijhoff, 2014), 55.

[10] In Maitland's words (ibid. 19): 'Equity was not a self-sufficient system, at every point it presupposed the existence of common law. . . . Equity without common law would have been a castle in the air, an impossibility.'

intervention is the case of the debtor who gave his creditor a deed
(a document bearing a formal seal) as evidence of the debt, and who paid
the debt but neglected to recover or destroy the deed. If the creditor now
sued at common law, the deed was effectively incontrovertible evidence of
the debt. In the application of what we might now describe as rules of
evidence, a deed could not be contradicted by oral evidence; and in any
event, the parties to an action at common law were not competent to give
evidence. If the common law case were to proceed to judgment, the debtor
would lose and would have to pay the debt a second time. To prevent this,
the debtor would commence a proceeding in Chancery, where the rules of
evidence were different. The Chancellor would investigate what had
happened (including via the sworn testimony of the parties), and if he
were convinced that the debtor had paid, he would order the creditor to
hand over the deed and to cease the proceeding at law. In understanding
the relationship between the common law and Equity, it is crucial to
understand that the Chancellor did not make any order that was intended
to bind, override, or contradict the common law courts. He had no
jurisdiction to do that. He made orders against the parties.

When Equity came to be viewed as a system of law, it was perhaps
natural that conflicts with the royal courts of common law would arise.
When there was an issue as to jurisdiction between a royal court of
common law and an inferior court, such as a local court or an ecclesiastical court, it was the royal courts of common law that held the whip
hand; they made the final decisions about jurisdiction, and could forbid
the other courts from proceeding. As between the royal courts of
common law and Equity, however, there was no clear hierarchy. It was
possible to sue at common law for unlawful vexation in Chancery.[11]
More often, the pressure was in the opposite direction. Since Chancery's
original function was to address the failings of the common law, it must
necessarily issue orders that, for example, forbade someone from enforcing a common law right, as in the example of the deed that was given in
the last paragraph. Those who defied such orders could be imprisoned
until they complied.[12] There is a temptation to say that the Equity rule

---

[11] Baker (note 2) p. 174.

[12] In *Attorney-General v Day* (1748) 1 Ves Sen 218, 27 ER 992, 224, 996, Lord Hardwicke
LC mentioned an extreme case: Chancery can order a party to convey an interest in land;
'[b]ut if he will not, choosing to lie all his life in prison, as Mr. *Savil* did, the court cannot
carry it into execution...'

Again, to underline the absence of a formal hierarchy, it was possible (though rare) for
such a person to be released by the common law courts via *habeus corpus* on the grounds

prevailed over the common law rule; and this is a norm that ended up in legislative form, when the two court systems were combined into one.[13] But of the English provision, Maitland said to his students that while 'it may well seem to you that those are very important words', nonetheless, thirty years after its enactment, 'it has been practically without effect'.[14]

Patrick Glenn might have said that this legislation was based on a mistakenly binary view that one system must 'win' over the other.[15] It is certainly true that such a binary view is misleading, when the matter is viewed in historical perspective. As the old maxim has it, 'equity supplements but does not contradict the common law'.[16] This statement is, at the same time, deeply true and fundamentally false. It is false inasmuch as the whole point of Equity was to contradict the common law; it is true inasmuch as the contradiction had always to be indirect in order for the creation and growth of Equity to be something other than a kind of civil war. That is what Maitland meant when he said the provision was without effect: it addresses itself to conflicts, and properly understood, common law and Equity do not conflict.[17]

It was the maxim's falseness that gave rise to tensions in different periods.[18] But these tensions were usually linked to strong personalities on one or both sides. The systems could operate in harmony. It was the truth encapsulated in the maxim that allowed the two systems to co-habit in peace for most of several centuries. Indeed, in some ways they cooperated.[19] A new phase began in the 1870s, via the Judicature

---

that the imprisonment was unlawful (according to the common law): Baker (note 9) p. 109.

[13] For example, the Ontario *Courts of Justice Act*, RSO 1990, c C.43, s 96(2): 'Where a rule of equity conflicts with a rule of the common law, the rule of equity prevails.'

[14] Maitland (note 9) p. 16.   [15] Glenn (note 1).

[16] This traditional apothegm was recited in *Rhone v Stephens* [1994] 2 AC 310, 317.

[17] Compare Glenn (note 1), discussing how it may rightly be said that laws do not conflict.

[18] Baker (note 2) pp. 174–182, discussing conflicts during his period that ends in 1558. The most dramatic conflict occurred in 1616; see Baker (note 9) pp. 108–109; Bryson (note 9) pp. xliv–xlvii.

[19] Since the earliest times, the Chancellor would occasionally consult the common law judges before reaching a decision. It is also true that the judges of the common law, when they chose to enforce the law strictly (as in the example of the debtor who paid but did not recover the evidence of the debt), knew perfectly well that litigants had recourse to Chancery. See B Rudden, *Equity as Alibi* in S Goldstein (ed), EQUITY AND CONTEMPORARY LEGAL DEVELOPMENTS (Jerusalem: Greene Fund for Equity Studies, 1992) 30. Another example of cooperation is that (contrary to a common misconception) the courts of common law, in resolving common law disputes, did not ignore the institution of the trust, even though it was entirely a creation of equity and in that sense might have

Acts.[20] These instituted a reform of the court structure that combined
the previously separate courts (three royal courts of common law and
one of Equity, as well as the Court of Probate, the Court for Divorce
and Matrimonial Causes, and the High Court of Admiralty) into one
court (with multiple divisions). The reform was procedural inasmuch as
it was not understood to change the rights of citizens or the results of
disputes; it was designed to simplify the ways in which rights were
enforced and disputes were resolved. The effect of this reform is a
matter of some ongoing controversy, in relation to whether it should,
in the end, be understood to have changed the substance of the law and
not just its procedures.[21]

3   Chunk and Permeate

Patrick Glenn was interested in whether the relationship between
common law and Equity could be understood in terms of non-classical
logic. In this section, I ask whether that relationship can be captured by
the non-classical logic called 'chunk and permeate', which is explained by
Graham Priest in his contribution to this volume.[22] Described abstractly,
in chunk and permeate there are multiple chunks, each of which contains
information. The information in one chunk may be inconsistent with
that in another. This is why they need to be seen as separate chunks. But
if a filter is applied, *some* information may be allowed to pass from one
chunk into another in a way that does not create an inconsistency and
allows a useful result.

Applied to multiple legal orders, we might say that each legal order is a
chunk. Certain rules apply within each chunk, but the rules in one chunk
are not the same as the rules in other chunks and to this extent there are
inconsistencies. In some situations, however, the rules of one chunk are

been thought to be irrelevant to disputes at common law. See L. Smith, *Tracing in Taylor v. Plumer: Equity in the Court of King's Bench* [1995] LMCLQ 240; L. Smith, *Simplifying Claims to Traceable Proceeds* (2009) 125 LQR 338. A brief explanation of the trust will be offered below (text around note 42).
[20] In the United States, this development took place earlier, and first in New York, in 1846: K. R. Funk, *Equity Without Chancery: The Fusion of Law and Equity in the Field Code of Civil Procedure, New York 1846–76* (2015) 36 JLH 152, 161–162. In the Australian state of New South Wales, it did not take place until 1970.
[21] See the essays in Part I, The Fusion Debate, of S. Degeling and J. Edelman (eds), EQUITY IN COMMERCIAL LAW (Sydney: Thomson/Law Book Co., 2005).
[22] At p. 168. My assumption is that my reader has read that essay before this one.

allowed to permeate into another chunk to provide information that assists legal reasoning in that chunk. The role of the filter that controls permeation is crucial, because if everything were allowed in, the receiving chunk would be simply applying the legal order of the sending chunk, and would not be logically (or, in this context, normatively) distinct. One of Priest's examples (Example 3) is from the subject called private international law.[23] Parties to a contract may choose that any dispute about the contract will be governed by the law of jurisdiction C, and speaking generally, this will be effective. A court in another jurisdiction, A, will do its best to apply this (foreign) law of contract. But the court in A is also applying its own law: for example, it applies its own law of procedure.[24] Moreover, it is not all of the substantive law of C that permeates; only the law of contract. And indeed we might say that this happens only because the law of A contemplates it. It is the private international law of A that provides that effect shall be given to the choice of a foreign law. It permits the permeation and it creates and defines the filter.

One of the challenges of applying chunk and permeate to multiple legal orders is that it is not always clear what are the chunks, and what is the information. In his discussion, Priest supposes an output chunk that contains all matters of fact. The other chunks contain rules of multiple legal orders. The filters control which rules pass from each chunk into the output chunk. In the output chunk, the rules are applied to the facts and conclusions are drawn. This is not exactly how a jurist would be likely to envisage the example discussed in the preceding paragraph.[25] The jurist would have some trouble in seeing the decision-making process of the court in A as accepting information (rules) from another chunk which

---

[23] In the common law, sometimes called 'the conflict of laws'; but see Glenn (note 1).

[24] Jurists frequently distinguish between substantive law and procedural law. Substantive law covers such questions as: what counts as a crime? How do you make a contract, and what counts as a breach of contract? When must you compensate someone for harm to their person or property? Procedural law (sometimes called adjectival law) covers such questions as: how do you start a lawsuit? What can you do if the defendant refuses to participate in the lawsuit? What evidence is admissible to prove one's allegations of fact? Substantive law is about the rights and obligations of the parties, abstracted from the courtroom process; procedural law is about how the substantive law is put into operation.

[25] In his paper, Priest notes that there are many ways to implement the chunk and permeate structure, including in relation to how many chunks there are, and where the facts are understood to be located.

contains the laws of A. The more natural view is that the court in A finds
the facts and applies the law of A. It so happens that the (private
international) law of A provides that in general, parties may choose the
law applicable to their contract, and this is why the court applies the
contract law of C rather than the contract law of A. The court in A
understands itself to be doing nothing but applying the laws of A, even
when exceptionally those laws dictate that the laws of C should be used
for some issues. This seems more like a two-chunk structure (as envisaged by Priest as a possible understanding of his Example 2). One chunk
thus includes both facts and rules; some rules are allowed to permeate
from another chunk.

Because the contract law of A is not applicable to the resolution of the
dispute, one could say that it is necessary to see three chunks. Thus the
court of A, in resolving the dispute, applies some but not all of the laws of
A (leaving out A's contract law); so the decision-making chunk should be
seen as notionally separate from the laws-of-A chunk (as well as from the
laws-of-C chunk). In this view, it is still possible to see the filters as
constituted by the 'choice of law' rules of the private international law of
A. Choice of law rules are, in a sense, meta-rules or rules about rules.[26]
They do not resolve the case directly, but rather they tell the judge which
legal order's rules apply to an issue. Examples of such rules are: (i) if the
issue is about an allegedly non-contractual wrongful act (like negligent
harm to property), the governing law is the law of the place where the act
occurred; (ii) if the issue is as to the formal validity of a will,[27] the
governing law is the law of the place where the will was executed; (iii)
if the issue is as to the consequence of a breach of contract, the governing
law is the law chosen by the parties[28]; and so on.

In Priest's articulation of the notional three-chunk view, the facts are
in the decision-making, output chunk. One difficulty with this is that the
filters themselves are shaped by the facts, as the examples in the previous
paragraph show. Putting the facts inside a chunk (and so apart from the
filters) thus seems inappropriate. Perhaps the facts need to be seen as
common to all chunks, and indeed to the filters, thus lying in the

---

[26] See also the essay by Jaap Hage in this volume, at p. 89, Sections 5.3 and 5.4.

[27] That is, whether it was made in the right form, including such things as whether it needed
to be signed, witnessed, and so on. Form, in this context, is distinguished from substance
or content; a different legal system might govern the will's 'substantial validity', which
includes questions such as whether the testator is allowed to disinherit her family.

[28] Of course such a rule needs to be supplemented by another rule in case there is no choice.

background of the whole structure of chunks and filters. That structure, then, addresses itself more to the application of legal rules to the facts.[29]

Assuming that the facts do not belong to any particular chunk, another complication is that the 'information' in the chunks may not only be legal rules but also legal results. Assume that person a has successfully sued person b in the courts of jurisdiction A, and obtained a judgment ordering b to pay a $10,000. If b does not live in A and has no assets there, this judgment might not be very useful. Assume that b lives in B and has assets there. The order of the court in A is not directly enforceable in B by the legal officials of B; in B, it is an order of a foreign court. It would be possible for a to start a new lawsuit against b in B, but this would require a range of risks and expenses that a has already incurred in A. Thus a might show to the court in B the judgment of the court in A and ask the court in B to 'recognize' it. If the court in B does so, it will make its own order that b pay a $10,000; this order will be a new judgment, directly enforceable in B via the legal officials of B. The subject of the recognition and enforcement of foreign judgments is also considered part of private international law. This part, however, does not involve choice of law rules but rather rules and principles that are based on comity but that also aim to protect citizens against unfair foreign judgments.[30] In this example, the 'information' passing from one chunk to another is neither a rule nor a fact, but a judgment, which is the result of the application of (foreign) rules to facts. Since a judgment as such is particular to the parties, it is rather like a fact for the analysis: not being a general norm, it can be seen as outside all the chunks and filters.[31] It is something important that has happened in the past. In this example, the

---

[29] This approach might also be necessary to understand some aspects of the relationship between common law and Equity in historical perspective. As we have already seen with the example of the debtor who was asked to pay twice, the two systems had different rules for getting at the facts: different rules of evidence, we might say today. The result is that 'the facts' were not necessarily seen the same way in the two different settings.

[30] For example, the court in B might not recognize the judgment from A if it concluded that the court in A never should have heard the case, or if it concluded that b was not given proper notice of the claim. Between many jurisdictions, there may be rules that may make recognition and enforcement almost automatic. These may be constitutional rules within a federation, or they may be rules based on inter-jurisdictional agreements.

[31] A judgment that orders b to pay $10,000 to a is normative, but it does not impose a general norm. Of course, in systems in which court decisions are a source of law, a decision of a court can be read as creating one or more general norms. Such norms are found via interpretation of the reasoning, not in the order made at the end. This precedential or source-of-law aspect of a judgment is not the aspect with which I am here concerned; it is itself a rule of the relevant legal system, of the kind discussed earlier.

rules governing which foreign judgments can or must be recognized are the relevant filters.

If all of this be right, we can adopt Priest's three-chunk implementation for these examples from private international law (choice of law, and recognition and enforcement of a foreign judgment). The court's decision-making role is seen as belonging to a separate chunk from the norms of its own legal system; this is because some of those norms may end up being inapplicable in that process. Perhaps modifying Priest's implementation slightly, the facts (possibly including outputs from previous legal processes) do not belong to any chunk but lie in the background of all the chunks and filters. The chunks and filters contain general norms. The filters, in these examples, are the rules of private international law (of the legal system of the deciding court). If the legal systems of more than two jurisdictions were applicable, there would be more than three chunks.

4 Common Law and Equity as Chunk and Permeate

Applying all of this to the relationship between common law and Equity is interesting, but difficult. It is difficult partly because, as we have seen, that relationship evolved over the centuries.

We start with the early days of Equity, when it is evolving into a system of legal norms. As was mentioned above, the common law was a complete system of law in the sense that it was apt to give an answer to any legal question.[32] It is generally assumed that the courts of common law did not pay any attention to rules and principles of Equity. From the perspective of the common law courts, therefore, there was no plurality of legal orders in relation to Equity.[33]

From the perspective of Equity, it was rather more like the choice-of-law example from private international law. How much of the common law, and how much Equity, should be permitted to permeate into the Chancellor's decision (the decision-making chunk)? At least some common law had to permeate, because Equity was not a complete system

---

[32] Not necessarily a satisfactory answer; that was why Equity arose; but an answer.

[33] This is not entirely accurate; see Smith (note 19). In the nineteenth century, for example, a plaintiff who was owed an ascertained sum of money by the defendant under a trust could obtain a judgment at common law, even though the trust was entirely the creation of Equity. In this sense, the courts of common law gave some recognition to the rules of Equity, perhaps according to the same logic of private international law that might lead them to give some effect to the rules and judgments of a foreign legal system.

of law. To take two examples, Equity needed to know who was the owner of property 'at law' before it could, or might, subject that person to some order or obligation regarding that property. Again, as was mentioned earlier, Equity did not have its own system of power-conferring rules for contract formation; for the Chancellor to know whether there was a contract or not, he had to apply the common law rules.[34] The rules of the common law were the starting point of the parties' juridical relationship.

It was not in every case, however, that *any* of the rules of Equity permeated into the Chancellor's decision. Let us start from a historical truth: originally, every petition to the Chancellor had to recite that the petitioner could not obtain justice from the courts of common law.[35] Part of the story of the origin of Equity was that it arose to address such injustices. But the other side of the coin is that if the Chancellor thought that the common law courts were able adequately to deal with the issue, he would not intervene. Right up until the nineteenth century fusion of the courts, a plea that could be made in response to any claim for Equitable relief was 'want of equity'.[36] This was an argument that the plaintiff was not entitled to what he was claiming, even if the facts he alleged were true; and one reason this might be the case was that he had an adequate remedy at common law. If, in such a case, the conclusion was that there was no need or room for the Chancellor's intervention, the plaintiff's claim would be dismissed (without prejudice to his or her rights at common law).

In the many cases where the Chancellor did intervene, the grounds for intervention were various. In modern terms, we might say they were a mix of procedural and substantive reasons.[37] Applied historically, however, this distinction has to be treated with some care, because it can

---

[34] Unless there was already a judgment of a common law court so deciding. However, Chancery intervention in cases that were already decided (as opposed to pending) was one of the causes of friction between the systems (see note 18).

[35] Some early petitions are in W. P. Baildon (ed), SELECT CASES IN CHANCERY 1364–1471 (London: Selden Society, 1896). In a case from 1457, the plaintiff's bill (petition), addressed to 'the reuerent fadir [reverend father] in God and right gracious lorde Erchebisshop of Caunterbury, Chanceler of Engeland' (at p. 143), concludes by asking (at p. 145): 'Wherfor please hit your gracious lordeship the premysses tenderly to considre, and for as moche as your seide [said] Besechers [the petitioners] by cours of the comen lawe may haue noon recover ageynst the seide Nicholas ...'

[36] S. J. Hunter, AN ELEMENTARY VIEW OF THE PROCEEDINGS IN A SUIT IN EQUITY, 6th edn by G. W. Lawrance (London: Butterworths, 1873), 29, 280–281; Langdell (note 9), 102.

[37] See note 24.

easily be anachronistic. Consider the example mentioned earlier, of the debtor who paid his debt but failed to destroy the deed that was the evidence of the debt. The creditor sues at common law. The defendant cannot tell his story in the court of common law, for what we could call procedural reasons: he cannot give evidence himself (because no party is allowed to give evidence at common law); nor can anyone else give oral evidence that is inconsistent with the deed. The common law courts were aware of the risks of individual injustice created by their rules, but in some cases, preferred to protect other values. Thus, in this kind of case, the importance of preserving the sanctity of deeds, and of avoiding the risk of perjury by conflicted witnesses, were considered paramount.[38] As we have seen, the Chancellor had different rules for getting at the truth. The Chancellor would not deny the legal validity of the deed; but the creditor would be told that even though he had a legal right to be paid again, it would be unconscionable for him to insist on it. In terms of chunk and permeate, we might say that in this case, the filter lets in the rules about the validity of the deed; but it also let in some Equity, that forbade this particular creditor from enforcing his (valid) deed. This was how Equity could be said to supplement the law without directly contradicting it.

During the nineteenth century, it was popular to organize Equitable jurisdiction according to three heads: exclusive, concurrent, and auxiliary.[39] The auxiliary jurisdiction was said to be activated where a party engaged in litigation at common law had need of some procedural device that was only available in Chancery, such as 'discovery of documents'.[40] The concurrent jurisdiction operated where the plaintiff had some right

---

[38] For reasons relating to certainty of proof, it was decided in the fourteenth century that the royal courts of common law would not enforce promises unless they were evidenced in sealed deeds (a decision that was circumvented by later developments in the sixteenth century). When counsel objected, in a 1321 case involving the carriage of hay, that people could not be expected to execute deeds for such everyday transactions, Herle J. said: '...for a cartload of hay we shall not undo the law.' See Baker (note 9) p. 319, and, for a transcription of the case, J. H. Baker and S. F. C. Milsom (eds), SOURCES OF ENGLISH LEGAL HISTORY: PRIVATE LAW TO 1750 (London: Butterworths, 1986), 285–286. Of course, the judges in the royal courts of common law knew that claims could be made in other courts, including local courts (for everyday contracts) and Chancery (see note 19 and Baker [note 9] p. 320).

[39] See M. Macnair, *Equity and Conscience* (2007) 27 OJLS 659, 664–665.

[40] This procedure requires the other party to disclose all relevant documents in his possession or control. The unified law of civil procedure of the modern world preserves most of the elements of Chancery procedure.

at common law but sought to invoke Equity's intervention in order to obtain a desired remedy unavailable at common law. For example, the remedy for breach of contract at common law was compensatory damages. The courts of common law did not actually order people to perform their contracts, unless the performance involved merely the payment of a sum of money.[41] A plaintiff could go to Equity to seek a decree of specific performance, by which the defendant would be ordered to perform the contract and not just to pay damages. Finally, the exclusive jurisdiction referred to those legal institutions that were the entire creation of Equity. The core illustration is the law of trusts. In a trust, property is held by one person (the trustee) for the benefit of another (the beneficiary). The trustee is usually the owner of the property according to the common law, but is obliged to ensure that the benefits of the property (through its enjoyment or investment) accrue to the beneficiary.[42] The rights of the beneficiary exist only in Equity. In this sense, it is clear that the beneficiary has no adequate remedy at common law, because he has no rights at common law.

Already in Maitland's time, in the early twentieth century, this classification was said to be obsolete as a result of the fusion of the courts.[43] Certainly the auxiliary jurisdiction makes no sense when procedural law has been unified. There remains, however, a distinction between the other two that is arguably still relevant; this distinction might be described as the threshold question for Equitable intervention. When a plaintiff seeks a decree of specific performance, he must in principle show that monetary damages would be inadequate.[44] If he cannot, he will not get the decree. In this sense, and for other reasons, the power to grant such a

---

[41] At least, not since very early times (ceasing after the fourteenth century): Baker (ibid.) pp. 318–320.

[42] 'Usually' the legal owner because any rights can be held in trust, and this includes the rights that go with being the beneficiary of a trust; you can be a beneficiary of a trust, but hold those rights as a trustee, in another trust, for the benefit of another. Such structures, involving layers of trusts, are very common in certain commercial contexts. Only at the top layer does the trustee hold common law rights in trust.

[43] Maitland (note 9) pp. 20–21: '...no longer useful'.

[44] The same is true in another example of the concurrent jurisdiction: where a plaintiff seeks an injunction, which is an order to do or not to do something other than to perform a contract. For example, a plaintiff might claim that the defendant is trespassing on the plaintiff's land and seek an injunction that the defendant cease. In principle, the plaintiff must show that monetary damages would be inadequate as a remedy. For both specific performance and injunctions, I say that 'in principle' the plaintiff must show that damages would be inadequate; this is because many would argue that in practice, modern judges tend to discount this requirement.

decree is said to be discretionary. But the exclusive jurisdiction is different. A trust beneficiary could not be required to show that monetary common law damages are inadequate, because speaking generally, such a beneficiary has no rights at common law. And it has never been suggested (or at least not since the fifteenth century) that when the beneficiary wishes to enforce a trust, this is a matter of discretion for the judge. Trusts are always specifically enforceable. One way to make sense of this difference is that in the concurrent jurisdiction, the plaintiff has a non-discretionary right to compensatory damages, coming from the common law. Thus, if she gets nothing from Equity, she will still be fully compensated so far as this is possible with money. In the exclusive jurisdiction, by contrast, if the plaintiff gets nothing from Equity, she gets nothing at all, because she has no rights except Equitable rights.[45]

It might be possible to interpret this difference as a difference in the filters of a chunk and permeate structure. The 'adequacy' threshold does not apply in the exclusive jurisdiction but it does apply in the concurrent jurisdiction. If it applies but is not satisfied, Equity does not change the outcome. Alternatively, if applies and it is satisfied, Equity may make an order which could not have been obtained from a common law court, such as a decree of specific performance. The modern court that applies both common law and Equity could be understood as represented by Priest's three-chunk structure, with Chunks 1 and 2 being the common law and Equity, and Chunk 3 being the decision-making forum. The filters that control how much Equity gets into Chunk 3 can, again, be

---

[45] When a court declares that property is subject to a trust that was not created intentionally, the trust may be called a 'constructive trust' because it arises from the law's construction of the circumstances. For decades there has been disagreement about whether the constructive trust is 'just a remedy' or whether it is a 'genuine trust'; see L. Smith, *Common Law and Equity in R3RUE* (2011) 68 WASHINGTON & LEE L REV 1185, 1197–1201. One way to understand this disagreement is that some commentators have mentally aligned the constructive trust with injunctions and specific performance (in the discretionary concurrent jurisdiction), while others have aligned it with intentionally created trusts (in the non-discretionary exclusive jurisdiction). In parallel to this, in some cases courts may say that a constructive trust cannot be awarded unless a money order would be inadequate, suggesting that the trust is discretionary (e.g. *Kerr* v. *Baranow* [2011] 1 SCR 269, 2011 SCC 10, [50]–[53]); in other contexts, such trusts are awarded without reference to any adequacy threshold or to discretion (e.g. *Boughner* v. *Greyhawk Equity Partners Limited Partnership (Millenium)* (2012) 111 OR (3d) 700 (SCJ), affirmed 2013 ONCA 26). One possible reason for this dissonance is that both classifications may make sense in different situations: in some situations the plaintiff will have a non-discretionary money claim even if no trust is found, but in other situations, she will have no rights at all if no trust is found.

understood to be different as between the exclusive jurisdiction and the concurrent jurisdiction.

5   Conclusion

Earlier I suggested that the key to understanding the relationship between the common law and equity lies in the paradoxical maxim that 'equity supplements but does not contradict the common law'. So far from being only of historical interest, in my view both the truth and the falsity of this statement are crucial in comprehending the modern relationship between the two sets of norms.[46] In this sense, chunk and permeate may offer a helpful way of formalizing the relationship between the common law and Equity, since it provides a way to understand how bodies of information that are inconsistent with one another can be integrated in a manner that avoids inconsistencies.

---

[46] Hohfeld was more impressed by its falsity than by its truth: W. N. Hohfeld, *The Relations Between Equity and Law* (1913) 11 Mich L Rev 537, 543–544; W. N. Hohfeld, *Supplemental Note on the Conflict of Equity and Law* (1917) 26 YALE LJ 767. He argued that any inconsistency between common law and Equity could be understood as an effective repeal of the common law. This may be correct as a way of understanding the outcomes of particular cases, but it is not adequate conceptually, if only because common law property rights have different characteristics from what are usually called Equitable interests. Thus even in the modern law, if one wished to abolish the language of law and Equity, one would still need some replacement labels to describe accurately the juridical position where different parties hold common law property rights and Equitable interests in the same asset: see Smith, ibid. Hohfeld promised for the future a 'more complete' analysis of the rights of the beneficiary under a trust (W. N. Hohfeld, *Fundamental Legal Conceptions as Applied in Judicial Reasoning-II* (1917) 26 YALE LJ 710, note 2, republished in W. N. Hohfeld, FUNDAMENTAL LEGAL CONCEPTIONS AS APPLIED IN JUDICIAL REASONING, 3rd printing with new foreword by A. L. Corbin (New Haven: Yale University Press, 1964), 65, note 2, but this did not appear before his untimely death.

PART III

The Logical Debate

10

Do Inconsistent Laws Deliver Gluts?

J. C. BEALL*

1 Introduction and Background

I am a conservative glut theorist. A *glut*, in this context, is a 'truth value glut', a true falsehood, a truth whose negation is also true. A good example, in my view, is the liar paradox: 'this sentence is not true'. It's a sentence that is both true and false, and so a glut. While I am a glut theorist, I am a very conservative one: the gluts do not go beyond the peculiar paradoxical phenomena involving 'true' or other so-called semantic vocabulary.

But glut theorists are often not so conservative. Indeed, Graham Priest, perhaps the most prominent glut theorist, has long argued that there is a strong source of gluts to be found in the normative, non-semantic realm. In particular, Priest has long argued that *legal inconsistencies* – negation inconsistencies in the law – provide very strong grounds for the existence of gluts [2].[1]

My aim in this paper is to confront the question square on: do legal inconsistencies – cases of inconsistent laws – give us good reason to accept that there are gluts? Priest [2, §§ 13.1–13.3] argues that legal inconsistencies do provide sufficient grounds for glut theory. My aim is to evaluate Priest's arguments.

My discussion mirrors the structure of Priest's argument. In § 2 I briefly rehearse the idea of 'inconsistent obligations', as a generic form of the target legal inconsistencies. § 3 discusses Priest's case for

* An early version of this paper was delivered at the *Logic and Politics* conference in Paderborn, Dec. 2013. I'm grateful to that audience, and especially to Franca D'Agostini, Elena Ficara and Graham Priest for helpful discussion.
[1] Indeed, at a recent conference commemorating Priest's book IN CONTRADICTION, Priest reaffirmed his view that the strongest, most direct case for glut theory ('dialetheism', as Priest calls it) comes from cases of inconsistent laws, rather than standard paradoxes. My own view has long been just the opposite: the best – and, in my view, only strong – case for glut theory comes from the standard truth-theoretic paradoxes, but my aim here is not to discuss my own glut theory [1].

(at least the possibility of) gluts arising from the law – the case for 'the possibility of the production of legal [gluts]' [2, p. 184]. My evaluation of Priest's argument comes in § 4. In turn, § 5 provides an additional – though ad hominem – objection based on 'legal gaps'.[2]

2   Inconsistent Obligations

To set terminology, an *inconsistent obligation* involves an obligation both to do x and not to do x. Priest begins his argument with a background account of *inconsistent (legal) obligations*.

A simple case is sufficient for present purposes. Priest gives one thus:

> I contract with party X to be present at a certain spot at a certain time. Separately, I contract with party Y not to be present at that spot at that time. Both contracts are validated in the usual way, by witnessing, etc. ...In such circumstances I am legally obliged both to be and not to be at [the given] spot at [the given] time. (And if it be suggested that this is not a case of inconsistent obligations *simpliciter*, since I am obliged to X to be at [the given] spot and obliged to Y not to be, just take X and Y to be the same person.) [2, p. 182]

As Priest says, a sufficient condition for being legally obliged to do x is that you'd be in default, according to a relevant court, were you not to do x. And so it seems fairly clear – and common – to have inconsistent obligations, so understood.

While some might object to the existence of inconsistent obligations (so understood), I do not. I agree with Priest that there are many (or at least many possible) cases of inconsistent legal obligations; and, indeed, I agree that legal authorities and legal systems can fairly easily produce such inconsistent obligations.

But the question at hand is not the existence of inconsistent obligations as such; the question, as Priest agrees, concerns *legal gluts* – actual gluts arising from the law. *Legal gluts* are gluts (truths of the form $\varphi \wedge \neg\varphi$) that are produced from the legal systems – from the law. Priest argues that there are such legal gluts. Let us turn to his principal cases.[3]

---

[2] I should note that the main gist of my objection to Priest's argument is in my book SPANDRELS OF TRUTH [1, Ch 5]; but I extend the discussion here, especially with respect to the important parity-of-reasoning argument with respect to 'legal gaps'.

[3] Actually, Priest is happy to concentrate only on the possibility of gluts arising directly out of legal systems. But I think that his cases are plausible enough to make the step to actuality fairly easy. (If we remain at the level of mere possibility, then Priest's argument for glut theory based

3   Priest on the Production of Legal Gluts

Priest's chief aim is to show that 'legal systems are wont to produce not only inconsistent obligations', but outright legal gluts. This would be straightforward if legal obligation commuted with negation, that is, if $O(\neg\varphi)$ is true just when $\neg O(\varphi)$ is true. In that case, we could take any inconsistent pair of legal obligations

- $O(\varphi)$
- $O(\neg\varphi)$

and transform the second $O(\neg\varphi)$ into its equivalent $\neg O(\varphi)$, and we'd have an outright contradiction – a legal glut: $O(\varphi) \wedge \neg O(\varphi)$. But Priest rejects the step from $O(\neg\varphi)$ to $\neg O(\varphi)$ [2, § 13.2, p 184; § 13.3, p. 195]. His chief reason is that if a legal system does in fact oblige one to do the inconsistent (so to speak), then it need not be that the legal system *also* does *not* oblige one to do the inconsistent.[4]

3.1   The Case from Construction

The case for legal gluts doesn't go directly via inconsistent legal obligations to legal gluts. What, then, is the case for the production of legal gluts? Priest points to examples, implicitly relying in the background on a 'positivist' account of the law: the existence of laws is independent of their merits (or lack thereof); their existence requires only certain social structures of governance; law is *posit*ed – hence, the term 'positivistic'. In a slogan: we are the makers of our laws. Another slogan: laws are constructed, not discovered. And this, of course, is a big difference between social-political laws and the laws of physics, or the laws of metaphysics, or perhaps even the laws of logic: we are not the makers of logical laws, or metaphysical laws, or physical laws; but we are the makers of our social-political laws.

---

on merely possible legal gluts requires some modal principles that we need not go into – such as that $\neg\Diamond(\varphi \wedge \neg\varphi)$ is necessarily true. I ignore this issue here.)

[4] Priest also gives an Ockham-style reason: namely, that if the given equivalence principle is imposed, then if $O(\varphi \wedge \neg\varphi)$ requires $O(\varphi) \wedge O(\neg\varphi)$, as Priest thinks, then every legal inconsistency delivers an outright legal glut: commute negation in $O(\neg\varphi)$ via the equivalence to get $\neg O(\varphi)$, and conjunction behavior delivers $O(\varphi) \wedge \neg O(\varphi)$. This, Priest suggests, is too much inconsistency – or at least more than what the prima facie legal inconsistency ought deliver. I leave further discussion of this Ockham-style argument aside.

Details notwithstanding, I agree with the general thrust of legal positivism (or constructivism or etc.), so understood; and I am happy to
concede it as a background assumption. This makes it very easy to see the
strength of Priest's examples (which are hypothetical, though Priest
notes – and I agree – that they are not at all implausible, and that there
may well be historical examples conforming to the examples).

3.2   Case 1: Voting Rights

Priest's first case involves a constitutional parliamentary system which
has a constitution that states:[5]

1. No female has the right to vote;
2. All property holders have the right to vote.

It turns out that, in the twisting contingencies of time, a female named
'Jan' obtains property – and is eventually recognized by the legal authority as property owner. After the law changes its stance on 'property
owner' to admit Jan ito its extension, Jan heads to the polling booth.
She stands before the voting authority with her badge of property
ownership, and thereby with the right to vote. But, of course, the constitution still contains the other clause: namely, that no female has the right
to vote – hence, Jan does not have a right to vote. Conclusion:

· Jan does and does not have the right to vote.

While some might dance many interpretative dances to avoid the given
conclusion, I do not. I concede Priest's case to be what it is: a legal system
full of gluts. According to the given legal system, Jan does have the right
to vote and does not have the right to vote.

3.3   Case 2: Traffic Priority

The twisting contingencies of time or social cultures is not necessary for
the production of legal inconsistencies. To show as much, Priest gives
another case that doesn't involve changes in the law [2, § 3.2, p. 185].
In particular, consider a legal system governing traffic priority at intersec-
tions. Suppose, in particular, that the following clauses are part of the
law – part of the legal definition of 'priority' (with respect to traffic, etc.):

---

[5] See Priest's discussion, which I paraphrase: [2, § 13.2, p. 184].

1. Any female driver has priority over any male driver.
2. Any older person has priority over any younger person.
3. If X has priority over Y, then Y does not have priority over X.

Now meet Mr X, age 40, and Ms Y, age 30. When Mr X and Ms Y meet at an intersection, the going legal system delivers *both* that Ms Y has priority (being female) and that Mr X has priority (being older). But since Mr X has priority over Ms Y, Ms Y does not have priority over Mr X. Conclusion:

. Ms Y both has priority over X and does not have priority over X.

The same conclusion applies to Mr X.[6]

As with the first case, I concede that the case is what it appears to be: a legal system full of gluts. According to the given legal system, someone both has traffic priority and does not have traffic priority.

3.4   Summary of Priest's Case

Priest has given two very plausible cases in which legal systems produce inconsistencies. According to the first system, someone both has a right to vote and does have it. According to the second system, an agent both has and does not have traffic priority. These cases – and there are clearly many more such cases – are eminently plausible, and certainly possible. (Indeed, I think that some such cases are actual. But I will leave this aside.)

Priest concludes, on the basis of the given cases, that there are not only inconsistent legal obligations, but that there are legal gluts. But this, I shall argue, is a mistake.

4   Arresting *According to Law* Behavior

Priest summarizes his proceedings thus:

> The contradictions in question [re Jan and Ms Y] follow simply from a few contingent facts and certain statements of legal obligation, right, etc. Given

---

[6] Priest takes this case to be a clear counterexample to *ex contradictione quodlibet*: 'It is also clear that we have a counter-example to *ex contradictione quodlibet*. It does not follow from this contradiction [involving Ms Y having and not having priority] that the [given] law is consistent!' [2, p. 185]. As will be clear from my evaluation of Priest's overall argument, I think that this claim about ECQ ('explosion') is too swift, or at least ambiguous. By my lights, it's certainly true that the given legal system – perhaps most legal systems – are not closed under ECQ; but to get a counterexample to ECQ we need at least outright gluts, or at least outright possible gluts. And this is where I think that Priest's argument comes short of establishing, as I argue below.

that the contingent facts are not at issue, *and that the reasoning is valid* [ital. mine], the only way to reject the truth of the contradiction is to reject the truth of the statement of legal obligation, right, etc. [2, pp. 185–186]

By 'valid', in this context, Priest means *truth-preserving over all (relevant) possibilities.*[7] While I concede the other premises of the argument, I reject that the argument is indeed truth-preserving. The problem, in short, is that Priest is sliding over an implicit *according to the law* operator; and this operator does not 'release' in the required fashion. Let me explain.

4.1   Review of 'Release' Behavior

Let us set some terminology. Let $\mathbb{O}$ be a unary sentential operator (i.e., it takes a sentence and delivers a new sentence). We say that $\mathbb{O}$ *releases* – or *exhibits release behavior* – iff for any sentence φ, there is no relevant possibility in which $\mathbb{O}(\varphi)$ is true but φ untrue. The idea is that $\mathbb{O}$ 'releases' the information in φ when applied to φ.

Common operators that release are necessity, knowledge, and truth. Common operators that don't release are possibility, *according-to-fiction* – and, I shall argue, *according-to-law.*

Parenthetical note. I note, only in passing, that truth (say, $\mathbb{T}$) is unique in also 'capturing', that is, going in the other direction: there's no relevant possibility in which φ is true but $\mathbb{T}(\varphi)$ is untrue. Neither necessity nor knowledge 'capture' in this sense. *End note.*

4.2   According-to-Law Does Not Release

Quite often, what we care about in philosophy – and in many activities in philosophical logic and the philosophy of logic – is the behavior of sentential operators. One key sort of operator is an *according-to-X* operator. Common such operators are according-to-fiction operators. Thinking briefly about such according-to-fiction operators is directly relevant to the current topic of legal systems – and, in particular, *according-to-law* operators.

Question: are there inconsistent fictions? Answer: of course! *We are the makers of fictions*, and we can – knowingly or not – make them inconsistent. In general, when a system is a *constructed* or *posited* system, it is very

---

[7] He doesn't mean 'logically valid', since, e.g., 'legal authority' etc. is not part of logical vocabulary.

easy to produce inconsistencies. That is why it is difficult to reject the first leg of Priest's argument: namely, that legal systems (at least on a basic positivist picture) can easily produce inconsistencies. Such legal systems carry much more weight and consequence for societies than fictions sometimes do (though perhaps not always – depending on the weight that societies place on the fiction, e.g., religious fictions, etc.); but both are as susceptible to system-internal inconsistencies – system-internal gluts.

But that's the rub for Priest's case: one gets from legal inconsistencies (legal-system-internal gluts) to outright legal gluts – actual gluts that transcend the system – only if the *according-to-the-system* operator releases. But we have no reason to think that legal 'according to' operators release any more than literary 'according to fiction' operators release.

In fact, we have common counterexamples to the release behavior of such operators. The counterexamples in the case of fiction operators (i.e., according-to-fiction) needn't be spelled out. The counterexamples to the legal operators (i.e., according-to-law) are not much harder to find. Indeed, Priest's cases of *voting rights* and *traffic priority* are themselves common counterexamples to release behavior. Consider the traffic topic:

. According to Australasian law, drivers drive on the left side of the road.

But, of course, this produces no hint of actual contradiction, despite many other legal systems where it is legally obligatory to drive on the right side of the road. And the topic of voting rights delivers the same sort of counterexample to the release behavior of *According to Australasian law*.

The reason that no actual contradiction – no actual legal glut – is delivered is that the operator *According to Australasian law* does not release! And this is not a peculiarity of Australasian law. Priest's case for legal gluts – for gluts that are beyond system-internal inconsistencies – requires a case for the general release behavior of *According-to-law* operators. But he has not provided one; and I think that common counterexamples suggest that one is not going to be found. Hence, that Priest's argument is valid (in the sense of truth-preserving over relevant possibilities) is incorrect.

4.3　What of God's Law?

One might think that *God's law* is what will do the trick: namely, that *According to God's law* might well exhibit release behavior. Maybe so. But this raises other problems for Priest's case.

One (obvious) problem is the very existence of God's law, which turns on the very existence of God. There are many, many philosophical and theological arguments for the existence of gods, but none are strong.

Suppose that the existence problem is solved. Another problem emerges: we now need an argument that *God's law* is inconsistent. Appealing to the release behavior of *According-to-God's-law* delivers actual gluts only if there are (internal) gluts in the given (godly) legal system to begin with. But once we depart from a *constructivist* or *positivist* picture of legal systems – as we do in the target appeal to God's system – the cases of stipulated inconsistent laws is no longer plausible. (I am not saying that an account of God's law, whatever it is, cannot be inconsistent in some sense; I'm saying only that the ease with which inconsistent laws are generated from *constructed* legal systems disappears.)

I conclude that while *According-to-God's-law* might release, this operator itself does not clearly help the case for actual legal gluts.

5   By Parity of Priest's Reasoning: Legal Gaps

Even if none of the foregoing considerations are telling in general, there's a problem with Priest's strategy – at least an ad hominem problem for excluded-middle-endorsing logicians (qua logical law). In short: just as we can come up with gluts within legal authorities (cases of legal overdetermination), so too gaps (cases of legal underdetermination).

Consider, for example, cases in which we have a new entity (e.g., an android like Data from Star Trek) of which no laws are true or false – the entity simply wasn't in the domain over which the laws quantified. Or take standard cases like 'is a child', where the law must decide whether x is in the (legal) extension or (legal) antiextension of the term. Until the decision is made, we have laws that are gappy with respect to x, that is, neither φ nor $\neg\varphi$ is true of x, and so $(\varphi \vee \neg\varphi)$ is not true of x. In such cases, the law has to decide things so that at least one of $O(\varphi(x))$ and $O(\neg\varphi(x))$ is true. But until then, neither $O(\varphi(x))$ nor $O(\neg\varphi(x))$ is true.

By parity of Priest's reasoning, we should acknowledge the existence of *legal gaps*. In short: just as we should acknowledge the existence of inconsistent obligations – wherein both $O(\varphi)$ and $O(\neg\varphi)$ are true – so too the dual 'incompleteness' situation, wherein neither $O(\varphi)$ nor $O(\neg\varphi)$ is true. Indeed, such cases of *underdetermined law* are commonly recognized; these are cases where the legal system needs to make a decision both about the (legal) extension and (legal) antiextension of certain terms.

I agree with Priest that the cases of *overdetermined law* are just as common as those of underdetermination, certainly just as possible to produce, even though – as Priest discusses – many philosophers are wont to try to dismiss them. Where Priest goes wrong is arguing from the legal inconsistencies to actual gluts. At the very least, any philosopher (like Priest) who accepts excluded middle as a logical law should reject Priest's step from legal overdetermination to actual gluts; for the step also goes from legal underdetermination to actual gaps – something ruled out by excluded middle.

6 Closing Remarks

The realm of normativity, generally, and law in particular provides a great source of inconsistency. But whether such inconsistencies deliver support for glut theory turns on whether the given *according to* operators exhibit 'release' behavior. Priest has convincingly reminded us of the ease with which legal systems produce (or can produce) inconsistent laws; but such inconsistency needs to be 'released' from the system before it delivers actual gluts. My own view is that the same holds of all normative notions, but this is too large to cover here.

References

1. J. C. Beall, SPANDRELS OF TRUTH, Oxford University Press, Oxford, 2009.
2. Graham Priest, IN CONTRADICTION, Oxford University Press, Oxford, 2nd edn, 2006. First printed by Martinus Nijhoff in 1987.

11

The Applications of Bivalent Logic, and the Misapplication of Multivalent Logic to Law

ANDREW HALPIN

1 Introduction

One of the delights of engaging in academic debate with Patrick Glenn was meeting up with him some time after the disagreement had appeared in print[1] to be greeted with a warm smile and an enthusiasm to continue the discussion, with a genuine expectation that each side had something worthwhile to contribute. Generosity and openness characterized Patrick as a person and as a scholar. Informed by these characteristics, his scholarship was always rich, with an extraordinary diversity of sources and an expansive range of stimulating commentary to provoke fresh insights. The process of disagreeing with him always left one feeling that what had been learned by engaging with his work far exceeded the particular contribution offered in making a criticism of it.

So it is with Patrick's enthusiasm for examining the relevance of the new logics, or paraconsistent logic, to law, and for opening up the discussion, which commenced in 2010 at the Netherlands Institute for Advanced Study, to such a variety of expertise. I have learned far more from being associated with his project, than I anticipated from my own narrow interests in the field. My own contribution is critical of Patrick's position, but still much informed by his enthusiasms. The sad loss of the opportunity to continue the discussion with Patrick after this appears in print is slightly offset by the possibility of engaging more fully with his own ideas which were expanded after the NIAS workshop in his book,

---

[1] For a sequence of disagreements, see Glenn, LEGAL TRADITIONS OF THE WORLD: SUSTAINABLE DIVERSITY IN LAW, 2nd ed (Oxford: Oxford University Press, 2004) [now, 5th ed, 2014]; Halpin, *Glenn's Legal Traditions of the World: Some Broader Philosophical Issues* (2006) 1 JOURNAL OF COMPARATIVE LAW 116; Glenn, *Legal Traditions and Legal Traditions* (2006) 1 JOURNAL OF COMPARATIVE LAW 69; Halpin, *A Rejoinder to Glenn* (2007) 2 JOURNAL OF COMPARATIVE LAW 88.

THE COSMOPOLITAN STATE, published in 2013.[2] I shall refer extensively below to chapter 14 of that book, entitled *Cosmopolitan Thought*.

The setting of the cosmopolitan state for Patrick's treatment of the new logics, or paraconsistent logic, clearly reveals his own motivations for dealing with the subject. The particular ambitions and challenges of the cosmopolitan state are seen as needing a different type of support, a different type of reasoning, to that required by conventional Westphalian notions of the state. Hence, in the final sentence of the concluding chapter of his book, Patrick affirms "[t]he new paraconsistent logics" as "an important ally" in the process of establishing the cosmopolitan state.[3] So close is the perceived connection between the two that the new logics become retitled as "cosmopolitan logic."

What precisely the cosmopolitan state requires from logic is expressed quite simply in an email sent by Patrick at the time he was planning the present book[4]:

> I'm hoping to edit a volume [on] law and the new logics, in which I explore application of new forms of non-dichotomous logic. They are variously known as multivalent, paraconsistent or non-monotonic and do not adhere to the classic rules of non-contradiction and the excluded middle. . . . The underlying thesis [of a paper he was sending] is that no opposition can capture all the dimensions of any relationship; or that no contradictions can be seen as absolute. I call these conciliatory as opposed to conflictual forms of logic.

The cosmopolitan state is seen as a state that rises above the conflicting interests of independent nation-states, and the contradictions between different cultures and value systems, and yet the enterprise of building or recognizing the cosmopolitan state is undertaken in our present world where these conflicts and contradictions are present. What is required, then, is a resource that can acknowledge the differences without allowing them to turn into conflict, a "conciliatory" form of logic to represent the contradictions without requiring them to be resolved to the advantage of one side at the expense of the other.

Politically, this is a noble aspiration but a severely demanding one. However, to make this a specifically legal aspiration is even more

---

[2] H Patrick Glenn, THE COSMOPOLITAN STATE (Oxford: Oxford University Press, 2013). [Hereinafter referred to as TCS.]

[3] TCS, 291.

[4] Recirculated in an email from the editor, Lionel Smith to the contributors, 1 September 2015.

exacting, in a way that relates to the very core of law. Or, at least, the core of a dominant notion of law which prevails at the municipal and international levels in the present world, and which figures in Patrick's own discussion of the application of paraconsistent logic to law.[5] At the core of this prevailing notion of law lies its role of settling disputes arising from a conflict between the parties, by giving judgment to the advantage of one side at the expense of the other. That is not to say that law does not perform other, facilitative roles, to the mutual advantage of both parties. But passing judgment in disputes with a resultant winner and a loser is fundamental to the practice of the law that is germane to our current interests. Politics may be advanced through compromise, but when matters come to law conciliation is not an expected outcome. A conciliatory form of logic is, accordingly, more than a demanding aspiration for law to accommodate. It is a deeply awkward aspiration.

I stress the awkwardness of conciliation for law at the outset, because much will be made of this subsequently. As the discussion unfolds, I will attempt a more refined assessment of just where the awkwardness of conciliation occurs for the practice of law, and of what implications this has for the role of law in establishing the cosmopolitan state; together with a reflection on the place of the new logics in responding to these concerns. However, I shall also attempt to show how considering the application of logic to law can provide an illuminating study on the nature of, and the relationship between, classical logic and the new logics – more precisely, between bivalent logic and multivalent logic. Getting this relationship right, in turn, provides the resources to clarify a variety of issues arising in the cosmopolitan or global context of law,[6] which Patrick's discussion in *Cosmopolitan Thought* deftly identifies. Or, so I shall argue.

The argument of this chapter proceeds in the following way. In Section 2, I shall set out my understanding of the relationship between bivalent

---

[5] I add the qualification to avoid the implication that I am advancing a singular uniform concept of law in this chapter, or that I am closing off exploration of ideas of law or the practice of law that do not possess the core feature. That this core feature is central for present purposes is evident in that, were it to be wholly absent we would not need to draw on paraconsistent logic to resource the cosmopolitan state: law would have already provided the resources from within itself.

[6] I take a cosmopolitan outlook in the setting that concerns us to be one possible, rather optimistic, response to the global context in which law now operates. Even a less optimistic outlook has to grapple with the issues present in that global context, which cosmopolitanism responds to.

logic and multivalent logic.[7] The key suggestion made here is that the generally accepted limitations of bivalent logic, which proved a spur for the move into multivalent logic, can be overcome by recognizing the need in some circumstances for a dual application of bivalent logic (the plural applications in the title of this chapter). I show how this dual application leaves open, within a bivalent framework, the uncertainties and possibilities that multivalent logic seeks to address. This has implications for the relationship between the two. More importantly for our present concerns, it provides within the expanded bivalent framework the possibility of recognizing resolved and unresolved states of the primary entity that is subject to the initial bivalent analysis. It is then a simple matter to extend this framework to cover a number of entities, whose ultimate manifestations are mutually exclusive, thus recognizing at one (unresolved) stage the presence of contradictory possibilities, while at the other (resolved) stage the emergence of one entity at the expense of the other(s). And all this within a bivalent framework. Section 2 emphasizes the advantages of this bivalent approach over a multivalent approach, raising the concern that a multivalent approach may distort our analysis of certain phenomena by disregarding the underlying bivalent possibilities, or choices, that confront us (the misapplication of the title).

Section 3 then surveys the different legal practices and phenomena discussed by Glenn in his *Cosmopolitan Thought*, as evidence of the application of multivalent logic, or of the inadequacies of bivalent logic, within law in general and the law of a cosmopolitan state in particular. These are divided into a number of topics, and for each topic I mount the argument that the multivalent (or new logics) perspective provides a distorted analysis, which the expanded bivalent framework can be used to correct. Within the introductory text of Section 3, a further technical matter is discussed, in establishing a distinction that is often elided between binary (bivalent) logic and a binary division (*divisio*). The significance of this distinction for the application of the bivalent framework flows into the subsequent discussion.

---

[7] This draws on material in ch. 5 of my REASONING WITH LAW (Oxford: Hart Publishing, 2001). (Those visiting the original material need to be alerted to two significant *corrigenda*:

(1) p. 93 line 25 should read: $Pp \lor P{\sim}p \lor ({\sim}Pp \land {\sim}P{\sim}p)$ [(1a) or (2a) or (3)]
(2) p. 94 line 27 should read: (2b) It is not resolved that a sea battle did not occur on such and such a date.)

Section 4 offers some concluding reflections on logic, law, and the cosmopolitan state as envisaged by Glenn; and, more speculatively, on how the present case study might be relevant to wider discussions of the new logics.

2   Reconsidering Bivalent and Multivalent Logic

2.1   Aristotle's Case of the Sea Battle Tomorrow That "cannot be true yet or false"

In this section, I adopt two interchangeable ways of representing the crux of bivalent logic, in terms of the bivalent values true/false, or in terms of the law of the excluded middle expressing no additional possibility between there being x or there being not-x. Aristotle's discussion of future events has been a significant provocation for considering the limitations of bivalent logic and gives some indication of the need to take account of a fuller picture, without offering a detailed portrayal of what that picture might be. He states in respect of the future alternatives, that a sea battle will occur or a sea battle will not occur[8]:

> Though it may be that one is more probable, it cannot be true yet or false.... For the case of those things which as yet are potential, not actually existent, is different from that of things actual.

I want to suggest that this fuller picture requires us to recognize that two issues are at stake: whether or not there is something (a sea battle), and whether or not it has been resolved that there is something or not (resolved that the sea battle has occurred).

In this more complex situation comprising the two issues we need to move beyond a simple application of the law of the excluded middle [bivalence], which is only capable of providing as the exhaustive possibilities:

{1}   (1a) There is a sea battle, or   [it is true that there is a sea battle, or]
        (1b) There is not a sea battle   [it is false that there is a sea battle]

Although this is fine if we are talking in the present or past tense and it can be assumed that what is happening (happened) has been resolved, it clearly does not adequately represent the two future possibilities, either of which remains possible; each of which "cannot be true yet or false."

---

[8] Aristotle, On Interpretation, IX. Translation is taken from the Loeb edition, in The Organon I, Harold Cooke (trans) (Cambridge, MA: Harvard University Press, 1938).

By combining the two issues we have identified in this scenario, we reach not the two possibilities at {1} but four permutations:

{2}   (1a) It is resolved that a sea battle occurred.
        (1b) It is not resolved that a sea battle occurred.
        (2a) It is resolved that a sea battle did not occur.
        (2b) It is not resolved that a sea battle did not occur.

(1a) and (2a) in {2} amount respectively to (1a) and (1b) in {1} where the resolution has been assumed, but the fuller analysis in {2} permits us to consider the possibilities that the occurrence or non-occurrence of the primary entity (x, a sea battle) has not as yet been resolved, which is precisely the conundrum Aristotle poses.

Since (1b) and (2b) in {2} are mutual implications, the four permutations there reduce to three significant possibilities:

{3}   (1) It is resolved that a sea battle occurred.
        (2) It is resolved that a sea battle did not occur.
        (3) It is not resolved whether a sea battle occurred or not.

Where (1) here amounts to (1a) in {2}, (2) to (2a), and (3) to both (1b) and (2b).

The three possibilities in {3} do not defy the law of the excluded middle, since they are the outcome of a dual application of that law at {2}. In relation to the key elements arising in the two issues we have identified, the law of the excluded middle [bivalence] separately applies to:

    is/is not a sea battle   [T/F(is a sea battle)]
    is/is not resolved   [T/F(is resolved)]

The third possibility, being an outcome of applying the law of the excluded middle [recognizing bivalence] twice, does not then produce a third position at variance with that law [bivalence]. It merely introduces a complication from recognizing the law [bivalence] operating with two factors at stake: the thing that is or not, and whether the occurring of that thing has been resolved or not. In Aristotle's terms, {3}(3) covers the complication of the "not yet"; but does so without challenging bivalent logic.

2.2   Łukasiewicz's Three-Valued Logic Provoked by Aristotle's Conundrum

Early in the twentieth century, the Polish logician Jan Łukasiewicz was stimulated by Aristotle's conundrum to develop a three-valued logic by adding to the bivalent true/false a third value representing a possibility.[9] So, regarding John being at home, we have, as in {1}:

>   (1a) John is at home, or   [it is true that John is at home, or]
>   (1b) John is not at home   [it is false that John is at home]

But, in addition, there are the possibilities that John will or will not be at home tomorrow:

>   (2)(a) John will possibly be at home tomorrow.
>   (2)(b) John will possibly not be at home tomorrow.

Whereas (1)(a) and (1)(b) are simple contradictories whose values, respectively, can be captured by the two values, true/false, Łukasiewicz (like Aristotle) denied that (2)(a) and (2)(b) were contradictories.

Łukasiewicz's solution was to recognize a third value for a possible state of affairs. In addition to true and false to which Łukasiewicz gave the values of 1 and 0 respectively, he designated a possibility by the value of ½:

{4}   It is true that John is at home.   1
       It is false that John is at home.   0
       It is possible John will be at home.   ½
       It is possible John will not be at home.   ½

Łukasiewicz's three-valued logic, despite being less sophisticated than other multivalent logics, can for present purposes be used as a representative of them to the extent that their sophistication only amounts to shades and variations of possibility or probability in the additional or non-bivalent values. If there is a flaw in ascribing an extra value to possibility/probability in the simplest case, the flaw will be reproduced in ascribing an extra value a number of times to different degrees of probability. Is there such a flaw?

Two significant problems have been noted. Quine observed that it is impossible to propose three truth values and maintain classical negation, as the three values cannot be arranged in a consistent linear form.[10] Prior pointed out that the disjunctive proposition (Either there will or there will not be a sea battle tomorrow) only has a value of ½ within

[9] Jan Łukasiewicz, *On Determinism* in SELECTED WORKS, L. Borkowski (ed) (Amsterdam, North-Holland Publishing Company, 1970).
[10] W. V. Quine, PHILOSOPHY OF LOGIC (Englewood Cliffs, NJ: Prentice-Hall, 1970; 2nd edn, Cambridge, MA: Harvard University Press, 1986) 84.

the three-valued logic of Łukasiewicz.[11] This departs from Aristotle's analysis under which it is true that (Either there will or there will not be a sea battle tomorrow). Intuitively, this seems to make more sense.

These problems can be understood as emanating from Łukasiewicz's insistence on collapsing the operation of two variables (John being at home, or not; it being resolved whether John is at home or not) into a single application of a set of three values, at {4}, when what is required is a dual application of two values across the more complex operation of the two variables, as seen in the permutations produced in {2}. The framework proposed as an outcome of that analysis at {3}, relying on a dual application of the law of the excluded middle, rectifies the two problems noted. In the first case, it upholds the law of the excluded middle and is wholly faithful to classical negation, requiring only that we discern which combinations of possible negations of the two variables we are dealing with. In the second case, within the framework analysis the proposition {3}(3), corresponding to Prior's disjunctive proposition, is in the form of the conjunction of two true negative propositions and so carries a truth value of 1 within bivalent logic, consistent with Aristotle's analysis and intuitive understanding.

2.3 A General Framework for the Dual Application of the Law of the Excluded Middle

The relationship between the two elements whose combinations go to making up the four permutations illustrated in {2} can be stated in general terms, as can the three resulting propositions illustrated in {3}. The second element indicates some form of resolution (or not) of the first element (or its negation). Taking p as the first element (e.g., sea battle) and P as the second element which may operate upon it so as to resolve its status (e.g., resolving whether there was an occurrence of), we may then formally represent the framework for the dual application of the law of the excluded middle as follows.

{5} $Pp \lor \neg Pp$ (1a) or (1b) in {2}
        $P\neg p \lor \neg P\neg p$ (2a) or (2b) in {2}
        which amount to
        $Pp \lor P\neg p \lor (\neg Pp \land \neg P\neg p)$ (1) or (2) or (3) in {3}

[11] A. N. Prior, *Three-Valued Logic and Future Contingents* (1953) 3 PHILOSOPHICAL QUARTERLY 317, 325–326.

This framework, as has been remarked above, upholds bivalence across p ∨ ¬p and P ∨ ¬P. It does not, however, support the illusion of (neither p nor ¬p). The framework leaves no room for a case to be described in terms of (neither p nor ¬p). Rather, it indicates how this expression misuses terms for representing alternative states of what actually is the case, either p or ¬p, in a misleading attempt to convey what is not yet the case. An accurate depiction would have to be in terms of (neither p yet nor ¬p yet). It is precisely this additional dimension of *yetness*, emphasized by Aristotle, that the framework offered here aims to capture.

2.4   Turning to the Use of Legal Materials

The general framework established at {5} can be applied to the process of using legal materials to reach a judgment over the legal status of a particular entity. A simple illustration would be where the legal materials are being used to determine whether or not we have an instance of a valid contract. Taking p as *a valid contract* and P as *resolving the legal status*, we would obtain, corresponding to the framework in {5}, the following possible states.

{6} Pp ∨ ¬Pp (1a) contract is resolved as valid, or
                                      (1b) contract is not resolved as valid
      P¬p ∨ ¬P¬p (2a) contract is resolved as invalid, or
                                      (2b) contract is not resolved as invalid
      which amount to
      Pp ∨ P¬p ∨ (¬Pp ∧ ¬P¬p)   (1) contract is resolved as valid, or
                                      (2) contract is resolved as invalid, or
                                      (3) contract is not resolved as valid or invalid

The analysis in {6} is compatible with a range of possible understandings of how law operates. On an extreme formalist understanding of law, where the legal materials are regarded as sufficient to decisively determine the outcome of a particular case, options {6}(1)&(2) will suffice to represent the possible states of the law regarding the specific contract. On a less formalist, or more realist, understanding, which allows for the legal materials being in such a condition that it is impossible to say what the legal outcome will be until judgment is given, option {6}(3) will also be required to cover all the possible states of the law regarding the specific contract.

It is not only doctrinal formalism that would limit the options to {6}(1) &(2). Ronald Dworkin's more sophisticated understanding of law's operation, involving judges reaching beyond narrow doctrinal material to construct a "political theory" in order to derive the answer to a case, nevertheless imposes a restriction to options {6}(1)&(2) in the belief that such a political theory can provide the right answer. Interestingly, Dworkin attempts to invoke the law of the excluded middle in order to support his right answer thesis. He argues that to deny the right answer thesis would amount to a breach of the law of the excluded middle (which Dworkin assumes is valid) because it would mean allowing for a third possibility beyond the exhaustive $p \lor \neg p$: a valid contract, or, not a valid contract.[12] To reduce the stages of Dworkin's argument for the present, he imagines as the implausible contender for this third possibility: a case of (neither p nor $\neg p$) in the form of an inchoate contract with a minor whose enforceability is a matter of judicial discretion. This, accordingly, gives us the possibilities of a valid contract, or an invalid contract, or an inchoate contract. However, it is clear from his argument that the inchoate contract has to be capable of being made into a valid or invalid contract; that is to say, it amounts to a contract that is not yet resolved as valid or invalid. This is *not* a case of (neither p nor $\neg p$) but a clear case of ($\neg Pp \land \neg P\neg p$), as in {6}(3).

Dworkin's failure to recognize this logical possibility, of legal materials being in a condition whereby the outcome as regards a particular case remains unresolved, undermines his argument for the right answer thesis. Acknowledging the possibility of this state of the law leads directly to the prospect of a no-right answer thesis. Whether the law in practice does or does not occur in the state indicated in {6}(3) is an empirical matter. It is not a logical one, and the attempt made by Dworkin to invoke logic to dispel the possibility is misplaced.

The misapplication of the law of the excluded middle, both by Dworkin and previously in Section 2.3 above, amounts to a false assertion of (neither p nor $\neg p$) to cover a case where we do seemingly have neither p nor $\neg p$ in a loose sense, but on a more rigorous analysis we have to recognize that what we have is a case of ($\neg Pp \land \neg P\neg p$). The not-yet case. Since it has been demonstrated that this not-yet case of ($\neg Pp \land \neg P\neg p$) comes about from the dual application of the law of the excluded middle, there is accordingly an upholding of bivalence in such a case. To this extent bivalence is upheld within the operation of the law, in the use of legal materials. Notably, this occurs at the two stages, or conditions, that the law can be in. First, where the condition of the law is in an unresolved state so as to fall under the not yet resolved case of ($\neg Pp \land \neg P\neg p$).

---

[12] Ronald Dworkin, *No Right Answer?* in P. M. S. Hacker and J. Raz (eds), LAW, MORALITY AND SOCIETY (Oxford: Clarendon Press, 1977) ch 3. Revised in (1978) 53 NEW YORK UNIVERSITY LAW REVIEW 1; reproduced as *Is There Really No Right Answer in Hard Cases?* in A MATTER OF PRINCIPLE (Cambridge, MA: Harvard University Press, 1985) ch 5, The argument using the law of the excluded middle appears at 120–134.

Secondly, when the law is in a resolved state so as to fall under the simpler options of Pp $\lor$ P$\neg p$. Taken together, these different conditions that the law might be in are represented by the dual application of the law of the excluded middle, illustrated at {6}.

2.5   The Complexity of Multivalued Legal Materials

The discussion in Section 2.4 proceeded on the basis that there was only one factor at stake whose legal status had to be determined, a valid contract, and that the legal materials were in a condition that could lead to the resolution of that status (one way or another – valid or invalid), or in a condition such that the status could not yet be resolved. It could reasonably be pointed out that this simplifies the operation of law, in considering only the one factor as being involved in the resolution of legal status: a singular issue of validity. Often, legal materials throw up a variety of values that are relevant to the determination of legal status. These multiple values can be used to generate different results across a number of cases. Abstract principles (freedom of speech) and broad synthesizing conceptions (negligence, unconscionable conduct) are commonplace in legal materials, but they do not characteristically operate through the consistent application of a single value.

If our argument for the retention of bivalence in the operation of the law effectively bars the recognition of multivalued law, then it must be considered flawed. The challenge is whether the more rigorous analysis of bivalence introduced for the use of legal materials in Section 2.4 can assist in producing a clearer picture of the practice of multivalued law. In general, the more rigorous analysis of bivalence found in the framework for the dual application of the law of the excluded middle relies on a discrimination between what options are available and whether those options have been resolved. Fundamentally, there is no reason why the same discrimination cannot be made between the availability of multiple values in legal materials, and whether each of those values has been exercised to determine the outcome of a particular case.

So, to take freedom of speech as an area of law that possesses a multivalued character. We first identify the different values present: p, q, r, etc. We then examine instantiations of those values in the resolution of particular cases. Where different values are indicated by p = freedom of speech, q = privacy, r = reputation, we may find different cases being resolved not simply along the lines of resolving a valid instance of freedom of speech, or not:

$$P p \lor P \neg p$$

but in more complex ways, ranging across possibilities such as:[13]

$$Pp \vee (P\neg p \wedge Pq) \vee (P\neg p \wedge Pr)$$

where, in the latter two possibilities, the law resolves that there is not a valid instance of freedom of speech but a legally recognized instance of protecting, respectively, privacy or reputation.

Across this range of *resolved* cases, for each value the basic alternative, $Pp \vee P\neg p$, holds. If our focus were on the legal protection of privacy or reputation, rather than on the legal protection of freedom of speech, we would want to supplement the case of Pp as either $(Pp \wedge P\neg q)$ or $(Pp \wedge P\neg r)$. Thus giving us $Pq \vee P\neg q$ or $Pr \vee P\neg r$, depending on our particular focus, across the range of resolved cases.

This still leaves open the unresolved case in a context of multivalued law. However, this can be accommodated by a simple adaptation of the unresolved condition with a single factor, found in {6}(3). Using the three values in the example above, we obtain:

$$(\neg Pp \wedge \neg P\neg p) \wedge (\neg Pq \wedge \neg P\neg q) \wedge (\neg Pr \wedge \neg P\neg r)$$

Pulling these findings together, we can offer as the standard form of the framework in dealing with multivalued legal materials an adaptation of {6}(1)–(3) above:[14]

{7} $Pp \vee (P\neg p \wedge Pq) \vee (P\neg p \wedge Pr)$ ... (1) speech is resolved as protected, or

(2a) speech is resolved as unprotected but privacy protected, or

(2b) speech is resolved as unprotected but reputation protected, or ...

...$\vee ((\neg Pp \wedge \neg P\neg p) \wedge (\neg Pq \wedge \neg P\neg q) \wedge (\neg Pr \wedge \neg P\neg r))$

(3) it is not resolved whether speech, or privacy, or reputation, is protected or unprotected

Note that since this is constructed on multiple dual applications of the law of the excluded middle with regard to p, q, and r, there is an upholding of bivalence for the operation of multivalued law. Note, in particular, that this remains so despite the presence of conflicting values in the law at (3). The presence of unresolved multiple conflicting values

---

[13] For simplicity, I take the different values to operate in a one-to-one conflict between freedom of speech, on the one hand, and an opposing value, on the other hand. However, once this simpler illustration is grasped, there is nothing to prevent the opposition occurring between a combination of values, on either side. For example, taking $s =$ unconstrained political debate, one might find a resolution: $(P(p + s) \wedge P\neg r)$.

[14] Bearing in mind the qualification as to simplicity mentioned in the previous note.

at {7}(3) is no more of a challenge to bivalence than the presence of the unresolved contradictory states of p was at {6}(3). All we have is a more elaborate example of the not-yet case. And again, despite the complexity, as at the close of Section 2.4 we can point to the two stages, or conditions, that the law can be in: an unresolved state, or a resolved state.

3   Topics from Glenn's "cosmopolitan thought"

3.1   A Preliminary Technical Point Regarding the Use of Binary

Within his chapter on cosmopolitan thought, Glenn offers a sweeping survey of classical Western thought centred on binary logic.[15] Among the connections Glenn makes here, there is one that has critical significance for his own call for a move from bivalent logic to multivalent logic, and is also more widely subscribed to (including among the other contributors to this book). This is the connection assumed to exist between binary logic and binary division. As a preliminary to the discussion of other topics addressed by Glenn, I want to point out the confusion between two quite different uses of binary in these terms, which invalidates the connection Glenn and others make between them. Once the confusion is cleared up, it becomes apparent that a claim for the need to break out of a binary division does not amount to a rejection of binary logic, and, equally, does not justify a turn to multivalent logic.

Binary divisions in Glenn's discussion are traced back to the classical use of division (Greek *diairesis*, Latin *divisio*) employed in processes of definition and classification – public law/private law; and also located by him in dichotomous pairings or dualisms – law and morality, primitive/civilized.[16] There are essentially two objections Glenn has with binary divisions, objections that surface in the topics to be discussed below: the binary division sets itself up as being exclusive, permitting no further categories to be recognized; and, the binary division sets itself up as being rigid, allowing for no variation or scale of characterization adopting attributes from both sides of the division.[17]

For Glenn, these objections to binary divisions amount to objections to binary logic, and hence require the turn to multivalent logic. However, if we look more carefully at what might be involved in a binary division, and at what precisely each objection finds fault with, issues of binary and multivalent logic are quite beside the point.

---

[15] TCS, 260–65.   [16] TCS, 261.   [17] For illustrations, see TCS, 269–71.

Let us first clarify the relationship between binary logic and a binary division. Take the law of the excluded middle to represent binary logic, giving us:

$$p \lor \neg p$$

One way of forming a binary division is to make it turn on whether p is present or not, which appears to simply reproduce the disjunction of binary logic: we have p or we do not have p. That all private legal obligations are contractual or non-contractual appears to follow this form. On closer scrutiny, however, this is not the case. For in this binary division we have as a starting point, the subject matter we wish to divide, private legal obligations. So if p represents a contractual legal obligation, the other side of the division is not $\neg p$, which could be the case if we had a morally (but not legally) binding agreement, or if we had a barking dog. The other side of the division has to be (other private legal obligations which are not contractual). Let these be represented by r. So what we have for the binary division is:

$$p \lor (\neg p \land r)$$

Another way of forming the binary division is to commence with something definite on the other side, rather than the negation of the former side. So if p represents public law, and r private law, the binary division appears from the outset as:

$$p \lor r$$

where we understand the two to be mutually exclusive, and so by implication the negation of each is present with the affirmation of the other, thus upholding bivalent logic for each item:

$$p \lor \neg p, r \lor \neg r$$

It is clear now that although a binary division implicates binary logic, it is not the product of binary logic. We can go so far as to suggest that the second form of a binary division we considered is the standard form. Unless we wish to countenance the trite and insignificant division between p and all the things in the world that are not p,[18] we will find that the first

---

[18] Which is, obviously, not the case in all of the examples considered by Glenn. There is a point (TCS, 262) at which Glenn suggests that identity of A is bound up with "radical separation of A from all that is not-A". More than can be discussed here lies behind that comment, but the point at issue here is that when a distinction is made between one thing

form turns out to be more rigorously represented as $p \lor (\neg p \land r)$, or, more briefly, $p \lor r$. This then gives us as the standard relation between a binary division and binary logic:

{8} $p \lor r$ binary division, upholding
        $p \lor \neg p, r \lor \neg r$ binary logic

Note that the choice of r in the binary division, as opposed to s, t, u, etc., as other things in the world that are not p, is not a matter of bivalent logic but a matter of what division is material in the subject we are studying.

Now consider the two objections to a binary division noted above. The objection of exclusive categorization, and the objection of rigid classification. It can now be shown that each of these objections can be answered without challenging bivalent logic. In the case of an objection to exclusive categorization, the offence is caused by representing all cases of the subject we are dividing as falling exclusively into either p or r. Accept this as a misrepresentation of the subject matter, and acknowledge the additional category, s.[19] This gives us:

$$p \lor (\neg p \land r) \lor (\neg p \land s)$$

or, more simply:

$$p \lor r \lor s$$

And so for a case of multiple division, we can simply expand the binary division at {8}:

{9} $p \lor r \lor s$ multiple division, upholding
        $p \lor \neg p, r \lor \neg r, s \lor \neg s$ binary logic

noting that the move from a binary division to a multiple division has nothing to do with binary logic. What it does have to do with is our perception of the subject matter that we wish to divide (categorize, classify).

What about the objection of rigid classification? This appears to be a stronger challenge to binary logic by directly confronting $p \lor \neg p$ through insisting that there is something in between: suggesting the

---

and another (even if the ultimate purpose is to establish some sort of connection between them) that distinction is set within a specific context that narrows the concern with the other to something more specific than everything else in the world.

[19] Or any number of additional categories: r, s, t, u, etc.

bogeyman of (neither p nor $\neg p$). In this setting, it is important to realize we are not dealing with a rerun of the argument for recognizing (neither p nor $\neg p$) considered above at Section 2.4, with Dworkin placing an inchoate contract in between a valid contract and an invalid contract. There the spurious assertion of (neither p nor $\neg p$) turned out to be a case of ($\neg Pp \wedge \neg P\neg p$) – the unresolved, or not-yet case. Here, however, the argument turns on an established category existing in between p and $\neg p$.

The first point to make in addressing this argument is the one made above with regard to the standard form of a binary division, where it was pointed out that the apparent categorization into $p \vee \neg p$ turns out on a more rigorous analysis to be a categorization into $p \vee r$. Nevertheless, the objection could still be made that in between the rigid classification into p or r there exists a case that is not-quite p and not-quite r, or even that is both p and r. Take as an example, the classification into public law or private law. The objection to this may not simply be that this fails in its claim to exclusivity (that there is a third category missed out by these two); the objection may be that this classification is too rigid (that some instances are a hybrid of public and private law). Even with the modification of treating the classification as $p \vee r$, as in {8} above, the recognition of the hybrid case appears to shatter the binary logic affirmed in {8}, since it amounts to a case (call it s) that is both p and r. Since r amounts to a case of $\neg p$, and s amounts to a case of both p and r, in s we have both p and $\neg p$, which certainly would deny binary logic.

However, a crucial step has been overlooked by this argument. What the recognition of the hybrid case informs us about is not a failing of binary logic but a failure of our initial classification. Suppose we start classifying animals according to their sex as either male or female, a rigid classification into p or r. And then we come across an animal that is hermaphrodite. And say we recognize the hermaphroditic condition as satisfying both criteria we were previously using to classify animals as male or female. So the hermaphrodite, s, is both p and r, and we appear to be on our way to a denial of binary logic, in the manner given at the end of the previous paragraph. What is being overlooked is that our initial classification into exclusively male or female has proved faulty. Empirically, we have discovered that we need a triple classification into wholly male or wholly female or both-male-and-female. If we use the terms p and r as we did before in denoting our exclusive binary classification, then our new triple classification would be represented as a more elaborate

example of the multiple division found at {9},[20] where $s = (p \land r)$; and
would similarly uphold bivalent logic;[21] giving us as a variation on {9}:

{10} $(p \land \neg r) \lor (\neg p \land r) \lor (p \land r)$ non-rigid multiple division, upholding
       $(p \land \neg r) \lor \neg(p \land \neg r), (\neg p \land r) \lor \neg(\neg p \land r), (p \land r) \lor \neg(p \land r)$ binary logic

Or, to put it less formally, all animals are: wholly male or not wholly
male, wholly female or not wholly female, a combination of male and
female or not a combination of male and female. And to return to our
primary concern with the case that turns out to be a hybrid of both public
and private law, this follows precisely the same analysis. There, too, we
have to abandon our preliminary classification into a rigid binary division as faulty, in the face of the empirical evidence of hybridity, and
embrace a new non-rigid multiple division. This does not require embracing a new logic, since the new classification also upholds binary logic.
Moreover, the impetus for changing our classification is not adherence to
a particular logic, but empirical recognition, or perception,[22] of the
inadequacy of the rigid classification.

We may conclude this preliminary discussion with the observation
that whereas binary in binary logic limits the available values for the
presence of any entity to two (T/F), binary in binary division amounts to
a recognition of two classificatory entities. The existence of binary division does not preclude the possibility of multiple divisions based on
more than two classificatory entities. However many classificatory
entities we end up with is a matter of how we see (or wish to see) the

---

[20] This illustration has been worked out with a hybrid that satisfies both of the elements in
the initial binary division, a case that is both p and r, rather than of a case of not-quite p
and not-quite r. Where we have an instance of the latter, the new triple classification
would amount to: $(p \land \neg r) \lor (\neg p \land r) \lor (\neg p \land \neg r)$, that is, wholly male or wholly female
or neither-fully-male-nor-fully-female. In the case of a variable classification, any signifi-
cant step in that variation that was employed in practice would yield a new parenthetical
classification, with its distinctive proportions of p and r, adding to the complexity of the
options available.

[21] And similarly, for the alternative considered in the previous note: $(p \land \neg r) \lor \neg(p \land \neg r)$,
$(\neg p \land r) \lor \neg(\neg p \land r), (\neg p \land \neg r) \lor \neg(\neg p \land \neg r)$. And if we take instances of a variable
classification, then these, in turn, would add to the number and variety of the items
separately subject to binary logic.

[22] I provide the alternative here to acknowledge the possibility that the recognition of
inadequacy may arise not from a common (undisputed) assessment of a case falling
outside the established classification, but from an individual, ideological, disagreement
with the established classification. This is particularly pertinent to perceptions of the
public law/private law divide. Even so, an ideological shift in classification is not dependent on, nor furthered by, a shift in logic.

subject matter that is to be divided. Whether we end up with two or more than two classificatory entities, binary logic will apply to each one of them.[23] There is no specific connection between binary logic and binary division.

3.2   Logic and Conciliation

One of the topics found in Glenn's approach to cosmopolitan thought is the use of the new logics to bring about conciliation between otherwise conflicting norms or outlooks.[24] On closer examination, however, what is being advocated is a more discriminating use of what might previously have been regarded as a rigid adherence to one norm or outlook always at the expense of the other. A phenomenon that is particularly apt when a body of legal materials is expanded to recognize different conflicting norms, or, even, norms emanating from different systems of law, as is increasingly the case in the cosmopolitan, or global, context. So, we are told:[25]

> [Conciliatory recognition] also resorts generally to non-monotonicity, or defeasance in Neil MacCormick's language, since none of the contradictory laws can be seen as monotonic in application or constantly binding.

and that:[26]

> 'specification' of particular solutions can take place for specific reasons in the process of conciliation of norms.

But the process of conciliation, so described, does not amount to an eradication of conflict, it simply provides for a more subtle habilitation of conflicting norms, sometimes choosing the one, sometimes choosing the other, as appropriate. Indeed, it may even be possible in some contexts to find circumstances where the generally conflicting norms can be harmonized, but this is not what Glenn is claiming for every case.[27]

All we have here is a case of multivalued law as represented at {7} above, embellished with a recognition of non-rigid multiple division as

---

[23] Taking "the presence," or instantiation, of a classificatory entity to occur when an item is recognized as falling under that classification.
[24] TCS, 259, 268, 275, 283. Echoing the email comment recorded above at note 4: "conciliatory as opposed to conflictual forms of logic."
[25] TCS, 275.   [26] TCS, 283.
[27] TCS, 281 and n153, considering the possibility of harmonizing state law and federal law in certain cases, but not all cases.

found at {10} above. Neither of these features requires recourse to multivalent or other forms of the new logics. We have seen that bivalent logic prevails throughout.

What is interesting in Glenn's depiction of these phenomena is first the awareness that the state of legal materials may be such as to host conflicting norms or outlooks within them, and then the recognition of a need to select or choose the outcome from that material for the case at hand. However, this state of conflicting norms does not represent the condition of resolved law for that case,[28] and as such does not threaten bivalent logic, as noted in {6}(3) and {7}(3). This leaves us to consider the significance of choice.[29]

3.3   Choice

One thing that is clear is that the exercise of choice in determining how different, conflicting norms apply to a specific case is not a matter of syllogistic logic, as would be so if a single norm determined how a case that fell under it was to be disposed of.[30] However, Glenn wants to go further than this in suggesting that the choice available is a matter of a choice of logics.[31] By this he seems to mean that at times courts can make a decision based on a single norm and at other times they can make a decision based on a number of norms – sometimes bivalent logic, sometimes multivalent logic – and it is up to the court to decide which to use.[32] But if the court has a choice whether to decide a case under a single norm (to use bivalent logic), then it is not the norm that determines the outcome; rather it is the court's choice to place the case under that norm.

There is no difference in the nature of the choice exercised here from the choice exercised when being confronted by a number of norms, and

---

[28] As mentioned, the law as resolved in the particular case will be the instantiation of one norm at the expense of the other, the instantiation of the other norm at the expense of the first, or a finding of a situation where both can be harmoniously accommodated.

[29] TCS, 267 (non-definitive; more nuanced), 272 (non-bivalent), 275, 276 (non-univalent choice between norms), 285 (voluntary), 286 (choice and defeasibility), 288 (between incompatible texts).

[30] TCS, 259–260.   [31] TCS, 268, 272, 281.

[32] "Choice amongst the full range of logics is an ongoing one and none is excluded by previous choices. . . . Put slightly differently, multivalent logic is necessarily inclusive of bivalent logic. That which is used will depend on that which is more adequate or appropriate." – TCS, 268–269.

the decision is made on a particular occasion to employ one of the norms rather than another in determining the outcome of the case; or, from a choice to find that otherwise conflicting norms can be harmonized in their disposal of the case. On each occasion, the outcome is determined by the choice of the court rather than the norm eventually selected as appropriate. So Glenn's insistence on a choice of logics would do more than defeat syllogistic or bivalent logic. It would preclude that and any other form of logic from disposing of the case.

To consider the matter more fully, we are back to our earlier distinction between unresolved law and resolved law, that pertains throughout situations of single norms or multivalued law, as seen in {6} and {7}; and which upholds bivalent logic (whether the multivalued law produces discrete or non-rigid classifications, {9} and {10}); but which does not give any role to logic in determining how a case is to be resolved.[33] Nevertheless, Glenn's insistence that logic has a part to play in widening the scope of choice surfaces again in his notion of "both-and" logic.

3.4   The Use of Both-and Logic

According to Glenn, the choice informed by the new logics permits one to resolve a conflict not by deciding in favour of one side to the disadvantage of the other, but by accommodating the two sides: choosing both the one and the other. He describes this as the use of both-and logic, and provides a number of illustrations. One example is the conflict over sovereignty between King and Parliament. This conflict is resolved by holding that sovereignty is held by both King and Parliament.[34] But this resolution in fact accommodates neither side to the original conflict, where what was sought on each side was exclusive sovereignty. There is no need to invoke new logics here. This is the simple strategy adopted by the parent dealing with squabbling children, who gives neither child what is demanded (exclusive use of the toy) and persuades each child to be satisfied by getting something but not everything (sharing the toy). The success of the strategy depends upon the persuasive powers of the parent in getting the children

---

[33] Recall that if no choice is given to the court, then (as the commentary following {6} indicated) the legal materials will be sufficient to decisively determine the outcome of a particular case, and options {6}(1)&(2) will suffice to represent the possible states of the law, avoiding the case of unresolved law. Similarly, with options {7}(1), (2a)&(2b), where the applications of the different values is already settled in the legal materials.

[34] TCS, 280.

to back down from the initial excessive demand. Sometimes it works; sometimes it doesn't. Logic has nothing to do with it.

Another example furnished by Glenn is the conflict between the validity of national constitutional law and the validity of EU constitutional law.[35] The use of both-and logic here is invoked to hold together these admittedly contradictory claims to validity. On this occasion, however, each side is not persuaded to back down from its excessive demands. Glenn cites Nicholas Barber as approving an override of the law of non-contradiction through "each side show[ing] institutional restraint," and thus "the constitutional dilemma can remain unresolved."[36] Here, it is a matter of each child claiming to be the toughest, but never putting it to the fight. In Glenn's words, "Both sides may claim victory; neither side must admit defeat . . .".[37] The unresolved condition of the conflicting claims fits simply under {7}(3), adapted for two values: $((\neg Pp \wedge \neg P\neg p) \wedge (\neg Pq \wedge \neg P\neg q))$, it is not resolved whether national constitutional law or EU constitutional law is ultimately valid. Once again, no challenge to bivalent logic.

If, however, the point being made is that we can be sure that neither side will ever put it to the fight, we are effectively ruling out {7}(1)&(2): the unresolved state will never get resolved, one way or the other. The not-yet gives way to never. In that case, it becomes redundant to talk of the issue not being resolved. The initial claim to have supreme validity over the subordinate validity of the other side is an empty one. Neither side is serious in the claim being made, and so there will never be any conflict between them.[38] We do not need fuzzy logic to account for this state of affairs. Political fudge will do.

3.5 Abandoning Uniform Concepts

While on the subject of constitutional matters, Glenn suggests that another advantage of subscribing to the new logics is that they introduce

---

[35] TCS, 289.

[36] TCS, 289 nn 211 & 213, citing N. W. Barber, *Legal Pluralism and the European Union* (2006) 12 EUROPEAN LAW JOURNAL 306, 327, 328. (See further, Nick Barber's contribution to this volume.)

[37] TCS, 289.

[38] This is moot. For a serious assessment of the conflict, see Jo Murkens, *Bundesverfassungsgericht (2 BvE 2/08): 'We want our identity back' – the revival of national sovereignty in the German Federal Constitutional Court's decision on the Lisbon Treaty* [2010] Public Law 530.

the possibility of breaking free from the straightjacket of uniform concepts, notably, a restrictive concept of the state.[39] The topic of challenging, and even abandoning, uniform concepts, is one on which I can
happily find considerable agreement with Glenn.[40] The dissent comes,
unsurprisingly, when the role of logic in this process is considered.

Glenn suggests that[41]:

> The logic here is cosmopolitan and multivalent, since there is ongoing
> appreciation, evaluation, and choice amongst earlier models and prior
> aggregations of normative information, all measured against present need.

He also suggests that the greater diversity of understandings of the state
locate themselves within "a large and included middle."[42] That is to say,
between the existence and non-existence of the rigid traditional concept
of a state, there can be found a host of different forms of the state,
possessing some and losing others of the characteristics associated with
that concept, even encompassing examples of so-called failed states.
Significantly, the impetus for recognition of this diversity of forms of
the state comes from "present need," as the excerpt above indicates, or
from "constitutional experience."[43]

Breaking out from an established concept is no more difficult than
breaking out of an exclusive categorization, as recently considered in
Section 3.1. The established concept of p distinguishes p from all other
contenders for p on a uniform set of grounds. Let us use p to refer to a
genuine state, recognized in accordance with this uniform set of grounds,
and r to refer to any contender that fails under these grounds.[44] As we
saw when breaking out of the exclusive categorization at {9}, the push for
doing so came from our perception of the subject matter that we wished
to categorize, so too the push for abandoning the uniform concept comes

[39] TCS, 276–79.
[40] See Andrew Halpin, *The Creation and Use of Concepts of Law when Confronting Legal
and Normative Plurality* in Seán Patrick Donlan and Lukas Heckendorn-Ursheler (eds),
CONCEPTS OF LAW: COMPARATIVE, JURISPRUDENTIAL, AND SOCIAL SCIENCE PERSPEC-
TIVES (Farnham: Ashgate, 2014); *Questioning a Uniform Concept of Public Law*, (2016) 16
JUS POLITICUM 91.
[41] TCS, 277.   [42] TCS, 276.
[43] "The [rigid traditional] nature of constitutionalism breaks down in constitutional experience." – TCS, 276.
[44] Similar to the use of r in the binary division in Section 3.1, r here denotes a more
restricted set than everything else in the universe that is $\neg p$. Barking dogs are also not
considered as contenders for states.

from how we view the subject matter we wish to conceptualize – the impetus of "need" or "experience."[45]

The difference is that where we previously had a recognized subject matter that we wished to categorize, we now are dealing with a conceptualization that carves up the subject matter: between genuine and rejected contender. The motivation differs slightly, then, in that we perceive that what was exclusively attributed to the uniform concept is more accurately recognized as existing in different forms sharing different attributes from the uniform concept, or similar attributes to that concept, and so bringing in some previously rejected contenders.[46] The process of breaking out, accordingly, is not so much the move from $p \lor r$ at {8} to $p \lor r \lor s$ at {9}, but rather:

{11} $p \lor r$ as division between uniform concept and failed contenders

is modified to

$(p_1 \lor p_2 \lor p_3) \lor r_1$ as recognizing multiple concepts and amended failed contenders

Yet still this will uphold binary logic, as at {9}, with:

$$p_1 \lor \neg p_1, p_2 \lor \neg p_2, p_3 \lor \neg p_3, r_1 \lor \neg r_1$$

As for Glenn's suggestion that we now have "a large and included middle" between $p \lor \neg p$, occupied by the multiple $(p_1 \lor p_2 \lor p_3)$, this is another instance of the error previously noted in Section 3.1, when discussing the move to a non-rigid classification at {10}. This is the error of ignoring the failure of our initial classification. In this setting, $(p_1 \lor p_2 \lor p_3)$ does not sit between $p \lor \neg p$; it replaces p; and, as seen in the line preceding this paragraph, generates its own sequence of applications of bivalent logic.

We may, therefore, make similar concluding remarks here to those found at the end of Section 3.1. However many concepts of p we end up with is a matter of how we see and divide (or wish to see and divide) the subject matter that concerns us. Whatever number of multiple concepts we end up with, binary logic will apply to each one of them. The recognition of multiple concepts does not require embracing a new logic;

---

[45] For further discussion on the rejection of concepts that collide with empirical data, particularly with the recognition of transnational or global legal phenomena, see Andrew Halpin, *Conceptual Collisions* (2011) 2 JURISPRUDENCE 507.

[46] For an illuminating example relating to the subject that sparked off this discussion, see Tony Anghie's argument on the need to break out of an imperialist concept of a sovereign state which obstructed the recognition of Third World states, in his IMPERIALISM, SOVEREIGNTY AND THE MAKING OF INTERNATIONAL LAW (Cambridge: Cambridge University Press, 2005).

and the impetus for changing from a uniform concept is not adherence to a particular logic, but empirical recognition, or perception, of the inadequacy of a rigid uniform conceptualization.

4   Concluding Reflections

It is incontrovertible that contemporary law has become more complex and more diverse, with far greater cross-pollination between an increasing variety of normative orders affecting the practices of both municipal and international law. It is common ground, then, that legal materials store a number of potentially conflicting values within the principles, precepts, rules and guidelines that they contain. This in itself is not a new thing. Part of law's genius has always been to hold different values together in tension, awaiting the finer determination of those points of tension (or conflict) by the jurist or judge in the setting of a concrete dispute. What is new in the present global setting is that sharply conflicting values from different legal (or other normative) orders are brought into close proximity in the sort of disputes that now cross previously established cultural and national divides.[47]

To some extent the disagreement I have expressed in this chapter with Glenn could be minimized by replacing his invocation of multivalent logic with my recognition of multivalued law,[48] including the supplementary acknowledgement of non-binary and non-rigid multiple classifications and concepts. However, that would not really get to the heart of the matter. The point of establishing the capacity of dual or plural applications of bivalent logic to cover the different legal situations surveyed in this chapter, with the corresponding demonstration of the redundancy (or misapplication) of multivalent logic, has not been to vindicate a

---

[47] There is a suggestion from Glenn, TCS, 276, that the emergence of conflicting values and their being settled in established legal orders is a cyclical matter – although my language of conflicting values and settled values is represented by Glenn's preferred vocabulary of multivalent logic and bivalent logic:

> The multivalence of the logic that prevailed throughout most of the legal history discussed in this volume yielded to bivalence in some measure during the time of national legal construction. Bivalence will continue to be operative, though it may be some time until it reaches the pre-eminence it obtained in some jurisdictions in recent centuries. In the foreseeable future it will be more obviously challenged by the logics of cosmopolitan ways.

[48] See previous note for an example of this.

terminological preference. The point of the exercise has been to inquire into the nature of law and its practice in this contemporary setting, and to clarify the potential and limitations of the role law can perform here.

The critical focus of the disagreement, accordingly, is not on the greater complexity or sophistication of legal materials, but whether law in facing the challenges of its current circumstances has gained some additional resource enabling it to address more varied and possibly deeper conflicts of interests and values found in the contemporary global setting. Glenn, as we saw in Section 1, sees this resource in new and conciliatory forms of logic. Equipped with this resource, he suggests, cosmopolitan law can hold together contradictory values and provisions without ending in conflict. Glenn's comprehensive account of this resource gives it work to do at the two stages or conditions of law. At the stage of unresolved law, or raw legal materials, a greater variety of potentially conflicting material is brought together. At the stage of resolved law, or judicial determination of a case, a greater variety of dispositions is effected which need not cohere around a single value.

Put in those less strident terms, Glenn's agenda does not require multivalent logic at all. At the unresolved stage where each value only has a possible influence on the legal determination of conduct, the coexistence of conflicting values does not reach a point of contradiction and bivalent logic is respected, as we have demonstrated at {7}, {9}, and {10}. However, it should be stressed that the prospect of holding conflicting values or contrary norms together at this stage does depend on their legal applicability to determine a specific situation remaining unresolved. That is only a practical prospect in a limited number of circumstances. The vast majority of general legal norms that are relied on for guidance in recurring everyday situations are not found in an unresolved condition subject to competing with contrary norms existing alongside them within the legal materials. At the resolved stage, if all we discover is that different cases are resolved in accordance with different values or different amalgams of those values, again, applications of bivalent logic can provide an account of what is going on, as we saw at {7}, and as amplified by {10}.

The invocation of multivalent logic is only necessary if a more ambitious agenda is maintained. Glimpses of such an agenda occur when Glenn claims that the logic of cosmopolitan law can overcome contradiction so as to avoid conflict.[49] If this is a serious claim, it has to be

---

[49] See email excerpt at note 4; TCS, 267, 276, 285.

realized at the resolved stage. There are a number of devices employed in the process of reasoning from legal materials containing multiple and conflicting values, which give the impression of taking into account and so respecting both sides of a normative divide. Proportionality, margin of appreciation, and balancing are such devices that Glenn cites (in the company of others) in support of an approach to resolving cases that depends on multivalent logic.[50] However, these devices are misleadingly named if that is what they suggest.[51] In practice their use may result in a wider range of dispositions, but each disposition will result in a particular determination of instantiated value/s that is selective of one option and dismissive of others, in accordance with the analysis at {7}–{10}. The claim of harnessing multivalent logic to overcome conflict is unfounded.

The favouring and dismissal of conflicting normative options at the point of resolved law brings us back to the awkwardness of conciliation for law, raised in the Introduction. Whether the conflict is seen as conflict between normative options or conflict between parties to a dispute, legal judgment settles it to the advantage of one side at the expense of the other. This is what law does – and what there has been, and continues to be, a need for law to do. The real test for the claim that paraconsistent logic provides law with the power to overcome conflict would be satisfied only when legal judgment could simultaneously award each party to the dispute satisfaction of their respective contradictory claims. Neither Glenn nor any of the contributors to this volume has suggested that as a possibility.[52] This teaches us much about law, and possibly something about the new logics.

---

[50] TCS, 281–283, 288–290. See also, other contributions to this volume.

[51] On the use of balancing, the work of Stuart Macdonald is particularly insightful. See Stuart Macdonald, *Why We Should Abandon the Balance Metaphor: A New Approach to Counterterrorism Policy* (2009) 15 ILSA JOURNAL OF INTERNATIONAL AND COMPARATIVE LAW 95 (criticizes the balance metaphor for assuming a shared understanding of security and liberty, and argues that many of the key issues actually stem from different under-standings of what these values require, at 99–100, 123–125); *The Unbalanced Imagery of Anti-Terrorism Policy* (2009) 18 CORNELL JOURNAL OF LAW AND PUBLIC POLICY 519 (takes the image of a set of scales at face value and applies it, concluding that it has no value as an analytical aid and can even result in perverse conclusions, at 529–533); *Understanding Anti-Terrorism Policy: Values, Rationales and Principles* (2012) 34 SYDNEY LAW REVIEW 317 (constructs an alternative framework, using values, rationales and principles, and argues that indeterminacy is inevitable, at 318–332).

[52] The closest Glenn gets is in discussing *res judicata*, TCS, 271. However, each case clearly upholds a judgment in favour of one party at the expense of the other, no matter how many cases are brought on the matter; if paraconsistent logic had prevailed at any point, there would have been no need for the losing party to try again. As for reaching a point

In considering these wider lessons, first with respect to paraconsistent logics, it is interesting to speculate whether they find significance only at the point of the subject matter they address being in an unresolved condition. If we return to the initial motivation for multivalent logic, Aristotle's conundrum with the sea battle tomorrow, it is no longer a conundrum once tomorrow comes. We can then state in straightforward bivalent terms that either there is a sea battle or not. The aim of my suggestion for a dual application of bivalent logic, taking in not only the sea battle but also whether its occurrence has been resolved, was to show that the conundrum could be captured without exhausting the resources of bivalent logic. This expanded use of bivalent logic also has the advantage of offering a bridge between the unresolved and resolved conditions of the subject matter, as seen in the general framework at {5}, whereas paraconsistent logic is limited in its scope to dealing with the unresolved condition: either providing a representation of the chances of its potential fulfillment at that point of non-fulfillment (multivalent logic); or, consigning inconsistent possible resolutions to different possible worlds (modal logic). If that is so, one needs to ask just what exactly is gained by applying paraconsistent logic to the subject matter of interest. Very little, it would appear, if the subject matter is going to reach a resolved condition.[53] As is the case with law.[54]

As for law, the conclusion of this chapter is that paraconsistent logic has nothing to offer; a conclusion in part supported by Graham Priest in his contribution to this volume, when he considers the move from the existence of contradictory norms within legal materials to their

---

where two court decisions contradict in favouring different parties, this is resolved not through paraconsistent logic but a battle between the courts, as seen in *Earl of Oxford's Case* (1615) 21 ER 485.

[53] In the case of multivalent logic, where its previous fractional value proves to be an inaccurate account of its resolved (binary) value of 0 or 1. In the case of modal logic, if one of its possible states is going to put in an appearance in our actual world. There thus seems to be a bias in the applicability of modal logic to dealing with possible states that did not occur in our world. In the more ambitious uses of other possible worlds, this is nevertheless used to draw conclusions on what can be said about the nature of our world – notably in the metaphysics of David Lewis (on which, see Ned Hall, *David Lewis's Metaphysics* in THE STANFORD ENCYCLOPEDIA OF PHILOSOPHY (Edward N. Zalta ed, 2012), http://plato.stanford.edu/archives/fall2012/entries/lewis-metaphysics/); and more recently by Timothy Williams, MODAL LOGICS AS METAPHYSICS (Oxford: Oxford University Press, 2013).

[54] Taking the basic business of law not to be the manufacturing and purveying of political fudge – text following note 38.

resolution at the point of judgment.[55] At that point, Priest suggests a role for "chunk and permeate" logic, in tracking the influence of normative material from one normative order on another. But as he acknowledges, this only operates after the event, crucially after the "chunks" and "filters" have been chosen, so transferring attention to the extra-legal factors at play in selecting the chunks and setting up the filters.[56] This does not make a new form of logic into an extra resource to open up fresh possibilities for law in tackling the more varied and possibly deeper conflicts of interests and values it is confronted with, so as to support the emergence of a conflict-free cosmopolitan state.

Recognizing tensions or conflicts within legal materials, such that the materials themselves are incapable of determining the legal regulation of conduct in certain cases, need not impel us towards a new logic. The condition can be recognized from a legal realist perspective,[57] which then emphasizes the wider social influences at play in resolving law.[58] Maybe some of the new logics can play some part in modelling the outcomes produced by these extra-legal social factors, in ways that contributors to this volume have suggested. However, this is very much a secondary role for logic. To elevate any form of logic to a primary legal resource, and make it a resource that can banish conflict from the way in which law resolves normative contradictions and personal disputes, is dangerously misleading, about the nature of law, and the prospects of a cosmopolitan state.

---

[55] Graham Priest, *Where Laws Conflict: An Application of the Method of Chunk and Permeate*, this volume.

[56] "Something must determine what the relevant chunks and filters are." (this volume, 176). See also, Graham Priest, IN CONTRADICTION: A STUDY OF THE TRANSCONSISTENT, 2nd edn (Oxford: Oxford University Press, 2006) 188, acknowledging the need to use "extra-legal (socio-political) grounds" at the point of judgment when dealing with contradictory legal norms (as cited by Glenn, TCS, 274).

[57] See Hanoch Dagan, RECONSTRUCTING AMERICAN LEGAL REALISM & RETHINKING PRIVATE LAW THEORY (Oxford: Oxford University Press, 2013), on a realist understanding of law incorporating three fundamental tensions (between power and reason, science and craft, and tradition and progress).

[58] In his book, Dagan himself argues for embodying a plurality of values within a moderately perfectionist structure in filling out these wider social influences – a specific normative position that I argue is only one possible normative complement for his realist outlook, in my review of *Reconstructing American Legal Realism* in (2014) 11 No FOUNDATIONS 138. The key point being that a realist perspective opens up investigation of the normative positions that do (or do not) get to influence the legal outcome.

12

Fuzzy Law

A Theory of Quasi-Legality

OREN PEREZ*

Law is everywhere.[1] We are exposed to multifarious forms of legality, which permeate ever more realms of our social lives. In this extensively juridified world, quasi-legal or "soft law" schemes occupy an important place. Quasi-legal schemes can be found in such diverse fields as transnational environmental governance,[2] administrative best practice guidelines,[3] corporate codes of conduct,[4] ethical clinical codes,[5] and the regulation of academic life.[6] The prevalence of these multiple quasi-legal structures poses a challenge for legal theory. What exactly is the nature of the norms elaborated in these quasi-legal environments? How

---

* I would like to thank Patrick Glenn, Michael Helfand, Gabriel Lanyi, Tim Meyer, David Schiff, Lionel Smith, Graham Priest, and Gunther Teubner for helpful conversations on the ideas articulated in this article. This paper draws on my paper *Fuzzy Law: A Theory of Quasi-Legal Systems* (2015) 28 CAN JL & JUR 343–370; I would like to thank the publishers and the editor for giving me permission to use the materials here.

[1] Lars Chr Blichner & Anders Molander, *Mapping Juridification* (2008) 14 EUR LJ 36.

[2] See, e.g., the Global Reporting Initiative (GRI), *Sustainability Reporting Guidelines* G3.1 (2011), online: www.globalreporting.org/resourcelibrary/G3.1-Guidelines-Incl-Technical-Protocol.pdf; International Standards Organization *(ISO)*, ISO 14001: Environmental Management Systems (1996) [ISO 14001]; Forest Stewardship Council, *Certification Scheme*, online: www.fsc.org/certification.html.

[3] D. Zaring, *Best Practices* (2006) 81 NYUL REV 294.

[4] See, e.g., Walmart, *Standards for Suppliers* (January 2012), online: www.corporate.walmart.com/global-responsibility/ethical-sourcing/standards-for-suppliers. For further examples see Kevin McKague & Wesley Cragg, COMPENDIUM OF ETHICS CODES AND INSTRUMENTS OF CORPORATE RESPONSIBILITY (Toronto: York University, 2003).

[5] See, e.g., American College of Emergency Physicians, *Principles of Ethics for Emergency Physicians*, online: ACEP www.acep.org/Content.aspx?id=29144; Australian Medical Council, *Good Medical Practice: A Code of Conduct for Doctors in Australia*, online: www.amc.org.au/images/Final_Code.pdf.

[6] See, e.g., Indiana University Bloomington, *Code of Academic Ethics*, online: www.indiana.edu/~vpfaa/academicguide/index.php/Policy_I-1.

should we conceptualize the priority relations between soft legal norms and non-legal reasons, and between competing soft legal norms? What is the dynamic of deliberation or argumentation in social contexts involving quasi-legal norms? Traditional legal theory has failed to produce a theory that adequately captures the structure and dynamics of quasi-legal systems. To a large extent, this failure reflects traditional legal theory's continued commitment to a binary conception of law which views the phenomenon of law through the binary frames of lawlessness and complete legality (lawlessness/lawfulness). The article responds to this challenge by developing a theory of quasi-legality which I term "fuzzy law."

Quasi-legal structures that lie between the poles of lawlessness and complete legality represent an increasingly prevalent phenomenon, which challenges the either/or approach of legal positivism.[7] The article addresses this conceptual challenge by developing a theory of fuzzy law.[8] The model embraces two critiques of the binary framework of traditional legal theory. The first critique is conceptual: drawing on the extensive philosophical study of the notion of vagueness,[9] the article argues that more consideration should be given to the possibility of reinterpreting the fundamental concepts of legal theory (e.g., validity, bindingness) in a nuanced fashion. The second critique is empirical: the article argues that the binary model fails to satisfactorily account for the deliberative and institutional dynamics underlying the diverse legal-like phenomena documented by the soft law literature. The model of fuzzy law replaces the either/or framework that has dominated traditional legal theory with a dynamic framework based on a degree-theoretic interpretation of legal normativity. The model is built on three theoretical pillars: the theory of complementary pairs (TCP), developed by Scott Kelso and David Engstrom; fuzzy-set theory; and the concept of defeasible reasoning.[10]

[7] Oren Perez, *Purity Lost: the Paradoxical Face of the New Transnational Legal Body* (2007) 33 BROOK INT'L LJ 1; Sally Engle Merry, *Global Legal Pluralism and the Temporality of Soft Law* (2014) 46 J LEGAL PLURALISM 108.

[8] My paper differs from Graham Priest's chapter (*The Logic of Conflicting Legal Traditions*) in that he is interested in conflict between norms associated with different but completely valid legal systems, while I'm interested in unfolding the role of partially valid norms (associated with quasi-legal systems) in deliberative settings. The papers can therefore be seen as complementary. We both agree however that the techniques of non-classical logic can be useful in analyzing legal-like phenomena.

[9] See, e.g., Max Black, *Vagueness* (1937) 4 PHILOSOPHY OF SCIENCE 427; Giuseppina Ronzitti, VAGUENESS: A GUIDE (Vol. 19)(Springer, 2011)

[10] See J. A. Scott Kelso & David A. Engstrom, THE COMPLEMENTARY NATURE (Boston: MIT Press, 2006); Didier Dubois et al. *Fuzzy Sets: History and Basic Notions* in Didier Dubois

Although the question of legal vagueness has been explored in the legal literature, most of the writings in this area considered it from the perspective of the semantic content of legal statements, neglecting the potential implications of vagueness for the concept of legality itself.[11] This neglected path is pursued here.

The article proceeds as follows. Section 1 explores the binary underpinnings of traditional legal theory, focusing on the writings of three key scholars: John Langshaw Austin, H. L. A. Hart, and Joseph Raz. Section 2 examines the theoretical and empirical challenges facing the binary account of law. Sections 3 and 4 develop the model of fuzzy law. My argument proceeds in three steps. First, I outline a theoretical framework that allows us to conceive legal normativity (or bindingness) as a fuzzy predicate that can be realized in degrees (Sections 3.1 and 3.2). Second, I analyze the meaning of nuanced bindingness in a deliberative setting, linking the fuzzy model of law with the literature on defeasible reasoning (Section 3.3). Finally, I consider the sociological implications of the model based on an analysis of the coordination dynamics of quasi-legal systems (drawing on the theory of complementary pairs) (Section 4). Section 5 concludes the discussion.

1   The Binary Underpinnings of Traditional Legal Theory: John Langshaw Austin, H. L. A. Hart, and Joseph Raz

In this section I want to expose the binary underpinnings of traditional legal thought, focusing on the writings of three key legal and philosophical theorists: J. L. Austin, H. L. A. Hart and Joseph Raz. An old Mishnaic story concerning a dispute between Rabban Gamaliel of Yavneh, the president (Nasi) of the Sanhedrin of Yavneh[12] and Rabbi Joshua provides a nice illustration of the binary underpinnings of traditional jurisprudence. The dispute focused on the question of the exact date of the Day of

---

& Henri Prade, eds, FUNDAMENTALS OF FUZZY SETS (Springer, 2000) 21; Jaap Hage, *A Theory of Legal Reasoning and a Logic to Match* (1996) 4 *AI & L* 199, s 16.

[11] See, e.g., Andrei Marmor, 'Varieties of Vagueness in the Law', USC Legal Studies Research Paper No. 12–8, online: SSRN www.ssrn.com/abstract=2039076 (2012); Timothy Endicott, VAGUENESS IN LAW (Oxford: Oxford University Press, 2000). Some writers have conflated the two dimensions of vagueness into a single doctrine of soft law – a move which I find unhelpful. See, my critique of Abbott et al.'s work at the end of Section 2 (Kenneth W. Abbott et al., *The Concept of Legalization* (2000) 54 INTERNATIONAL ORGANIZATION 401).

[12] The Great Sanhedrin was the supreme court of ancient Israel, head by a Chief Justice called *Nasi*.

Atonement (Yom Kippur).[13] Yom Kippur is the most solemn of Jewish religious holidays. Its central themes are expiation and repentance and a search for reconciliation with God. It is marked by a day long period of fasting, meditation and prayer.[14] The Mishnah begins with the statement that Rabban Gamaliel possessed pictures of the moon in its various phases, which he had used to examine witnesses testifying to sightings of the new moon. The Mishnah then tells us how on two occasions Rabban Gamaliel accepted the testimony of witnesses despite apparent contradictions in their testimony. Rabban Gamaliel relied on these testimonies to determine the dates of the Jewish sacred holidays. His acceptance of these testimonies was criticized by Rabbi Joshua. Rabban Gamaliel recognized that Rabbi Joshua was making a cogent argument, but nonetheless has chosen not to engage in an argument with him, but rather used his authority to order Rabbi Joshua to appear before him on the day of Yom Kippur (according to Rabbi Joshua's calculations) carrying his stick and his money-bag.

The story appears in the Mishnah as follows:[15]

> Rabban Gamaliel sent to him [to Joshua], "I decree that you appear before me with staff and money on the day which according to your reckoning is the day of Atonement". Rabbi Aqiva went and found him [Joshua] upset. He [Aqiva] said to him [Joshua]: "I must deduce that whatever Rabban Gamaliel did is done [i.e., valid]. For it is written [Leviticus 23:4], 'These are the appointed times of the Lord, holy assemblies, which you shall proclaim', Whether in their [proper] time or not in their [proper] time. I have no appointed times but these [which you proclaim]". He [Joshua] came to Dosa son of Harkinas. He [the latter] said to him: "if we are going to examine the court of Rabban Gamaliel, then we would have to examine every court which has arisen from the days of Moses till now. As it is said [Exodus 24:9], 'And Moses and Aaron, Nadav and Avihu' and 70 of the elders of Israel went up ...' And why were the names of the elders not specified? In order to teach that every body of three which has arisen as a court over Israel, it is like the court of Moses" He [Joshua] took his staff and his money in his hand and went to Yavneh to Rabban Gamaliel on the day which according to his reckoning was the day of Atonement. Rabban Gamaliel arose and kissed him on his head, saying to

---

[13] Mishnah Rosh Hashanah, 2:8–9.

[14] On the importance of Yom Kippur in Jewish tradition, see: *Yom Kippur* ENCYCLOPEDIA BRITANNICA. 2010. Encyclopedia Britannica Online. 15 Aug. 2010 www.britannica.com/EBchecked/topic/653569/Yom-Kippur.

[15] The English translation is from: David, Goodblatt, THE MONARCHIC PRINCIPLE: STUDIES IN JEWISH SELF-GOVERNMENT IN ANTIQUITY (Tubingen: J. C. B. Moher (Paul Siebeck), 1994) 204.

him: "Come in peace, my master and my disciple. My master in wisdom; my disciple in that you accepted my words".

By forcing Rabbi Joshua to appear before him on the day of Yom Kippur – 'transforming' it through his legal order into a 'normal' day – Rabban Gamaliel sought to establish the authority of the legal institutions of his period. Once Rabban Gamaliel issued his ruling, it displaced the original arguments and became a new source of duty. I will return to this text after analysing the writings of Austin, Hart and Raz.

I start the analysis with J. L. Austin doctrine of infelicities. The doctrine plays a critical role in Austin's distinction between constatives and performatives, which he introduced in his book HOW TO DO THINGS WITH WORDS. The term "constatives" is used to depict statements of fact that can be true or false; "performatives" refers to sentences that do not describe, report, or constate anything but their utterance "is, or is a part of, the doing of an action."[16] The doctrine of infelicities refers to those types of cases in which something goes wrong in the execution of the performative, leading, in Austin's terminology, to the utterance being "unhappy" or infelicitous.[17] My focus is not on the exact details of Austin's taxonomy of infelicities but on the way in which he conceptualizes the consequences of the infelicitous execution of a performative.[18] Austin views these consequences in a binary fashion, which assumes that a performative can either succeed or fail completely: "When the utterance is a misfire," Austin explains, "the procedure which we purport to invoke is disallowed or is botched: and our act (marrying, etc.) is void or without effect..."[19] An example of misfire is when I say "I appoint you," when I am not entitled to appoint, or when I try to name a ship but I am not a proper

[16] J. L. Austin, HOW TO DO THINGS WITH WORDS (Oxford: Oxford University Press, 1955, 1975) at 3, 5. Examples of performatives are the acts of marrying, betting, bequeathing, christening at 19, 33.
[17] Ibid. at 14–15.
[18] One of the prominent examples Austin gives for infelicitous execution is when a conventional procedure (e.g., marrying) is performed either incorrectly or incompletely (conditions B.1 and B.2 to his classificatory scheme): Ibid. at 15.
[19] Ibid. at 16. Austin does not deny that infelicitous performatives can have real implications in the world but he insists that they will remain void (talking about the act of marriage): "Two final words about being void or without effect. This does not mean, of course, to say that we won't have done anything: lots of things will have been done-we shall most interestingly have committed the act of bigamy-but we shall not have done the purported act, viz. marrying. Because despite the name, you do not when bigamous marry twice. (In short, the algebra of marriage is BOOLEAN.) Further, 'without effect' does not here mean 'without consequences, results, effects'": ibid. at 17.

person (do not have the capacity) to do so. In both cases, the action is void.[20] In short, the algebra of performatives is *Boolean*: it is binary or crisp and not fuzzy.[21]

Austin ultimately replaced the distinction between constatives and performatives with a more general framework, which distinguishes between locutionary, illocutionary, and perlocutionary acts.[22] Austin, however, continued to apply the binary scheme of "happiness/unhappiness" to this revised framework, arguing that this distinction applies to all utterances that possess some illocutionary force (that is, to both constatives and performatives).[23] Returning to the dispute between Rabban Gamaliel and Rabbi Joshua, the crucial point Austin would argue, is that Rabbi Joshua has failed to point out any flaws (infelicities) in the authority of Rabban Gamaliel; given this failure, his critique of the testimonies accepted by Rabban Gamaliel was simply irrelevant.

Austin's work is located at the intersection of philosophy of language and pragmatics, and it is not part of the classical corpus of works on jurisprudence. However, there are close links between his ideas and the works of Hart and Raz, as both share Austin's binary thinking.[24] Hart's theory of law is based on the thesis that the rule of recognition simultaneously establishes the validity of all the primary legal rules and determines the membership (or content) of a particular legal system.[25] Hart's analysis of the rule of recognition can serve as the foundation for a "set-theoretic" model of law, drawing a sharp distinction between members and non-members of a particular legal system.[26] The notion

---

[20] Ibid. at 34, 23.   [21] Ibid. at 17.

[22] Austin, *supra* note 16 at 94–103. See also, John R. Searle, *Austin on Locutionary and Illocutionary Acts* (1968) PHILOSOPHICAL REV 405 at 405–406.

[23] Austin, ibid. at 135–137, 147. A similar binary conceptualization can also be found in the work of John Searle on speech acts. See, John R. Searle & Daniel Vanderveken, FOUNDATIONS OF ILLOCUTIONARY LOGIC (Cambridge: Cambridge University Press, 1985) at 1–26, and John R. Searle, *A Classification of Illocutionary Acts* (1976) 5 LANGUAGE IN SOCIETY 1 at 14.

[24] Although Austin played an influential role in the life and scholarship of H. L. A. Hart; see, Nicola Lacey (2002) A LIFE OF HLA HART: THE NIGHTMARE AND THE NOBLE DREAM (Oxford University Press) 133–134.

[25] S. Shapiro, *What is the rule of recognition (and does it exist)?* (2009) Yale Law School, Public Law Working Paper No. 184, online: SSRN: www.ssrn.com/abstract=1304645 at 6, 11 [Shapiro (2009)]; Scott J. Shapiro, LEGALITY (Oxford: Oxford University Press, 2012) at 85 [Shapiro (2012)]; J. Dickson, 'Is the Rule of Recognition Really a Conventional Rule?' (2007) 27 OXFORD J LEGAL STUD 373 at 377.

[26] See, also, John M Rogers & Robert E Molzon, *Some Lessons about the Law from Self-Referential Problems in Mathematics* (1992) 90 MICH L REV 992 at 998.

of "law as set" assumes that the content of a particular legal system S_L can be depicted by using some predicate formula that captures the criteria articulated by the rule of recognition (enumerating in this fashion all the system norms).[27] There is no place under this account for vagueness or for borderline cases as far as the question of membership is concerned.[28] Hart's model provides another way to interpret the Mishnaic story. Rabbi Joshua might have made a cogent argument, but the reasons he offered were not legally valid under the relevant rule of recognition; allowing such attack could have undermined the authority of the whole court system. This point was emphasized by Dosa son of Harkinas in the text above: "if we are going to examine the court of Rabban Gamaliel, then we would have to examine every court which has arisen from the days of Moses till now."

Raz's argument regarding the content-independence and preemptive force of legal reasons similarly depends on a crisp understanding of legal authority and legal validity. Raz argues that to the extent that a legal regime meets the requirements of what he calls the normal justification thesis (NJT), legal rules provide their subjects with *protected reasons* for complying with the prescriptions of the law.[29] There are two features that qualify legal reasons as *protected reasons*. First, a legal norm provides a *content-independent reason* for complying with the rule. Content independence means that the law *displaces* the reasons that it is meant to reflect: "law, when it is binding, pre-empts the reasons which it should have reflected, and whether it successfully reflects them or not it displaces them, and is now a new source of duties."[30] Philip Selznick has captured this quality of law by noting that "[p]ositive law invokes a *suspension* of

---

[27] This formula would have the following structure: $S_L(x)$ {x | x has properties $(A_1, \ldots, A_m)$}, where x is a normative statement; Shapiro (2009), *supra* note 25 at 5.

[28] The rule of recognition differs from the law's other rules in that it "validates but is not itself validated"; it is a reflection of social convention. Shapiro (2012), *supra* note 25 at 84.

[29] Joseph Raz, *The Problem of Authority: Revisiting the Service Conception* (2006) 90 MINN L REV 1003 at 1022.

[30] Joseph Raz, BETWEEN AUTHORITY AND NORMS: ON THE THEORY OF LAW AND PRACTICAL REASON (Oxford: Oxford University Press, 2009) 7. Raz emphasizes that the considerations which establish that a rule is binding do not turn on the desirability of the acts for which the rule is a reason. The insightfulness and subtlety of a novel Raz argues are reasons for reading it because they show why reading it is good. But the considerations which show why a rule is binding, i.e. why it is a reason for complying with its prescription, turn on the desirability of having the affairs of the community being ordered by a legal institution; Joseph Raz, *Reasoning with Rules* (2001) 54 CURR LEGAL PROBS 1.

personal preference and judgment with regard to the specific issue."[31] In addition to being a content-independent reason for complying with a rule, the law also provides an *exclusionary reason* for not following reasons that conflict with the rule: it overrides "our inclination to follow reasons on the losing side of the argument."[32] Going back to the Mishnaic story, once Rabban Gamaliel issued his ruling it displaced the original arguments and became a new source of duty. The epistemic quality of the testimonies on which his decision was based did not matter anymore. This is consistent with Raz's account of the preemptory nature of legal rules.

2   A Critique of the Binary Conception of Law

TCP and fuzzy-set theory raise doubts about the binary underpinnings of Austin's, Hart's, and Raz's accounts of law and of illocutionary acts in general.[33] In the case of Austin, TCP and fuzzy-set theory question the idea that illocutionary acts are governed, in general, by a binary framework of happiness/unhappiness. TCP and fuzzy-set theory provide the theoretical framework for hypothesizing a third dimension that takes place between these opposite poles. In the case of Hart, TCP and fuzzy-set theory question the thesis that the rule of recognition allows us to determine unequivocally the identity of the legal system and clearly demarcate between what is legal and what is non-legal. The concept of fuzziness suggests that we should at least consider the possibility that applying the rule of recognition to a particular norm does not produce a binary output (valid/invalid) but an intermediate measure, lying somewhere in between these poles. To give a non-legal example: consider the set of all jazz pieces ever performed.[34] Is the music of George Gershwin part of this set? Or should it be assigned with some partial measure of

---

[31] Philip Selznick, *Sociology and Natural Law* (1961) 6 NATURAL LAW FORUM 84 at 99 [my emphasis]. William Edmundson has described this feature of legal reasons as their 'because I said so' quality; William Edmundson, 'Because I Said So' (27 October 2012). Georgia State University College of Law, *Legal Studies Research Paper*, online: SSRN www.ssrn.com/abstract=2165428.

[32] Raz (2006), *supra* note 29 at 1022. A protected reason to φ then is a "first order reason to φ and an exclusionary reason not to fail to φ for a certain range of excluded reasons." Joseph Raz, *On Respect, Authority, and Neutrality: A Response* (2010) 120 ETHICS 279 at 298.

[33] For a discussion of this issue in the broader context of illocutionary acts see, Oren Perez, *A Legally Inspired Degree-Theoretic Model of Speech Acts* (BIU working paper, 2015).

[34] S_J: $\{x \mid x$ is a jazz piece$\}$.

membership owing to its affinity with classical music?[35] TCP and fuzzy-set theory suggest that we should be sympathetic to the possibility of developing a degree-theoretic concept of legal normativity.[36]

A degree-theoretic understanding of legal normativity also questions Raz's either/or distinction between legal and non-legal reasons. Fuzzy-set theory points out the possibility of fuzzifying this distinction, opening up new possibilities for modelling the function of (fuzzy) legal norms in practical reasoning. Because Raz does not recognize the possibility of partial validity, he does not explore this path.

The foregoing argument suggests that conventional legal theory misses some important modelling options by disregarding the nuanced inter-pretative choices pointed out by TCP and fuzzy-set theory. There is strong empirical support for exploring these degree-theoretic options. There is extensive body of research that shows that soft legal instru-ments – that is, legal-like schemes that do not satisfy the conventional criteria of legal validity – have considerable success in changing social reality across a wide range of variables.[37] Studies of soft legal schemes also demonstrate that these systems, at least in some cases, are gaining significant autonomy, reflected by unique institutional dynamics decoup-led from corporate, economic, and political rationalities.[38] The binary vocabulary of legal positivism, which takes these multiple legal schemes as either fully valid or fully invalid, does not offer a convincing explan-ation of this widely documented reality. The empirical literature seems to contradict the approach of positivistic writers, such as Jan Klabbers, who consider the idea of soft law as a logical embarrassment. According

[35] G. Tzanetakis & P. Cook, *Musical Genre Classification of Audio Signals* (2002) 10 IEEE TRANSACTIONS ON SPEECH AND AUDIO PROCESSING, 293 at 300.

[36] This view is consistent with degree-theoretic approaches to truth. See Roy T. Cook, 'Vagueness and Meaning' in G. Ronzitti, ed, VAGUENESS: A GUIDE (Berlin: Springer, 2011) at 83, 86.

[37] See, e.g., Jacob E. Gersen & Eric A. Posner, *Soft Law* (2010) 61 STAN L REV AT 573, 575 (noting the fact that congressional soft law, despite of its lack of formal legal status, can ultimately have a real effect) and Andrew T. Guzman & Timothy L. Meyer, *International Soft Law* (2010) 2 J LEGAL ANALYSIS 171, 179–183 (noting the increasing use of soft law instruments at the transnational domain).

[38] Oren Perez, Yair Amichai-Hamburger & Tammy Shterental, *The Dynamic of Corporate Self-Regulation: ISO 14001, Environmental Commitment, and Organizational Citizenship Behavior* (2009) 43 LAW & SOC'Y REV 593, Gunther Teubner, CONSTITUTIONAL FRAG-MENTS: SOCIETAL CONSTITUTIONALISM AND GLOBALIZATION (Oxford: Oxford University Press, 2012) and Zumbansen, *Defining the Space of Transnational Law: Legal Theory, Global Governance, and Legal Pluralism* (2012) 21 TRANSNAT'L L. & CONTEMP. PROBS. 305.

to Klabbers, law cannot be "more or less binding."[39] Klabbers' approach seems problematic given the empirical evidence on the prevalence of non-conventional legal forms. If soft law does not have some independent normative weight (as suggested by Klabbers), why do people bother producing it?

Abbott, Keohane, Moravcsik, Slaughter, and Snidal (2000) offer a different approach to the question of legality, which is close in spirit to the degree-theoretic framework proposed in this article, in their article on the concept of legalization.[40] Abbott and colleagues explicitly embrace the theoretical possibility of graded normativity. They define hard law as a collage of three dimensions: precision, obligation, and delegation, and soft law as those legal-like social structures that do not rank high on one of these parameters. There are several difficulties with the account of Abbott et al. The first difficulty lies in the concept of obligation. As I argue below, the obligatory nature of a legal-like norm is a function of the institutional structure in which it is embedded and the societal meta-norms governing this structure. The obligatory nature of a legal-like norm is not simply a product of its syntactic structure (although having the form of a "norm" is prerequisite).[41] Further, one cannot assume a-priori that private instruments, associated with non-state institutions, cannot have an obligatory (or partially obligatory) nature. Ruling out, a-priori, the possibility that non-conventional institutions could produce obligatory (or partially obligatory) norms, such reasoning amounts to either the fallacy of *'affirming the consequent'* or the fallacy of *'begging the question'*.[42] The "obligation" dimension is therefore not an

---

[39] And "if something is not legally binding, it cannot be softly legally binding either"; Jan Klabbers, *Redundancy of Soft Law* (1996) 65 NORDIC J INT'L L at 167, 181; Jan Klabbers, REFLECTIONS ON SOFT INTERNATIONAL LAW IN A PRIVATIZED WORLD (CITY: PUB, 2006) at 4, online www.helsinki.fi/eci/Publications/Klabbers/JKSoft_law_and_public.pdf; see also Prosper Weil, *Towards Relative Normativity in International Law?* (1983) 77 AM J INT'L L 413 at 415, 417–418.

[40] Kenneth W. Abbott et al., *supra* note 11; see also, Harri Kalimo and Tim Staal, *Softness in International Instruments: The Case of Transnational Corporations.* (2015) 42 SYRACUSE J. INT'L L. & COM. 363, 387–388.

[41] Kalimo and Staal recognize this difficulty and note that the obligatory nature of a legal-like instrument depends both on the authority of the "author" of the instrument and on the mandatory quality of its language; ibid, at 396.

[42] For a discussion of these fallacies see, T. Edward Damer (2009) ATTACKING FAULTY REASONING, 6th edn. Belmont, CA: Wadsworth/Thomson Learning at 63, 78. Kalimo and Staal commit that fallacy by assuming that private instruments cannot be considered legally valid (ibid., at 423). But transnational legal theorists such as Teubner have explicitly rejected this claim. I think that Abbott et al. are more open to the idea that

independent criterion that can be used to assess the hardness/softness of certain legal instruments but the product of that inquiry. The dimension of "delegation" constitutes part of this institutional inquiry. A second difficulty in Abbott et al. account lies in the element of precision. Incorporating this element into the model of graded normativity forces us to treat vague norms that are part of state law as partially valid, although state law constitutes the prototype of crisp legality.[43] While it is true that vagueness may undermine the efficacy of a norm, it is not relevant to the question of validity. It is best to keep these issues apart.[44] Finally, the authors do not develop an explicit model of the argumentative dynamics associated with soft legal norms.

3 Fuzzy Law: A Theory of Quasi-Legality

I develop the model of "fuzzy law" in three steps. First, I outline a theoretical framework that allows us to conceive the bindingness of legal norms as a fuzzy (nuanced) predicate that can be realized in degrees (Sections 3.1 and 3.2). The intuition underlying this argument is that legal norms usually need to satisfy several criteria in order to be considered valid or authoritative.[45] In contrast to Austin and to legal positivists such as Klabbers, I argue that a failure to satisfy one or more of these conditions does not necessarily lead to a complete voidance of the legal act. Rather, it opens the possibility for a fuzzy interpretation of the normative force of such imperfect legal act. Second, I analyze the meaning of nuanced normativity in a deliberative setting, linking the fuzzy model with the literature on defeasible reasoning (Section 3.3). Finally, in Section 4 I consider the sociological implications of this model in an

---

non-state institutions may have the power to produce partially obligatory norms, although they do discuss it explicitly; see the discussion on p. 110.

[43] The term 'crisp' is borrowed from the literature on fuzzy sets in which it is used to distinguish between crisp and fuzzy sets; see: Lotfi A Zadeh, *Toward a Theory of Fuzzy Information Granulation and its Centrality in Human Reasoning and Fuzzy Logic* (1997) 90 FUZZY SETS AND SYSTEMS 111 at 113.

[44] Kalimo and Staal follow Abbott et al. by linking the issues of obligation and precision (supra note 40, at 396).

[45] Here is a common statement of this view "A systematic reconstruction of the law needs to identify set of properties that a norm must exhibit to be part of a certain legal system. . . . These properties are often called 'criteria of validity'" Pablo E Navarro & Jorge L Rodriguez, DEONTIC LOGIC AND LEGAL SYSTEMS (Cambridge: Cambridge University Press, 2014) at 118.

analysis of the coordination dynamics of quasi-legal systems (drawing on the theory of complementary pairs).

My argument brings together three theoretical frameworks: the theory of complementary pairs (TCP), fuzzy-set theory and the concept of defeasible reasoning. The theory of complementary pairs, developed by Scott Kelso and David Engstrom, provides an overarching critique of the either/or framework that dominates the field of jurisprudence. TCP recognizes the central role that contraries play in our life. But TCP argues that understanding how contraries operate requires us to replace the binary frames through which contraries are usually conceptualized (either/or, dualism, or monism) with a dynamic framework that seeks to reconcile these three basic frames[46] by treating them as "equally valid dynamical modes, tendencies, or dispositions of the complementary pair."[47] As Kelso and Engstrom note, this line of inquiry faces serious hurdles. They argue that one of the main stumbling blocks to progress in discovering a general principle of complementarity of contraries is "the tenacious human habit of dichotomizing life into contraries in the first place. Once human beings have fragmented life into dichotomies, contraries and opposites, they have a tough time putting them back together again."[48]

TCP seeks to uncover the dynamic nature of complementary pairs.[49] To emphasize this feature of complementary pairs, Kelso and Engstrom propose to denote them using the tilde symbol (~) instead of the more common forward slash (/). To have a complementary pair, a system must be minimally capable of producing both sides of the pair (e.g., legal~illegal, science~pseudo-science, segregation~integration, whole~part, valid~invalid, soft law~hard law). In exploring the dynamics of complementary pairs, we should recognize that complementary aspects can behave both as "tendencies" or "dispositions" and as well-defined

---

[46] The either/or frame represents two different frames because it can be interpreted as valorizing one side of the distinction (e.g., legal/illegal, good/bad) which brings the different possible interpretations of a complementary pair to four; Kelso & Engstrom, *supra* note 10 at 50.

[47] See Kelso & Engstrom, ibid. at 51.

[48] David A. Engstrøm & J.A. Scott Kelso, *Coordination Dynamics of the Complementary Nature* (2008) 30 GESTALT THEORY 121 at 123.

[49] Kelso & Engstrom, *supra* note 10 and J.A. Kelso, *The Complementary Nature of Coordination Dynamics: Toward a Science of the In-Between Uncertainty and Surprise in Complex Systems* in R. McDaniel & D. Driebe, eds, UNCERTAINTY AND SURPRISE IN COMPLEX SYSTEMS: QUESTIONS ON WORKING WITH THE UNEXPECTED (Berlin: Springer, 2005) 77.

states.[50] In many systems, contrary tendencies coexist simultaneously, exhibiting what Kelso and Engstrom term as *metastability*. The science of coordination dynamics seeks to unfold the mechanisms generating this metastability.[51]

Applying the abstract vision of TCP to the realm of law requires the development of a new vocabulary that would allow us to analyze the coordination dynamics of law as a non-crisp phenomenon, that is, to reach beyond the conventional thinking that considers law through mutually exclusive, either/or dichotomies (e.g., legal/illegal; valid/invalid; soft law/hard law).[52] This vocabulary can be found in the fields of fuzzy-set theory and of defeasible reasoning. Fuzzy-set theory, which was pioneered by Lotfi A. Zadeh in 1965, constitutes an extension to classical set theory.[53] In classical set theory, the membership of elements in a set is assessed in binary terms according to a bivalent condition: an element either belongs or does not belong to the set. By contrast, in fuzzy-set theory membership can be gradual or partial. This is described with the aid of a membership function valued in the real unit interval [0, 1]. Fuzzy-set theory provides a strict modeling language for studying vague phenomena.[54] The modeling language of fuzzy set theory provides a conceptual framework for reframing the idea of legal normativity as a fuzzy predicate that can be realized in degrees.[55]

Defeasible reasoning is a branch of logic that deals with dialectic reasoning. It develops a formal understanding of the way in which

[50] Kelso & Engstrom, *supra* note 10 at 73.
[51] The coordination dynamics associated with complementary pairs is informational in nature, which means that information is actively used to coordinate things. Engstrøm & Kelso, *supra* note 48 at 125. Metastability provides a description of the influence exerted by interconnected parts and processes when pure synchronization – phase and frequency locking – does not exist. "Metastability" reflects therefore a system's dynamics that lies beyond such attractor-bearing regimes. As a result, components are able to affect each other's destiny without being trapped in a sustained state of synchronization, a collective state where no new information can be created. See, Emmanuelle Tognoli & J. A. Scott Kelso, *The Metastable Brain* (2014) 81(1) NEURON 35, at 37
[52] Kelso & Engstrom use their framework to the study the brain and their detailed model cannot therefore be applied as such to the legal context.
[53] See Lotfi A. Zadeh, *The Birth and Evolution of Fuzzy Logic* (1990) 17 INTERNATIONAL JOURNAL OF GENERAL SYSTEMS 95.
[54] See Lotfi A. Zadeh, *Is There a Need for Fuzzy Logic?* (2008) 178 INFORMATION SCIENCES 2751 at 2753.
[55] For a similar application in the medical field, see e.g., Rudolf Seising, *From Vagueness in Medical Thought to the Foundations of Fuzzy Reasoning in Medical Diagnosis* (2006) 38 ARTIFICIAL INTELLIGENCE IN MEDICINE 237.

reasons and norms can overcome conflicting reasons and norms or be defeated by them. In particular, what distinguishes defeasible arguments from deductive ones is that they are not foolproof. Whereas in deductive argumentation an argument is valid if the truth of its premises guarantees the truth of its conclusion, defeasible arguments can be defeated by counter arguments. In other words, the addition of information can dictate the retraction of the conclusion of a defeasible argument without mandating the retraction of any of the premises from which the retracted conclusion was inferred (drawing on exception-permitting generalizations).[56] Defeasible reasoning consists therefore of "constructing arguments, of attacking these arguments with counter-arguments, and of adjudicating between conflicting arguments on grounds that are appropriate to the conflict at hand."[57] Combining the fuzzy-inspired idea of graded normativity with the notion of defeasible reasoning provides a framework for studying the deliberative dynamics of fuzzy legal systems.

3.1   Two Types of Legal Vagueness: Atomic and Institutionally Generated Vagueness

In thinking about the notion of fuzzy law, it is useful to distinguish between "atomic vagueness" and "institutionally generated vagueness." Most of the discussion in the legal literature has focused on the first type of legal vagueness.[58] Atomic vagueness refers to the inexact nature of the terms and concepts used in legal statements, or what Hart has described as the problem of legal "penumbra."[59] The terms vagueness and fuzziness refer to notions that have imprecise boundaries. The relationship

---

[56] Thus, for example, police officers commonly draw on the following generalization in making judgments about guilt: "fleeing from the crime scene indicates consciousness of guilt." However, this general statement can be defeated if in a particular instance the police officer finds out that the suspect was an illegal immigrant who wanted to avoid the police fearing deportation. See H. Prakken & G. Sartor, *A Logical Analysis of Burdens of Proof* in H. Kaptein, H. Prakken & B. Verheij, eds, LEGAL EVIDENCE AND PROOF: STATISTICS, STORIES, LOGIC 223 at 237 (Aldershot: Ashgate, 2009).

[57] Prakken & Sartor, ibid. at 229. See also Robert Koons, *Defeasible Reasoning*, THE STANFORD ENCYCLOPEDIA OF PHILOSOPHY (Spring 2014), Edward N. Zalta, ed, online: www.plato.stanford.edu/archives/spr2014/entries/reasoning-defeasible/.

[58] See Jeremy Waldron, 'Vagueness and the Guidance of Action' NYU School of Law, Public Law Research Paper No. 10–81, online: SSRN www.ssrn.com/abstract=1699963 (2010). See also Marmor, *supra* note 11, Endicott, *supra* note 11 and Kalimo and Staal, *supra* note 40.

[59] See H. L. A. Hart, *Positivism and the Separation of Law and Morals* (1958) 71 HARV L REV 593 at 606–615. This inexactness reflects, first, the fact that the linguistic conventions that determine the meaning of words are not fully determinative. Second, law creates further

between such vague terms and the objects they refer to is not crisp and can yield borderline cases in which the correctness of the application of the term is in doubt.[60] Fuzziness in this sense is a property of predicates such as "tall" or "rich" and of general concepts such as "income" or "periphery."[61] In the legal context, fuzziness is often associated with the use of evaluative predicates (reasonableness, good faith). Fuzzy terms are often used in conjunction with gradual predicates designating a degree (e.g., "substantial," "very," "quite," "almost not").[62]

A distinctive feature of atomic vagueness is that it can be dissipated by the relevant legal institutions. The law has a built-in institutional mechanism for dissipating vagueness: legal decisions. Andrei Marmor notes that in most cases, court decisions do not constitute an "instance of applying the law but of extending it or narrowing it, that is, adding a precification that goes beyond what the statute actually asserts."[63] The recent U.S. Supreme Court case of *Skilling v. U.S.*, which focused on the void-for-vagueness doctrine, provides a vivid example of this institutional capacity.[64] Skilling was convicted of conspiracy to commit "honest-services" wire fraud (18 U. S. C.§§371, 1343, 1346).[65]

---

semantic puzzles by superimposing its (potentially conflicting and inexact) principles on general linguistic conventions. See Frederick Schauer, *A Critical Guide to Vehicles in the Park* (2008) 83 NYUL Rev 1109. It is possible to distinguish in this context between transparently vague concepts, such as sorites predicates and extravagantly vague concepts such as the criminal offence of neglecting a child. Extravagantly vague concepts are more complex because "they designate a *multidimensional* evaluation with *incommensurable* constitutive elements"; see Marmor, *supra* note 11 at 4. Due to their underlying multidimensionality extravagantly vague concepts are much more resistant to precification.

[60] Marmor, *supra* note 11.

[61] This type of predicates produces the famous sorites paradox. Dominic Hyde, *Sorites Paradox*, THE STANFORD ENCYCLOPEDIA OF PHILOSOPHY (Winter 2011 Edition), Edward N. Zalta, ed, online: www.plato.stanford.edu/archives/win2011/entries/sorites-paradox/.

[62] Other types of linguistic inexactness, which I will not discuss here, are *ambiguity* (which refers to terms that have multiple meanings e.g., "bank," "cut," "park") and *generality* (which refers to terms that can be applied to a variety of situations and whose meaning may vary with context. e.g., "car," "property"). See J. A. Goguen, *The Logic of Inexact Concepts* (1969) 19 SYNTHESE 325 at 345.

[63] Marmor, *supra* note 11 at 10. Leo Katz notes similarly that "however unsure we are whether a defendant has acted in good faith or bad, reasonably or negligently, the law will eventually classify his actions in one of those two bins, good or bad faith, reasonable or negligent. It won't split the difference"; Leo Katz, WHY THE LAW IS SO PERVERSE (Chicago: University of Chicago Press, 2011) at 144. See further William Twining & David Miers, HOW TO DO THINGS WITH RULES: A PRIMER OF INTERPRETATION, 5th edn. (Cambridge: Cambridge University Press, 2010) at 169–171.

[64] (June 24, 2010) 130 S. Ct. 2896.   [65] Ibid. at 2907.

Skilling argued that §1346 is unconstitutionally vague and thus should be invalidated. The text of §1346 prohibits any "scheme or artifice to defraud," which was defined to include "a scheme or artifice to deprive another of the intangible right of honest services."[66] Justice Ginsburg emphasized that "[i]t has long been our practice, however, before striking a federal statute as impermissibly vague, to consider whether the prescription is amenable to a limiting construction."[67] In view of this general observation, the Court produced a limiting interpretation of §1346:

> In view of this history there is no doubt that Congress intended §1346 to reach *at least* bribes and kickbacks. Reading the statute to proscribe a wider range of offensive conduct, we acknowledge, would raise the due process concerns underlying the vagueness doctrine. To preserve the statute without transgressing constitutional limitations, we now hold that §1346 criminalizes *only* the bribe and-kickback core of the pre-*McNally* case law.[68]

The intrinsic vagueness of §1346 did not therefore leave the court paralyzed or helpless.[69]

A second form of legal inexactness, which I term *"institutionally generated vagueness,"* is a product of the institutional environment in which the legal communication arises. It is on this form of legal inexactness that my argument focuses. Unlike atomic vagueness, institutionally generated vagueness cannot be dissipated by the legal institutions associated with the legal communication. The literature on soft law has tended to confuse these two sources of legal vagueness.[70] Underlying the notion

---

[66] Ibid. at 2927.   [67] Ibid. at 2929.

[68] Ibid. at 2931. Drawing on this revised interpretation of §1346, the Court has affirmed the Fifth Circuit's ruling on Skilling's fair-trial argument, vacated its ruling on his conspiracy conviction, and remand the case for proceedings consistent with this opinion. Ibid. at 2935. For further discussion of this case see: Justin Weitz, *The Devil is in the Details: 18 USC Sec. 666 after Skilling v United States* (2011) 14 NYUJ LEGIS & PUB POL'Y 805.

[69] The capacity of law to resolve meaning disputes in concrete cases does not prevent future meaning conflicts because of the indeterminate nature of analogical reasoning. As Cass Sunstein notes: "The method of analogy is based on the question: Is case *A* relevantly similar to case *B*, or not? ... To answer such questions, one needs a theory of relevant similarities and differences. By itself, analogical reasoning supplies no such theory. It is thus dependent on an apparatus that it is unable to produce"; Cass R. Sunstein, *On Analogical Reasoning* (1993) 106 HARV L REV 741, at 773–774.

[70] This confusion is particularly apparent in the work of Abbott et al. and Kalimo and Staal (*supra* note 40) which brings together obligation, precision, and delegation as three dimensions of legality.

of institutionally generated vagueness[71] is the thesis that the meaning of legal-like (deontic) sentences[72] is a function not merely of their (deontic) syntax and semantic content but also of their level of bindingness (or validity). The bindingness of deontic sentences is a function of the institutional setting in which they were promulgated. We cannot therefore determine whether and to what degree deontic sentences constitute legal communication without collecting further data about the institutional context in which they were generated.[73] To make this argument in a somewhat different form, let us consider a text structured according to the deontic syntax (using, for example, the prohibitive form) but stripped of any contextual cues (time, place, participants' profile, and institutional background). Such text is not fully intelligible without further data about the institutional environment in which it was promulgated, because it is only through this data that we can determine what demands the text makes, i.e., its level of bindingness.[74]

Some clarification is in order regarding my use of the concept of bindingness. In talking about the bindingness of a rule I refer to the

---

[71] Andrei Marmor similarly distinguishes between semantic and conversational vagueness. In his opinion, an expression can be vague (or precise) with respect to a specific conversation independently of any semantic vagueness. This form of vagueness can be dissipated only after exposing the particulars of the context. Marmor, *supra* note 11 at 7.

[72] The deontic syntax is based on three basic forms: a *prescriptive* form (ought to, **OB**), a *permissive* form (may, **PE**), and a *prohibitive form* (impermissible that, **IM**). The obligatory form is commonly taken as basic and can be used to derive the other forms: $PEp \leftrightarrow {\sim}OB{\sim}p$; $IMp \leftrightarrow OB{\sim}p$. See Paul McNamara, Deontic Logic, THE STANFORD ENCYCLOPEDIA OF PHILOSOPHY (Summer 2010) Edward N Zalta, ed, online: www.plato.stanford.edu/arch ives/sum2010/entries/logic-deontic/ (2010). The law includes additional types of norms, such as competence norms and determinative norms. Eugenio Bulygin, *On Norms of Competence* (1992) 11 LAW & PHIL 201.

[73] Institutionally generated vagueness has both epistemic and metaphysical features. It is epistemic because it can be explained, in part, by our not knowing enough about the notion of legal bindingness and by the difficulty (as will be explained below) of articulating the social convention by which people relate certain institutional facts to levels of bindingness. But it also has a metaphysical feature because there is something intrinsically contingent about the idea of legal bindingness, as I elaborate below. For the distinction between epistemic and metaphysical vagueness see: Trenton Merricks, *Varieties of Vagueness* (2001) 62 PHILOSOPHY AND PHENOMENOLOGICAL RESEARCH 145.

[74] This point is also emphasized by Searle who notes that the force of declarations depends on extra-linguistic institutions and not just on linguistic conventions (although he makes this argument in the context of a crisp framework); see John Searle, MAKING THE SOCIAL WORLD: THE STRUCTURE OF HUMAN CIVILIZATION (Oxford: Oxford University Press, 2010) at 111–114.

normative force that second order observers[75] would expect first order (i.e., directly involved) agents to attribute to the rule, given the institutional structure in which the rule is invoked. It is a reflection therefore of mutual social expectations. This attributed normative force does not necessarily capture the psychological or behavioural force of a particular norm. For example, while an agent may recognize a certain norm as binding (and thus as constituting a content independent reason for action) he may nevertheless decide not to do what the norm obligates him to do, or to do what the norm prohibits him from doing.[76] The normative force of a rule does not therefore necessarily reflect its ultimate psychological effect or its ultimate behavioural consequences. Norms promulgated in different institutional settings can have varied claims for bindingness. Consider the difference between the Supreme Court of Israel and judges in a moot court trial. The rulings of the Supreme Court of Israel are fully binding in the sense articulated above. This claim remains intact even if it can be demonstrated that some Supreme Court rulings have not been implemented. In contrast, the ruling of a judge in a moot court trial has no valid claim for bindingness.[77] Demonstrating that some people attribute legal authority to such a tribunal does not change our view of its authority; rather, it reflects a mismatch between these agents' beliefs and prevalent social conventions.

3.2   A Model of Fuzzy Legality

The bindingness of deontic statements is a function of the social and institutional context in which such statements arise. Linking the meaning of deontic sentences to this social-institutional context opens up the possibility of conceptualizing the normative force (or bindingness) of a rule as a fuzzy predicate. It allows us to interpret legal normativity along a continuum bounded by the ideal types of "non-law" at one end and by "crisp (or absolute) law" at the other. What is at stake here is not the psychological or behavioural force of the norm but its proclaimed

[75] That is, observers that are not directly involved in the social interaction influenced by the rule.

[76] See further on this point: Searle (2010), *supra* note 74 at 128–129.

[77] While a judge in a moot court trial has some normative influence *within* that artificial process (e.g., she can declare one team as the winner), she has no influence *beyond* this process.

bindingness, as it is reflected in the mutual expectations of the relevant community.[78]

The idea of fuzzy sets, defined as sets that can have partial members, provides a theoretical framework for formalizing the notion of legal bindingness as a non-crisp predicate. In particular, the model of membership function provides an exact framework for interpreting the notion of legal bindingness in degree-theoretic terms. It is possible to construct a fuzzy membership function that receives as input data about the institutional structure associated with a particular legal-like sentence and produces a value that represents the relative bindingness of this sentence. This value represents the level of bindingness of the norms of the quasi-legal system,[79] relative to the norms of a hypothetical perfect legal system. Before I provide a more formal elaboration of this argument, a few more words about the meaning of the proposed fuzzy membership function are in order.

First, note that the proposed fuzzy membership function does not measure the membership of a certain rule in the fuzzy legal system itself (e.g., a certain corporate social responsibility (CSR) regime) based on some membership criteria.[80] Rather, it provides a measure of the *relative bindingness* of the norms of the fuzzy system, which is a function of the extent to which the structure of this system *fails to satisfy some projected criteria of perfect legality*. The relative bindingness of a norm constitutes a first step in determining the priority relations between the fuzzy norm and non-legal reasons, as well as between the fuzzy norm and perfect legal norms, and between the fuzzy norm and competing fuzzy norms. The idea of fuzzy legality therefore raises two meta-questions: (a) what is the structure of the fuzzy membership function associated with the system? and (b) what are the priority relations

---

[78] Charles Goodwin & John Heritage, *Conversation Analysis (1990) 19*, ANNUAL REVIEW OF ANTHROPOLOGY 283 AT 286 AND ALFRED SCHÜTZ, COLLECTED PAPERS: THE PROBLEM OF SOCIAL REALITY. Volume I § 1 (Berlin: Springer, 1982) at 11–12. The fact that a particular (fuzzy) rule may be disregarded in a particular interaction does not change its (fuzzy) normative value, although it may signal *a change in collective expectations.*

[79] I will use the terms quasi-legal system and fuzzy legal system interchangeably to designate soft legal schemes.

[80] The question of membership would be resolved through a conventional, sourced-based principle of legality, that is, whether the norm was created in accordance with a power-conferring norm that is part of the fuzzy system; See Navarro & Rodriguez, *supra* note 45 at 144.

between the fuzzy norms and competing non-legal, quasi-legal, and fully-fledged legal reasons?[81]

Second, the structure of the fuzzy membership function would usually not be determined explicitly by the constitutive texts of the quasi-legal regime (e.g., the constitutive texts of the CSR regime) or by an external legal source (e.g., the company bylaws). Rather, the rule of recognition that simultaneously determines the structure of the fuzzy membership function and the priority relations is an emergent social construct[82] that takes shape through the continuous invocation of fuzzy rules in multiple social interactions. In this context, fuzzy legal systems differ from conventional ones. In the paradigmatic case of state law, the priority relations between rules of the system are internally controlled: *law regulates the resolution of its own indeterminacies.*[83] In fuzzy legal regimes, however, there is no clear authority structure or meta-rulebook that resolves these questions. Rather, the fuzzy membership function and the meta-rule that determines the priority relations *emerge implicitly through the coordination dynamics of the particular fuzzy regime*, which depends on the external legal-social environment in which the regime is embedded.[84]

Below I develop this argument formally. I start with an analysis of the shape of the proposed fuzzy membership function. I then move to discuss the question of priority relations (Section 3.3). Readers who do not wish to engage with the technicalities of fuzzy set theory can skip the following text.

Fuzzy membership functions are constructed using five elements:[85]

---

[81] As John Horty notes "some of the most important things we reason about, and reason about defeasibly, are the priorities among the very defaults that guide our defeasible reasoning"; J. F. Horty, Reasons as Defaults (2007) 7 PHILOSOPHERS' IMPRINT 10. John Horty has developed a formal model of this process of meta-order reasoning: see J. F. Horty, REASONS AS DEFAULTS (Oxford: Oxford University Press, 2012) 111. I doubt, however, whether Horty's formal model can capture the implicit dynamic of fuzzy legal systems.

[82] R. Conte et al., *Manifesto of Computational Social Science* (2012) 214 THE EUROPEAN PHYSICAL JOURNAL SPECIAL TOPICS 325 at 328; S. Buckingham Shum et al., *Towards a Global Participatory Platform* (2012) 214 THE EUROPEAN PHYSICAL JOURNAL SPECIAL TOPICS 109 at 142; F. Giannotti et al., *A Planetary Nervous System for Social Mining and Collective Awareness* (2012) 214 THE EUROPEAN PHYSICAL JOURNAL SPECIAL TOPICS 49, at 62.

[83] Law authorizes the institutions ('courts') that resolve disputes about the meaning and application of rules. See Joseph Raz, *Sorensen: Vagueness has No Function in Law* (2002) 7 LEGAL THEORY 417.

[84] Engstrøm & Kelso, *supra* note 48.

[85] I. B. Turksen, *Measurement of Membership Functions and Their Acquisition* (1991) 40 FUZZY SETS AND SYSTEMS 5 at 8.

(a) A set of elements x ∈ **X** (e.g., a resident of Tel-Aviv);
(b) A linguistic variable **V** in a set of linguistic variables (e.g., the *height* of residents of Tel-Aviv), which serves as a label for an attribute of the elements in **X**;
(c) A linguistic term **A** (an adjective or an adverb) in a set of linguistic terms associated with the linguistic variable **V** (e.g., a *tall or short* resident of Tel-Aviv);
(d) A measurable numeric assignment interval **Z** ∈ [−∞,∞] that constitutes a referential set for the particular attribute label **V** (e.g., height) of the set of elements x ∈ **X** (e.g., [0, 2.40] for the height of residents of Tel Aviv);
(e) A *fuzzy membership function* fA(x) of the fuzzy set **A** (e.g., the set of tall male Tel-Aviv residents) in the space of points **X** (Tel-Aviv residents), is a function that maps each point in **X** onto the real interval [0, 1]. The value of fA(x) at x represents the "grade of membership" of x (a particular Tel-Aviv resident) in **A** (the set of tall Tel-Aviv residents). The grade of membership increases with fA(x).[86]

A possible membership function for the set of tall male Tel-Aviv residents could have the following form:

$$f(x) = 0 \,(for\, 0 \leq x \leq 1);$$
$$f(x) = 5x/4 - 5/4 \,(for\, 1 < x \leq 1.80);$$
$$f(x) = 1 \,(for\, 1.80 < x \leq 2.40)$$

Applying this formalism to the law requires a proper interpretation of the above constructs.

(a') The elements x ∈ **X** represent a stream *of rule-like sentences* (structured according to the deontic syntax) that occur in some social settings and can be linked to a particular norm-producing institution.
(b') The concept of *bindingness* serves as a label (**V**) for an attribute of the elements in **X** (rule-like sentences). (It substitutes "height" in the above example).
(c') The *extent* of the *bindingness* of a norm (*ranging between the poles of complete and null bindingness*) constitutes the linguistic term **A** associated with **V** (it substitutes "tall" or "short" in the above example).

[86] In other words, fA(x) represents the degree with which the use of the linguistic term **A** (tall) is compatible with the attribute **V** (height) of an element x ∈ **X** (a particular Tel-Aviv resident). Lotfi A. Zadeh, 'Fuzzy Sets'(1965) 8 INFORMATION AND CONTROL 338.

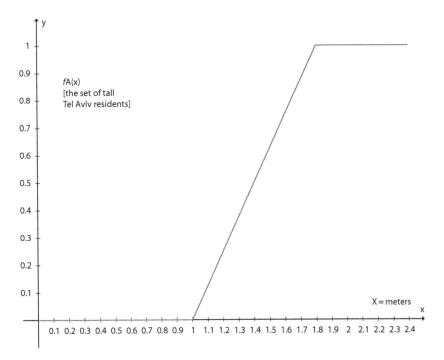

Figure 12.1:   Membership function of the set of tall Tel-Aviv residents

(d') Providing a measurable numeric assignment interval $Z \in [-\infty, \infty]$ as a referential set for *bindingness* (the particular attribute label V) is not appropriate for the legal context. I argue that Z should be conceptualized as a set of criteria that enumerates the attributes of perfect legal institutions, $B_{L\text{-perfect}}$ $(z_1 \ldots z_i)$. This set is context-specific and likely to change across cultures and time. The intuition underlying this argument is that a failure to satisfy one or more of these criteria does not necessarily lead to a complete failure of the legal authority (or the legal act).

(e') Given this conceptual structure, what would be the structure of a fuzzy membership function for legal-like sentences that arise within a particular legal system, A_L? The model I propose produces a membership value for a particular normative sentence, x, that arises in the domain of A_L, by examining the extent to which A_L satisfies a list of criteria that characterize a hypothetical perfect legal system, $B_{L\text{-perfect}}$, whose norms are completely binding. The membership function measures the "grade of membership" of a particular rule-like sentence

x that emerges in the discourse universe of A_L in $B_{L\text{-perfect}}$. In other words, it measures *the degree with which the use of the term "perfect legality" is compatible with the institutional attributes of this system* (A_L). This degree reflects the level of *bindingness* of the rules of A_L. This interpretation can be represented in the following format:

$$(1) f A_L = M\left(x, A_L, B_{L-\text{perfect}}\right)$$

Unlike simple predicates such as "tall" and "bald," which are defined based on a single variable (height, hair density), the proposed membership function is based on a rather complicated *aggregation function* that compares the institutional attributes of vector A_L with an attributes vector representing perfect legality ($B_{L\text{-perfect}}$), producing a single membership value for x. In other words, the function aggregates the scores of A_L on each of the attributes of perfect legality.[87] Constructing such a membership function requires us to decompose our understanding of a perfect legal system ($B_{L\text{-perfect}}$) into a vector of institutional attributes (including both hierarchical and procedural rules), such as the existence of a multi-level judicial system, the extent of the courts' independence, indicators of institutional reflexivity (e.g., the existence of an appeal procedure), enforcement procedures of court rulings, and more.[88] An aggregation

---

[87] This aggregation function would be composed in effect from multiple membership functions, one for each of the designated attributes of perfect legal system. The aggregation could be based either on arithmetic mean or on some weighted average (which could give more weight to some attribute, e.g., the level of independence of the court system). See Andrew Reid & Richard Frank, *Celerity in the Courts: The Application of Fuzzy Logic to Model Case Complexity of Criminal Justice Systems* in Vahid Dabbaghian & Vijay Kumar Mago, eds, THEORIES AND SIMULATIONS OF COMPLEX SOCIAL SYSTEMS (Berlin: Springer, 2014) 79 at 84–86 and Katz, Hagai, Anheier, Helmut, & Lam, Marcus, *Fuzzy Set Approaches to the Study of Global Civil Society* (2006) GLOBAL CIVIL SOCIETY, 7, 186–196.

[88] For different attempts to define this matrix see, e.g., L. P. Feld & S. Voigt, *Economic Growth and Judicial Independence: Cross-Country Evidence Using a New Set of Indicators* (2003) 19 EUROPEAN JOURNAL OF POLITICAL ECONOMY 497; Abbott et al., *supra* note 11; Joost Pauwelyn, et al., INFORMAL INTERNATIONAL LAWMAKING (Oxford: Oxford University Press. 2012); Martha Finnemore & Stephen J. Toope, *Alternatives to "Legalization": Richer Views of Law and Politics* (2001) 55 INTERNATIONAL ORGANIZATION 743; Sylvia I Karlsson-Vinkhuyzen & Antto Vihma, *Comparing the legitimacy and effectiveness of global hard and soft law: An analytical framework* (2009) 3 REGULATION & GOVERNANCE 400 and James Melton et al., *On the interpretability of law: Lessons from the decoding of national constitutions* (2013) 43 BRITISH JOURNAL OF POLITICAL SCIENCE 399 at 414. Feld and Voigt, for example, decompose the attribute of judicial independence into 12 de jure sub-variables and 8 de facto (sociological) variables. Feld & Voigt, *ibid* at 501–504.

function could be defined on this vector, given a designated range for each attribute (e.g., the extent of judicial independence), to produce a single measure of legality, ranging from a perfect legal institution to one lacking any legal powers (mapped onto the real interval $[0, 1]$). The fuzzy membership function linking the vector of institutional attributes to a scale of *bindingness* is a socially contingent meta-norm. There are no universal truths that establish *a priori* the structure of that function and the way in which it translates into measures of graded normativity.

Another way to construct a fuzzy membership function is to draw on prototypical understanding of absolute and void legality $[-\mathbf{P_Z}, + \mathbf{P_Z}]$:

$$(2) f\mathbf{A_L} = \mathbf{M}(\mathbf{x}, \mathbf{PA_L}, -\mathbf{P_Z}, +\mathbf{P_Z})$$

This function produces a membership value for a particular normative statement, *x*, relative to $\mathbf{B_{L\text{-}perfect}}$, but based on the distance between some salient feature(s) of the institutional setting in which *x* is embedded $(\mathbf{PA_L})$ and prototypical exemplars of absolute or void legality ($-\mathbf{P_Z}, +\mathbf{P_Z}$). An example of such a salient feature is the existence of a body responsible for resolving disputes. Two exemplars, representing full and void legality, are the Supreme Court of Canada and a moot court tribunal.[89]

It may be argued that the proposed application of fuzzy-set theory is unreasonable because the precision it imposes through the instrument of membership function is inconsistent with the idea of vagueness.[90] Although this argument presents a valid concern, I believe that the case for using fuzzy-set theory to model soft law is sound, subject to some qualifications.[91]

---

[89] Ibid. at 501–503. This interpretation assumes that in the legal context typicality (goodness of example) and vagueness (gradedness of membership) can be used as interchangeable concepts. For such an argument see James A. Hampton, *Typicality, 'Graded Membership, and Vagueness'* (2007) 31 Cognitive Science: A Multidisciplinary Journal 355 at 356 and Michael T. Hannan, *Partiality of Memberships in Categories and Audiences* (2010) 36 Annual Review of Sociology 159 at 164. One potential difficulty in this argument concerns the fact that soft legal structures may develop alternative forms of reflexivity which do not depend on central judicial institutions of the type found in traditional legal systems.

[90] The following quote from Rosanne Keefe is instructive: "[T]he degree theorist's assignments impose precision in a form that is just as unacceptable as a classical true/false assignment. In so far as a degree theory avoids determinacy over whether *a* is *F*, the objection here is that it does so by enforcing determinacy over the *degree* to which *a* is *F*. . . why should we suppose that propositions relate to the facts of the world in a neat infinite-valued way any more than in 'a neat two valued way'?"

[91] For a more general response to Keefe's argument, see Nicholas Smith, Vagueness and Degrees of Truth (Oxford: Oxford University Press, 2008) and Nicholas Smith, *Fuzzy Logic and Higher-Order Vagueness* in Petr Cintula, et al., eds, Understanding

First, the primary goal of the above model is not to generate numeric values that represent *actual* degrees of bindingness. Rather, the foregoing model can be used to produce an *ordinal scale* of degrees of bindingness.[92] What is critical about the assignments produced by the fuzzy membership functions presented above is the relative ordering of the values assigned – not their numeric value.[93] The ordinal view is better served by constructing the output of the fuzzy function using linguistic variables. The musical notation for distinguishing the loudness or softness of music offers an insightful analogy. The basic distinction is between *p* or *piano* for "soft" and *f* or *forte* for "loud." Adding *m* before p/f generates *mp* ("*mezzo-piano*") meaning "moderately soft" or *mf* ("*mezzo-forte*") for "moderately loud." It is also possible to reiterate *p* and *f*, creating *pp* ("pianissimo") for "very soft" and *ff* ("fortissimo") for "very loud," and so on.[94]

A second point is that the model of fuzzy law developed here is based on the idea of fuzzy "plurivaluationism," which argues that fuzzy sets are not governed by a single membership function but by a multiplicity of functions, which produce multiple and competing assignments for assertions of the type "*x* is *F*."[95] The structure of the fuzzy membership function that provides the best characterization of a particular quasi-legal system emerges through an implicit and reflexive process of contestation. This reciprocal and perpetually renewed process of meaning formation reflects, as Kelso and Engstrom argue, the dynamic of the complementary pair: legal~non-legal. Finally, the fuzzy framework developed above does not attempt to provide an accurate description of the socio-legal reality associated with quasi-legal systems, but rather seeks to provide a model or theoretical framework for thinking about the structure of quasi-legal systems.[96]

VAGUENESS: LOGICAL, PHILOSOPHICAL AND LINGUISTIC PERSPECTIVES (College Publications, 2011) at 1–19.

[92] J. A. Goguen, *The Logic of Inexact Concepts* (1969) 19 SYNTHESE 325 at 331–332 [emphasis in the original].

[93] Ibid.

[94] For a description of musical notation schemes, see George Langley, 'Musical Expression from the Performer's Point of View' (1911) 38 Proceedings of the Musical Association 1.

[95] Smith (2011), *supra* note 91 at 8. Further support for the pluralistic argument can be found in the literature on the elicitation of fuzzy membership functions. See, e.g., Charles C. Ragin, FUZZY-SET SOCIAL SCIENCE (Chicago: University of Chicago Press, 2000) 165; T. Bilgic & I. B. Turksen, 'Elicitation of Membership Functions: How Far Can Theory Take Us?' (1997) Proceedings of the Sixth IEEE International Conference on Fuzzy Systems.

[96] The argument for viewing the fuzzy theory of vagueness as a model is advanced by Roy T. Cook, *Vagueness and Mathematical Precision* (2002) 111 MIND 225 at 235–236; see further, Smith (2011), supra note 91, at 5.

3.3   The Deliberative Dynamics of Quasi-Legal Systems

3.3.1   The Priority Relations between Norms in Quasi-Legal Settings

In this section, I develop a model of legal argumentation in a fuzzy legal environment and link the argument with the broader question of the dynamics and reflexive structure of quasi-legal systems. What exactly is the role of fuzzy norms, such as those included in a social responsibility code (CSR) code, in social deliberations? The question can arise in the context of a conflict between quasi-legal norms (potentially of different regimes), non-legal reasons, and fully-fledged legal norms. In examining this question, I first focus on Raz's model of legal norms as exclusionary reasons. This model implies that a fully valid norm P trumps any (non-legal) reason that could be invoked to defeat it, irrespective of the strength of the substantive reasons that were used to support P when it was originally enacted or of the strength of any opposing, non-legal reason. P can be defeated only through the invocation of legally valid reasons. One cannot defeat an argument for tort liability by arguing that the tortfeasor is poor and that it would therefore be unjust to find him liable. Such morality-based argument can succeed only if it is trans-formed into legally valid reasons.[97] For example, one can argue that the standard of liability in torts is a function of the tortfeasor's socio-economic status.[98]

A conflict between two or more valid legal reasons is usually deter-mined by applying higher-order (legal) comparative principles. These may include hierarchical ordering, scope or time-oriented principles (*lex specialis derogat legi generali or lex posterior derogat legi priori*) or other balancing criteria (e.g., cost-benefit calculus).[99] The legal status of P is

---

[97] Oren Perez, *Regulation as the Art of Intuitive Judgment: Critique of the Economic Approach to Environmental Regulation*, (2008) 4 INT'L J LAW IN CONTEXT 291 at 298.

[98] T. Keren-Paz, *Egalitarianism as Justification: Why and How Should Egalitarian Consider-ations Reshape the Standard of Care in Negligence Law?* (2003) 4 THEOR INQ LAW. The distinction between moral and legal reasons has a long history. In *Donoghue* v. *Stevenson*, Lord Atkin noted that "acts or omissions which any moral code would censure cannot in a practical world be treated so as to give a right to every person injured by them to demand relief. In this way rules of law arise which limit the range of complainants and the extent of their remedy": [1932] AC at 580, [1932] All ER Rep at 11. See also *Home Office* v. *Dorset Yacht Co Ltd*, [1970] 2 All ER 294 at 307. John Kleinig makes a similar distinction between institutionalized and non-institutionalized desert claims; John Klei-nig, *The Concept of Desert* (1971) 8 AM PHIL Q 71 at 71, 74.

[99] Prakken & Sartor, *supra* note 56 at 232.

determined by legal reasons alone. An argument for not(P) can succeed only if its supporting legal reasons *defeat* the legal reasons that support P according to the applicable higher-order principles. The strength of the non-legal reasons supporting either P or not(P) is irrelevant to the success of the argument. Note that this model does not purport to capture the cognitive processes that an agent experiences when reasoning in a legal situation.[100] Rather, it describes the imaginary argumentative structure that is presupposed by the crisp (or absolute) model of law.

What happens when a norm can no longer be treated as fully valid because of the institutional framework in which it was created? According to Austin, Hart, and Raz, in such circumstances the norm loses its normative authority completely and has no content-independent normative power. Under this account, the norms included in soft legal instruments such as CSR codes have no independent normative force; their force depends exclusively and fully on their non-legal justification (ethical, economic, or other). An obvious implication of the positivistic model is that a conflict between two fuzzy norms (e.g., competing norms of two CSR codes that a firm has subscribed to) should be resolved strictly based on the strength of their underlying reasons and not on arguments that invoke their degree of bindingness.

The idea of fuzzy norms suggests a different dialectic. It asks us to imagine a reality in which norms such as those contained in CSR Codes, administrative best practice guidelines or clinical ethical codes possess *partial normative power*. What would be the argumentative structure when deliberating with fuzzy norms? I suggest two potential models of deliberation that capture the idea that fuzzy norms possess partial normative force: "threshold deontology" and "deliberative coherence." According to *threshold deontology*, certain acts "cannot be justified by their consequences unless those consequences reach or surpass some *threshold point of compellingness.*"[101] Applying this idea to the fuzzy context has three implications. First, in a conflict between *fuzzy norms* and *non-legal reasons*, fuzzy norms maintain their exclusionary force up

---

[100] For an attempt to analyse this cognitive process, See Searle, *supra* note 74 at 123–132 and Giovanni Sartor, *Defeasibility in Legal Reasoning* in J. Ferrer Beltrán & G. B. Ratti, eds, THE LOGIC OF LEGAL REQUIREMENTS: ESSAYS ON DEFEASIBILITY, Oxford University Press, Oxford, EUI Law Working Paper No. 2009/02 1, n 3.

[101] See Larry Alexander, *Scalar Properties, Binary Judgments* (2008) 25 JOURNAL OF APPLIED PHILOSOPHY 85, 85 [emphasis added] and Larry Alexander, *Deontology at the Threshold*, (2000) 37 SAN DIEGO L REV 893. This idea is also explored in Prakken and Sartor, *supra* note 56 at 232.

to a *certain threshold point of persuasiveness* in which the competing
non-legal reasons have the upper hand.[102] This construction can be
incorporated into the fuzzy formalism presented above by postulating a
function that maps the *bindingness* of a fuzzy normative statement onto a
scale of thresholds. As the fuzzy value of a norm comes closer to 1, the
value of the threshold increases. Take f_t to represent the threshold
function. Its structure is:

$$(3) f_t (f A_L(x))$$

The threshold function reflects *collective expectations* regarding the deliberative force of the norm. It is therefore a function of the level of the
norm's bindingness, as determined by $f A_L$.[103]

Interpreting bindingness in degree-theoretic terms has two further
implications for potential conflicts between fuzzy norms and fully-
fledged legal norms, and between fuzzy norms associated with distinct
regimes. In the former case, a fully-fledged norm always prevails over a
fuzzy norm because its bindingness level is taken to be 1. The latter case
is more interesting. Attributing partial normative force to fuzzy norms
means that a conflict between fuzzy norms is not resolved merely
according to the force of their underlying reasons but also according to
their relative degrees of bindingness. A potential meta-rule for resolving
such conflicts could determine that a norm with a higher degree of
bindingness always defeats a norm with a lower degree of bindingness.

Although the foregoing model is analytically coherent, there is tension between the rigidity of the threshold concept and the fluid nature
of legal deliberation. Particularly problematic is the assumption of the
model that beyond the threshold point the fuzzy norm loses entirely its
normative force. The idea of deliberative coherence, developed by Paul
Thagard,[104] provides an alternative conceptual framework for studying
the dynamics of reasoning in fuzzy legal environments, which may be
more compatible with this fluidity. Deliberative coherence is based on
the thesis that human cognitive processes are marked by a propensity

---

[102] Note that under this model the substantive reasons that were used (or could have been
used) to support P when it was originally enacted continue to be irrelevant to the
resolution of the conflict.

[103] See Section 3.2.

[104] E. Millgram & P. Thagard, *Deliberative Coherence* (1996) 108 SYNTHESE 63; P. Thagard
& K. Verbeurgt, *Coherence as Constraint Satisfaction* (1998) 22 COGNITIVE SCIENCE 1.

for consistency,[105] and that coherence is part of a suite of cognitive mechanisms that humans have developed for epistemic vigilance.[106]

Deliberative coherence depicts the process of deliberation in fuzzy legal environments as one of attainment of consistency. In contrast to the threshold model, fuzzy norms function as contingent constraints and not as rigid thresholds. The fuzzy norm constitutes a non-absolute constraint that must cohere with the other reasons offered in the discussion (e.g., non-legal reasons, conflicting quasi-legal norms, and possibly even fully-fledged legal norms). The invocation of a fuzzy norm in a deliberative interaction generates a coherence dilemma that requires the interlocutors to look for a solution that can restore the coherence of the deliberation, *taking into account the graded validity/bindingness level of the fuzzy norm,* as determined by $f\mathbf{A_L}$.

3.3.2   The Deliberative Dynamics of Quasi-Legal Systems: the Case of CSR Codes

To illustrate the foregoing model in a concrete environment, consider the case of CSR codes such as the ISO 14001 environmental management system, the SA 8000 (Social Accountability) standard, or the FTSE4Good sustainability index. CSR codes commonly contain various prescriptions that may conflict both with the economic concerns of the firm and with each other. Institutionally, such conflicts are likely to surface in deliberations within the decision-making bodies of the firm. According to the model of fuzzy law, such potential conflicts may be resolved through two different dynamics. First, according to the threshold model, the fuzzy norm (the code prescription) may be used against economic arguments up to a certain threshold. In the context of ISO 14001 or FTSE4Good regimes, such dynamics can occur, for example, in an argument for the purchase of green technology, the introduction of costly organizational procedures, or in an argument to cut some environmental expenses because of financial problems. Second, a conflict between two quasi-legal norms, associated with different CSR codes, may be resolved by developing a meta-rule (e.g., *lex posterior*).

Deliberative coherence models the dynamics of CSR norms somewhat differently. According to this view, the fuzzy norm acts as a constraint on

---

[105] Dan Simon & Keith J. Holyoak, *Structural Dynamics of Cognition: From Consistency Theories to Constraint Satisfaction* (2002) 6 PERSONALITY AND SOCIAL PSYCHOLOGY REVIEW 283 at 284.

[106] Dan Sperber et al., *Epistemic Vigilance* (2010) 25 MIND & LANGUAGE 359 at 376–377.

the deliberative processes that take place within the firm. In the context of ISO 14001, for example, this means that the interaction between ISO 14001 and corporate culture is one of continuous, bi-directional co-adaptation.[107] Conflicts are not resolved through the logic of the threshold but by introducing distinctions that seek to retain coherence. For example, if implementing one of the requirements of ISO 14001 becomes too costly because of unforeseen economic contingencies, the board can decide to delay implementation to the next year rather than fully reject the fuzzy obligation. In this way, the firm recognizes the normative validity of the CSR code but gives some prominence to its conflicting economic commitments.

As already noted, the priority relations between fuzzy norms and conflicting legal or non-legal reasons are rarely fixed in advance (e.g., in some meta-rulebook). It would be futile, for example, to look for a resolution of the kind of conflicts described above in the CSR code, in the corporation bylaws, or in the corporate law of the state in which the corporation is registered. Although corporate law and the corporation's bylaws are clearly relevant to such conflicts and provide the legal infrastructure that enables corporations to subscribe to a particular private code, they do not provide a detailed scheme for the resolution of normative conflicts involving fuzzy norms.[108]

Both the threshold model and the deliberative coherence model assume that fuzzy legal norms carry some normative force, which is independent of the reasons that were used to justify the adoption of the code in the first place (e.g., the potential contribution of a CSR code to the reputation of the firm). This intrinsic normative force is captured by the fuzzy membership function $f\mathbf{A_L}$.[109]

---

[107] Perez et al., supra note 38.

[108] In some cases, state law can provide external support to CSR norms, changing their degree of bindingness. Veronica Besmer describes the attempt to enforce Nike CSR commitments, drawing on California unfair competition law, alleging that Nike committed negligent or intentional misrepresentation by providing misleading replies to allegations about labour exploitation in its sub-contractors' facilities. These allegations, which eventually were proven as true, have been inconsistent with Nike's self-prescribed commitments on this issue (codified in a memorandum of understanding signed with its sub-contractors in 1992); Veronica Besmer, *The Legal Character of Private Codes of Conduct: More than Just a Pseudo-Formal Gloss on Corporate Social Responsibility* (2006) 2 HASTINGS BUS LJ (2006) 279 at 296–297.

[109] Studies of CSR codes have demonstrated the capacity of such codes to develop an autonomous dynamic that takes life of its own. Perez et al., *supra* note 38 at 617; Olivier

4 The Social Dynamics of Quasi-Legal Systems: Reinforcing Loops and Meta-stability

The model of quasi-legality developed above provides a more refined vocabulary for thinking about soft law than does the conventional positivistic model. A key challenge for this model concerns the specification of the social and institutional conditions necessary for the emergence and continuing operation of quasi-legal systems.

Note in this context, first, that the fuzzy law model makes no *a priori* assumptions about the institutional matrix that is necessary for the emergence of a quasi-legal system, or about the relation between that matrix and the projected bindingness of the fuzzy legal norms produced by it. This pluralistic approach is consistent with the literature on soft law, which pointed out the multiplicity of institutional structures associated with soft law schemes.[110] Second, the fuzzy law model is not deterministic. The socially contingent nature of the fuzzy membership function associated with grades of bindingness means that there is no necessary linkage between the existence of certain institutional components and the emergence of quasi-legal communication. Rather, the linkage should be viewed, following TCP, as a *potentiality*, which under certain social conditions can lead to the emergence of a sustainable quasi-legal structure.[111]

The fuzzy law model highlights two key aspects of the coordination dynamics of quasi-legal systems. First, the emergence of a sustainable

---

Boiral, '*Managing with ISO Systems: Lessons from Practice*' (2011) 44 LONG RANGE PLANNING 197 at 212.

[110] See, e.g. Paul Schiff Berman, GLOBAL LEGAL PLURALISM: A JURISPRUDENCE OF LAW BEYOND BORDERS (Cambridge: Cambridge University Press 2012), Oren Perez, *Private Environmental Governance as Ensemble Regulation: A Critical Exploration of Sustainability Indexes and the New Ensemble Politics* (2011) 12 THEOR INQ LAW 543 and Zumbansen, *supra* note 38.

[111] Indeed, even a developed institutional-legal structure does not necessitate the emergence of autonomous legal system. The former Soviet Union is a case in point. In that case the legal system constituted only a façade of legality, which was in realty completely controlled by the political party and its regime of power and fear. This point was nicely captured by Tom Rob Smith in his description of Lubyanka, the headquarters of the KGB: "An invisible borderline existed around the building ... Crossing that line meant that you were either staff or condemned. There was no chance you could be found innocent inside these walls. It was an assembly line of guilt." Tom Rob Smith, *CHILD 44* (New York: Grand Central Publishing, 2008) at 79–80. See further on the KGB and its regime of terror, J. M. Waller, Russia: Death and Resurrection of the KGB (2004) 12 DEMOKRATIZATSIYA-WASHINGTON 333.

quasi-legal system depends on the existence of *reinforcing communicative loops*. Thus, to use the example of clinical ethics committees, the establishment of a partial legal-institutional structure does not guarantee, in itself, the emergence of self-sustaining legal communication. For this to happen, fuzzy norms must be chosen by interlocutors as themes for communication. This occurs only if fuzzy norms are perceived to be carrying some intrinsic, content-independent normative force. In other words, they must be able to generate normative expectations.[112] There is a potential self-enhancing relation between the invocation of fuzzy norms in communicative interactions and their projected normative force. Fuzzy norms are invoked by interlocutors only if they are considered to have some degree of normative force. But such invocation, by itself, can facilitate further legal communication by signalling the existence of collective belief in the normative force of fuzzy rules, thus encouraging other interlocutors to rely on them in future interactions.[113] There is, therefore, a necessary linkage between the dialectic of reasoning with fuzzy norms and the sustainability of fuzzy legal systems as partially autonomous structures.[114]

But there is also something mysterious and uncertain about the emergence of these self-enforcing loops which ultimately determine the priority relations between fuzzy norms and non-legal reasons. Similar mysteries characterize other collective goods, such as trust and public participation. Eric Uslaner has noted, for example, that although trust is "the chicken soup of social life," facilitating all sorts of good things, "it appears to work somewhat mysteriously. It might seem that we can only develop trust in people we know. Yet, trust's benefits come when we put faith in strangers."[115] The emergence of collaborative knowledge production in online contexts raises similar puzzles. What are the distinctive social features that have turned Wikipedia into a success story, but

---

[112] Niklas Luhmann's distinction between normative and cognitive expectations is critical to this point. Normativity, Luhmann argues, means that certain expectations can be maintained even in the face of disappointment Niklas Luhmann, *Operational Closure and Structural Coupling: the Differentiation of the Legal System* (1992) 13 CARDOZO L REV 1419 at 1426. See also, Gunther Teubner, *The Two Faces of Janus: Rethinking Legal Pluralism* (1992) 13 CARDOZO L REV 1443 at 1449–4450.

[113] For a detailed study of the emergence of such self-enforcing dynamic in the context of ISO 14001 environmental management system, see Perez et al., *supra* note 38.

[114] Note that this process does not depend (at least not completely) on the capacity of fuzzy norms to change behavior.

[115] Eric M. Uslaner, THE MORAL FOUNDATIONS OF TRUST (Cambridge: Cambridge University Press, 2002) at 1.

caused the failure of its online competitor Citizendium? In retrospect, scholars have suggested various explanations, but these explanations have not been clear *ex ante* and remain somewhat incomplete even now, leaving the success of Wikipedia somewhat baffling.[116]

The second key aspect of quasi-legal systems, as predicted by the theory of complementary pairs, is their intrinsic instability. Fuzzy legal structures are potentially unstable in the sense that they have to cope with competing pressures that pull in different directions. The first tendency is toward the complete denial of the authority of the relevant institution to produce binding norms, leading potentially to the breakdown of the fuzzy legal system. The second tendency is toward the transformation of the fuzzy legal system into a crisp one through a series of institutional changes associated with fully binding norms. One of the key lessons of TCP is that social systems can cope with such conflicting and co-existing tendencies through the mechanism of meta-stability, that is, by continuously exploring potential social mechanisms through which such tensions can be resolved or attenuated, even if only temporarily.[117]

A good example of this dynamic comes from the evolving field of clinical ethics committees. Medical practitioners commonly encounter ethical dilemmas in their daily practice. The perceived need to ensure that decisions are ethically and clinically defensible has led to the development of a system of clinical ethics committees (CECs). CECs found in various jurisdictions, most notably in the United Kingdom, United States, and other European countries,[118] have a variety of functions: educating, developing policies and guidelines within institutions, providing advice in particular cases, and participating in matters relating to organizational ethics (for example, policies on eligibility for treatment or on the management of waiting lists). Among the issues CECs must address are the refusal of life-saving treatment, end of life issues, and

---

[116] J. Giles, *Internet Encyclopedias Go Head to Head* (2005) 438 NATURE 900; D. Karpf, *Open Source Political Community Development: A Five-Stage Adoption Process* (2011) 8 JOURNAL OF INFORMATION TECHNOLOGY & POLITICS 323 at 329.

[117] For further discussion of this dynamic see, Oren Perez, 'The Hybrid Legal-Scientific Dynamic of Transnational Scientific Institutions' EUROPEAN JOURNAL OF INTERNATIONAL LAW 2015 26 (2): 391–416.

[118] Royal College of Physicians, ETHICS IN PRACTICE – BACKGROUND AND RECOMMENDATIONS FOR ENHANCED SUPPORT: A REPORT OF THE WORKING PARTY ON CLINICAL ETHICS (London: Royal College of Physicians, 2005) [Royal College of Physicians].

the retention of organs.[119] CECs work in different ways and hold different positions within the organizations they serve. They may meet formally and regularly or be convened *ad hoc*. They may provide only non-urgent advice, but some may have a rapid-response facility. Membership and the range of expertise also vary.[120]

The role of CECs has been traditionally understood as providing advice rather than serving as a proxy decision maker. But some scholars argue that over the last decade CECs have acquired significant authority over treatment decisions.[121] As more and more hospitals have established CECs,[122] concerns about their structure and function have started to emerge, generating unstable dynamics. Some authors have argued that CECs constitute a due process wasteland, and that greater effort must be made to encourage and foster accountability and transparency in ethics support services.[123] Others have questioned the core competencies needed for CECs, arguing that they must acquire not only knowledge of basic concepts of ethical theory and clinical terminology but also basic *legal knowledge*, which includes relevant professional codes of ethics and statutory law (e.g., healthcare legislation, torts).[124] These concerns have led to polarizing dynamics involving at one end a *de facto* disregard of CECs as a source of authority and at the other end calls for the full integration of CECs into the formal legal system.[125]

---

[119] Gordon Duval et al., *A National Survey of U.S. Internists' Experiences with Ethical Dilemmas and Ethics Consultation* (2004) 19 JOURNAL OF GENERAL INTERNAL MEDICINE 251 and Royal-College-of-Physicians, ibid.

[120] Royal College of Physicians, *supra* note 118.

[121] Thaddeus Mason Pope, *Multi-institutional Healthcare Ethics Committees: The Procedurally Fair Internal Dispute Resolution Mechanism* (2008) 31 CAMPBELL L REV 257 at 257 and Anita J. Tarzian & ASBH Core Competencies Update Task Force, *Health care ethics consultation: An update on core competencies and emerging standards from the American Society for Bioethics and Humanities*, Core Competencies Update Task Force (2013) 13 AMERICAN JOURNAL OF BIOETHICS 3 at 3.

[122] G. McGee et al., *A National Study of Ethics Committees*, (2001) 1 AMERICAN JOURNAL OF BIOETHICS 60; A. M. Slowther et al., *Development of Clinical Ethics Services in the UK: A National Survey* (2012) 38 JOURNAL OF MEDICAL ETHICS 210; Duval et al., *supra* note 119.

[123] Sam McLean, *Clinical Ethics Committees: A Due Process Wasteland?* (2008) 3 CLINICAL ETHICS 99 at 101.

[124] V. Larcher et al., *Core Competencies for Clinical Ethics Committees* (2010) 10 CLINICAL MEDICINE, JOURNAL OF THE ROYAL COLLEGE OF PHYSICIANS 30 at 32; see also: Tarzian & ASBH Core Competencies Update Task Force, *supra* note 121 at 8.

[125] See Slowther, *supra* note 122 at 213 (noting the low referral rate in the context of UK CECs); R. F. Wilson, 'Rethinking the Shield of Immunity: Should Ethics Committees Be Accountable for Their Mistakes?' (2002) 14 HEC Forum 172 (arguing that CECs should

This instability also presents an opportunity for social innovation. Thaddeus Mason Pope, for example, argues that the current model of intramural CEC should be replaced by a multi-institutional CEC that serves several healthcare institutions. In his opinion, this could alleviate some of the tensions generated by the intramural model, because its detachment from any single institution would guarantee that it is more independent, and because its ability to reflect a diversity of voices and perspectives would addresses the problem of biased decision making and of lack of competence that characterize some intramural CECs.[126] Others, such as the ASBH Core Competencies Update Task Force, argue that CECs should maintain their hybrid structure but call for greater standardization in their structure and operation, focusing, for example, on the questions of CEC core competencies and working procedures (e.g., how to conduct and document case consultations).[127]

By highlighting this polarizing dynamic of quasi-legal systems, the model of fuzzy law also offers a way of thinking about the question of the beginning ~ end of law, articulating the dynamics by which systems of law can move between the states of void ~ perfect legality.

5   Conclusions

The model of quasi-legality elaborated above sought to provide an alternative conceptual framework for thinking about soft law. Understanding normative phenomena requires sensitivity to the space between legality and non-legality, which remains unaccounted for in the traditional jurisprudence literature. In thinking about the dynamics of this in-between space we are still facing significant theoretical and empirical challenges. Theoretically, more work needs to be done on the reflexive structure of fuzzy legal systems and in particular on the question of the priority relations between fuzzy norms and non-legal reasons. I argued above that the priority question could be resolved by two distinct deliberative dynamics, based on the ideas of

---

function as adjuncts to the courts, providing case consultation reviewable by the judiciary; in his opinion, the courts should have final authority in patient care decisions).

[126] Pope, *supra* note 121 at 316.

[127] Tarzian & ASBH Core Competencies Update Task Force, *supra* note 121 at 6–8.

threshold deontology and deliberative coherence. But more work can be done, for example, on the relation between these models. Another related direction concerns the potential conflict between overlapping fuzzy regimes. This direction seems particularly intriguing given the increasing number of firms that subscribe to multiple CSR codes.[128]

Empirically, more work is needed to uncover the institutional dynamics of quasi-legal systems. The fuzzy model points out the possibility for the emergence of legal communication based on institutional infrastructure that is less developed than the legal infrastructure of the modern state, or of treaty-based international institutions such as the World Trade Organization. But the question of the fuzzy dynamics of systems such as CSR Codes and Ethical Clinical Codes cannot be resolved simply by analysing the associated texts. Resolving this question requires a sociological analysis of the institutional apparatus in which such quasi-legal schemes are embedded and the communicative dynamics associated with it. A great deal of the work in the area of soft law, especially in the field of CSR codes, is based on econometric studies and panel data.[129] Such studies do not shed light on the sociological and psychological processes underlying these quasi-legal environments, especially the processes that take place within firms that adopt CSR codes or within the institutions in which these codes are created. To understand these dynamics, studies are needed that would explore the inner workings of the institutions and agents associated with these fuzzy legal structures. Such studies could follow various paths. One path could be based on "thick" examination of organizations that have subscribed to CSR codes such as ISO 14001, based on in-depth interviews and observations.[130]

---

[128] See Perez, *supra* note 110.

[129] Matthew Potoski & Aseem Prakash, *Covenants with Weak Swords: ISO 14001 and Facilities' Environmental Performance* (2005) 24 JOURNAL OF POLICY ANALYSIS AND MANAGEMENT 745; Richard Perkins & Eric Neumayer, *Geographic Variations in the Early Diffusion of Corporate Voluntary Standards: Comparing ISO14001 and the Global Compact* (2010) 42 ENVIRONMENT AND PLANNING A 347; D. Berliner & A. Prakash, *Signaling Environmental Stewardship in the Shadow of Weak Governance: The Global Diffusion of ISO 14001* (2013) 47 LAW & SOC'Y REV 345.

[130] See, for example, the work in Boiral, *supra* note 109, Perez et al, *supra* note 38 and Tim Bartley and Zhang Lu, 'Opening the 'Black Box': Transnational Private Certification of Labor Standards in China' (February 2012). Indiana University Research Center for Chinese Politics and Business, RCCPB Working Paper #18. Available at SSRN: www.ssrn.com/abstract=2169350.

Another path could take an experimental approach, relying, for example, on the method of comparative surveys and using vignettes. Such an approach may be used to study a multi-instrument regulatory environment by exposing subjects to various environments.[131]

---

[131] See Yuval Feldman & Oren Perez, *Motivating Environmental Action in a Pluralistic Regulatory Environment: An Experimental Study of Framing, Crowding Out, and Institutional Effects in the Context of Recycling Policies* (2012) 46 LAW & SOCIETY REVIEW 405. In this paper one of the questions we studied was to what extent the source of a legal prohibition – we distinguished between the state and two organizational settings: firm and academic institution – influences subjects' attitudes toward the act of recycling. See Ibid. at 421, 429–431.

INDEX

Lightning Source UK Ltd.
Milton Keynes UK
UKHW031051111120
372967UK00012B/51